EMPOWERING YOUR LIFE WITH
RUNES

Jean Marie Stine

ALPHA

A member of Penguin Group (USA) Inc.

International Standard Book Number: 1-59257-165-4
Library of Congress Catalog Card Number: 2003115221

06   05   04   8   7   6   5   4   3   2   1

Interpretation of the printing code: The rightmost number of the first series of numbers is the year of the book's printing; the rightmost number of the second series of numbers is the number of the book's printing. For example, a printing code of 04-1 shows that the first printing occurred in 2004.

Printed in the United States of America

Most Alpha books are available at special quantity discounts for bulk purchases for sales promotions, premiums, fund-raising, or educational use. Special books, or book excerpts, can also be created to fit specific needs.

For details, write: Special Markets, Alpha Books, 375 Hudson Street, New York, NY 10014.

Publisher: Marie Butler-Knight
Product Manager: Phil Kitchel
Senior Managing Editor: Jennifer Chisholm
Senior Acquisitions Editor: Randy Ladenheim-Gil
Development Editor: Lynn Northrup
Production Editor: Megan Douglass
Copy Editor: Molly Schaller
Illustrator: J.L. "Frankie" Hill
Cover Designer: Charis Santillie
Book Designer: Trina Wurst
Creative Director: Robin Lasek
Indexer: Brad Herriman
Layout/Proofreading: Rebecca Harmon, Mary Hunt, Katherin Bidwell

To Michael Valentine Smith (David McDaniel), Jillian Boardman (Jane Gallion), Jubel Hartshaw (Bruce Pelz), and the rest of that old gang of mine: Ed Baker, Owen Hannifen, Phil Castora, Jack Harness, Ken "Bear" Hedberg, Gail Knuth, and Lynn Styer ...
As we say in the Village, "Be seeing you."

Contents

Appendixes

Introduction

The 24 symbols and one blank stone known as runes are an ancient book of wisdom, filled with truths as valid today as they were two thousand years ago and more, when runes first came into the world. Follow that wisdom and you become your truest, best self—the person you were meant to be. Just think for a moment. What would your best self be like? What talents, abilities, lifestyle, friends, work, and rewards would you have? *Empowering Your Life with Runes* will show you how this age old set of symbols will help become that person—with every quality and asset you pictured, and more.

Empowering your life with runes isn't just a title. It is an approach to living that has brought happiness, success, and fulfillment to men and women for millennia. *Empowering Your Life with Runes* gives you all the tools and tips you need to get started using this ages old system to enjoy the same benefits in your life. You will learn what runes are, and more about the many different ways in which they can help you empower yourself to become the person you were meant to be. You will learn how to conduct rune readings to generate greater self-understanding, solve personal and professional problems, probe your future, and discover the best path to success. You will also receive guidance in how to use rune magic and meditation to attract love, money, health, and good fortune.

Many great thinkers over the years, such as Carl Jung and Marianne Williamson, and therapists, such as Carl Rodgers and Eric Fromm, have explored runes and have found them a valuable source of insight, inspiration, and personal empowerment. Runes can show the cure for what ails you, helping you enter and stay in recovery, find productive ways to manage and disburse anger, and overcome other self-destructive habits and compulsions. They also reveal your best qualities, assets, and abilities, and tell you just how to make the most of each. Once you begin working with runes, your whole life will begin to change for the better at a rate that will surprise you.

Empowering Your Life with Runes is divided into 12 chapters. Each chapter is self-contained. If you have a specific issue you want help with—such as career or love or money—you can skip right to that chapter. There you will find powerful rune reading techniques and magical rituals designed to help that you can use right away, without any prior experience or knowledge. However, you will benefit even more if you take the time to read Chapters 1 and 2 first, which give vital background that will make your work with the runes even more effective. Here's a description of what you'll find in each chapter:

- Chapter 1, "Putting the Power of Runes to Work for You," introduces you to the runes and their history, and shows you how to pick and learn from your personal Rune of Guidance.

- Chapter 2, "Runes of Self and Wholeness," acquaints you with the traditional Celtic design of three concentric circles on which runes are traditionally thrown for a reading, and presents brain-friendly step-by-step instructions that make it easy to conduct and interpret a reading.

- Chapter 3, "Runes of Solution and Insight," makes it simple for anyone to use the runes to solve difficult personal or professional problems and stimulate creative insights.

- Chapter 4, "Runes of Career and Destiny," offers four powerful methods of using runes to discover and fulfill your destined career and mission, whether it's business, the arts, or service to others.

- Chapter 5, "Runes of Health and Healing," presents ways you can diagnose illness and aid healing through rune readings, magic, and meditation.

- Chapter 6, "Runes of Conflict and Communication," gives you runic tools for resolving conflicts and enhancing communication with others, in personal, family, or business life.

- Chapter 7, "Runes of Finance and Prosperity," is all about increasing and ensuring abundance and prosperity and generating immediate solutions to financial woes with runes.

- Chapter 8, "Runes of Business and Success," teaches you runic secrets for avoiding the pitfalls and taking the wisest path to personal, professional, or business success.

- Chapter 9, "Runes of Love and Romance," details secrets of the runes of love and romance that can help you find your soul mate, increase intimacy, heighten sexual pleasure and attraction, trouble-shoot relationship problems, and even rekindle love when it seems lost.

- Chapter 10, "Runes of Power and Magic," explores runes' magical and mystical powers, and the essentials of creating potent rune spells, charms, and ceremonies are explained.
- Chapter 11, "Runes of Future and Fate," empowers you with ways of shaping your own fate and ensuring good-fortune through readings and runic energies.
- Chapter 12, "Living the Runes," shares tips for incorporating the wisdom of runes in your daily life.

Empowering Your Life with Runes offers you a unique opportunity to transform your life, and become all you can be and were meant to be. If you dream of a fulfilling life rich in the rewards that mean most to you, if you would follow your better self and not your worst, if you want happiness, prosperity, and love, runes will show you the way to all that—and more. The key is in your hand, all you have to do is turn it to unlock the secrets of runic wisdom and power.

How to Use This Book

In each chapter you will find four common elements:

- Profiles of individual runes (like the one shown below)
- Rune reading techniques
- Rune magic rituals
- Runic meditations

Each chapter profiles two runes, presenting the rune image, what it means, detailing some of its interpretations in readings, and listing what the rune is used for in magic and meditation, along with the Norse god who guards and can release the rune's energies, the rune's totem animals, and the herb and color most harmonious with that rune's energies.

Rune #0: Wyrd or Wishing Stone or Stone of Fate

Wyrd

Wyrd (pronounced we-erd) is your rune of dreams, fate, and the future. Throughout history, people have sought ways to represent the unknown, mysterious future—the fate awaiting us which is shaped by our dreams, hopes, desires. Often they chose the figure eight turned sideways—the infinity symbol of the Greeks. Runes capture this meaning with the blank stone, which like the future it represents has no image we can discern.

Rune Image: The blank, unknown future

In Rune Reading

Meanings: The past, the future, the past becoming the future, karma, decrees of fate, the unexpected, life being never the same again, wishes, desires, void, all and nothing, portal, gateway, other dimensions, cosmic realms, seeking after the unknown.

In Rune Magic

Use to: Create the destiny you want, make wishes into realities, discover the nature of anything hidden, mysterious or unknown

In Rune Meditation

Use to: Deepen inner acceptance of fate and the unknown, to see what can not be seen, to penetrate the veil of the unknown

Rune Gods: The Norns, Urd, Verdandi

Every chapter features unique rune reading techniques intended to shed light on the issues the chapter covers, as well as sample readings that help you understand how other people applied and interpreted their readings: the Intertwined Hearts reading for concerns of love and romance, the Mirror of Success reading for business and success, the Column of Health reading for identifying the cause and remedy of ill health, the Point of Agreement reading for resolving conflict and miscommunication, and nearly a dozen others.

Each chapter also features magical rune rituals that allow you to direct the runes' awesome benevolent energies to help yourself and others with health, prosperity, affairs of the heart, career—or whatever subject that particular chapter focuses on.

Finally, each chapter concludes with a runic meditation that will help you develop powerful insights into how you can best respond to the problems and issues the chapter covers.

Together, these four elements will empower you to set the legendary powers of the runes to work in your behalf and that of the people and institutions that mean the most to you.

Acknowledgments

Sometimes it seems to authors that their own efforts have the least to do with the successful completion and publication of their books. In my case, it is especially true. First, much credit for the existence of *Empowering Your Life with Runes* should go to my extraordinary agent (now retired) Bert Holtje and his equally extraordinary successor at James Peter Associates, Gene Brissie. Thanks, guys!

When candidates for sainthood are next considered, my vote goes to Randy Ladenheim-Gil and Lynn Northrup, who kept a light on in the window for the manuscript, long after it should have been blown out and the front door locked. Thanks, ladies! Thanks also to Molly Schaller, Megan Douglass, and the rest of the production team at Alpha Books.

Next, a big tip of the hat to Julia Case for coming to the rescue and replacing my hard drive when it crashed a week before my already stretched-thin re-revised deadline; and to Rachel Neulander for replacing my brain many times over. And a big hunk of gratitude to downtown Northampton, MA, especially The Haymarket (best mocha in the universe) and Jakes Café (for Sunday Eggs Benedict, and weekday everything else).

Finally, to the two wonderful teachers from whom I learned all the principles and lore that underlie this book, the late Deon Dolphin, author of *Rune Magic*, and Patrice Pilate. Thank you from the bottom of my heart.

Chapter 1

Putting the Power of Runes to Work for You

Runes are the letters of a miraculous, ages-old alphabet with amazing powers that can change your life. For thousands of years, they have been used as a source of guidance, solace, and insight. Runes have also been valued as a means of generating and directing magical power by many of the world's peoples and cultures.

The origin of runes is lost in the mists of history. But their importance to the peoples of antiquity cannot be denied. They have been found carved into monuments and rocks throughout northern Europe—as far south as Greece, as far north as Finland, as far east as Russia, and as far west as the shores of the Americas (much to the amazement of twentieth-century scholars).

The coming of the scientific age threw runes and other ancient systems of self-guidance and self-transformation—such as yoga, I-Ching, and tarot—into obscurity. Yet the visible presence of runes, mute and mysterious, at thousands of sites across Europe prevented them from being wholly forgotten. And such was their power to speak directly to the human heart and mind that they continued to stir curiosity and interest, until runes seemingly generated their own revival about three decades ago.

Today, there are dozens of books explaining the mysteries of runes. Each weekend hundreds of courses and workshops are offered in such subjects as rune magic, rune meditation, rune divination, rune lore, rune healing, and others throughout North America and Europe. Literally millions of people have used the power of runes to speed healing, deepen self-understanding, attract a soul mate, discover the pattern of future events, achieve financial success, and otherwise empower their lives for the better.

The Mysterious Origin of Runes

There are 25 runes (24 symbols and 1 blank rune, Wyrd, also called the Wishing Stone or Rune of Fate). Each is a letter in an ancient alphabet called Futhork. The word rune literally means "mystery," and the origin of runes remains a mystery to historians to this day.

Runes appeared suddenly about two millennia ago. Some say their origin was magical, a gift of the gods. Others say that they evolved from Phoenician or Greek. The only thing scholars agree on is that Futhork was in widespread use by 1600 C.E., particularly by the Germanic, Scandinavian, Danish, and Celtic nations.

According to tradition, as described in the Norse epic, *The Elder Edda*, the god Odin brought the gift of runes to the world in much the same way that Prometheus brought the gift of fire in Greek myths. Like Prometheus, Odin paid a heavy price for the knowledge he acquired. First, he had to pierce his side with his own magic spear, so that his sins could empty out freely with his blood. Next, he was suspended upside down by one leg from a limb of Yggdrasil, the Tree of Transformation, where he was lashed by hurricane winds.

The Source of Well-Being and Wisdom

Odin endured this torture (with its parallels to shamantic initiation and Jungian exploration of the unconscious), without food or drink, for nine days and nights, all the while scrutinizing the dark recesses of the underworld, searching for the secret runic wisdom concealed there. For this sacrifice, the Edda tells us, Odin won "well-being" (health and prosperity) as well as "wisdom."

I know I hung
On that windswept tree,
All of the nights nine
Wounded by Odin's own spear
Given to Odin
Myself an offering to myself:
Bound to the tree
That no man knows
From what roots it rises.
None gave me bread,
None the drinking horn.
Down into the deepest depths
I strained my eyes
Until I at last
I glimpsed the Runes.
With a roaring cry
I seized them,
Fell dizzy and fainting.
Well-being I won
And wisdom.
 —*The Elder Edda*

The Gift of Writing

Odin considered the secrets of the runes so powerful that he only shared
a part of rune lore widely—the exoteric or mundane aspect—the use of
runes as letters to form words. Northern European runic carvings are
testaments to this use of runes in writing. The Kingiktorsuak Stone, un-
earthed in Greenland in the early 1900s, baffled scholars for years, until
the recent revival of runic knowledge led to its translation. Believed to
be more than a thousand years old, this immense stone records that
"Elnikr Sigvatsson and Baane Tordsson and Enriki Osson, Saturday before
Rogation Day raised cairns here …" followed by an indecipherable date.

Runic Inscriptions

Another thousand-year-old runic inscription from Greenland explains
why the grave beneath it is empty. It memorializes "Gudvig," a woman

who died on an ocean voyage and whose body "was put overboard in Greenland's sea." A Viking mound at Maeshowe, in the Orkney Islands, decorated with runes, was signed by the proud iron-age artist, "Arnfithar the Cat raised these runes." At Hopperstad, in Norway, one of the thirty surviving ninth-century "Stave-churches" is covered inside with runic transcriptions of biblical passages, from the Lord's Prayer to the signatory: "Now is Palm Sunday eve/Lord bless the one who these runes cut/likewise the one who has them read." Even runic mail has been found engraved on sticks and bones (the notepads of the era). "To sister of Olav Haetus-vein," one is addressed, "in Bergen at a nunnery."

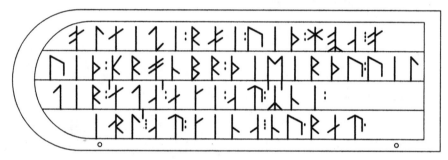

The runes engraved in this ancient bone fragment carry a message from a brother to his sister.

The Vitka

The rest of rune lore—the esoteric or mystical aspects—Odin imparted only to a small group of followers. Before receiving these secrets, each had to swear to employ the knowledge Odin imparted solely for the aid and benefit of humanity. The runic wisdom they gained was guarded zealously and passed down only to chosen students who had proved themselves above the temptation to misuse it.

Thus was born the mysterious guild of the Vitka or rune masters (singular, vitki). The Vitka were mighty in rune lore. They wielded the powers of runes as tools for divination, tools to unleash potent magic, and as a gateway to mystical realms and inner wisdom.

People brought to the Vitka their questions and troubles. A bride-to-be might wonder whether her married life would be a happy one. A vitki would have her cast or throw rune stones and, to eyes studied in rune lore, the patterns the stones formed would indicate the fate of the forthcoming union. A farmer whose wheat was failing might appeal to a vitki, in whose hands runes would become a focus for beneficial magic, directing fertilizing energy to boost the growth of his crops. Someone whose ungovernable temper was wrecking their family would seek out a vitki and be led through meditation on a Rune of Guidance that would slowly reveal and heal the inner wounds that caused their problem.

Women and Runes

Women held a coequal place with men in the traditional nature-based magical and mystical systems. Sometimes, it was because people believed women were closer to nature than men. Sometimes, because they believed women had greater psychic gifts. And, sometimes just because they believed women and men were equal.

That women were among the great practitioners of rune lore is shown in the *Saga of Erik the Red*. In the pages of this venerable Norse epic can be found an arresting description of a thirteenth-century vitki: "She wore a cloak set with stones along the hem. Around her neck and covering her head, she wore a hood lined with white catskins. In one hand she carried a staff with a knob on the end, and at her belt, holding together her long dress, hung a rune pouch. She wore calfskin shoes and catskin mittens to cover her hands all the time."

Today, many women are out of touch with their personal power to deal with day-to-day living, as well as their own magical power to transform themselves and their world. But, Freya Aswynn, author of *Northern Mysteries and Magick: Runes & Feminine Powers*, is one of many who believe that women have a special affinity for runes. This makes working with runes an ideal path for women seeking personal empowerment.

Wise was Kostbera
cunning in runes;
rune-staff she read
by fire's light.
　　—Rune Poem (trad.), Greenland

The Return of the Runes

About 500 years ago, runes and the Vitka began to fade from view, withdrawing into hibernation during the modern world's long love affair with technology. Then, in the 1980s—almost as if the runes felt that a growing disillusion with science and growing interest in psycho-spiritual tools like tarot, I-Ching, and ritual magic made the time ripe—they re-emerged. But, this time runes would share their powers, not merely with a chosen few, but with everyone.

When the runes broke their long silence and began speaking, it was to a California writer named Ralph Blum. Though his diminutive tome, *The Book of Runes*, was barely 100 pages long, and the subject matter unknown—such was the power of runes—it defied the odds and became a bestseller. Runes had successfully reintroduced themselves to the modern world.

To Blum, runes were primarily a method of divination, like astrology, tea leaves, and tarot, and secondarily a focus for meditation. And that is how they became familiar to the millions who read (or read about) his book. Runes proved their power to generate insights and accurately assess situations to those who tried Blum's system of rune reading. Word-of-mouth spread, and soon people everywhere wanted to learn all they could about these enigmatic symbols, and how they could benefit from runes.

In the years since, scholars have researched the scattered rune lore of Europe, reintroducing us to the lost art of rune magic, as well as furthering our understanding of runes as divinatory and meditation aids. Anyone interested in deepening their knowledge of runes can find books to guide them and teachers to instruct them. Runes have made themselves at home everywhere: billboard advertisements, magazine layouts, key chains, even in teen fashions at the mall.

What Runes Can Do for You

People who have worked with runes report runes helped them ...

- Increase self-understanding, exorcise personal demons and destructive habits, and achieve inner peace and wholeness.
- Spark insights, solve critical problems, and enhance their creativity.

- Discover their purpose in life, choose the right career path, and avoid dead-end jobs.
- Chart a path to maximum health, speed healing, and pinpoint personal health risks.
- Become conflict resolvers, locate areas of disagreement, and understand and reconcile seemingly irreconcilable points-of-view.
- Point their way to financial prosperity, attract money, and minimize personal financial weaknesses.
- Maximize professional success, identify opportunities others miss, and thrive on setbacks and come out ahead.
- Find soul mates, resolve romantic difficulties, enhance sex and intimacy, and recover from heartbreak.
- Develop psychic gifts, create spells of healing and good fortune, and ward off negative energies and emotions.
- Learn the form future events might take, see how their own actions will shape those events, and discover the wisest path through them.
- Use the runes as a day-by-day guide, uncover the secrets of critical monthly and yearly rune cycles, and benefit more and more from the wisdom of runes.

The step-by-step instructions you'll find in this book make it easy to get started reaping the benefits of rune power right away—without any prior training or experience.

How Do Runes Work?

How are runes able to work these wonders? Where does the mysterious power of these ancient symbols come from? In short, how do runes do what they do?

That's the same as asking how magic works, or how tarot or the I-Ching works. The truth is that—although there are many theories to explain it—no one really knows. One theory attributes the powers of runes to the gods, who gave them to humanity. Another theory holds that it is our own natural psychic powers that do the work, with runes, cards, and ceremonies merely serving to focus and direct these powers. The way in which patterns rule everything in the universe, from the largest level to the smallest, figures in yet a third explanation. A fourth leans toward the unconscious, which whispers to us when we concentrate on abstract symbols. Synchronicity—which favors vibrational affinities between rune stones and the reader or between the magician and crops on which a spell of fertility is being cast—was the favorite explanation of pioneer psychiatrist Carl Jung.

Secret of the Runes

The Vitka had their own answer. To these sages, runes weren't letters and Futhork was not a language—not in the sense we understand those terms today. Runes and Futhork were used in writing, of course. But, to the Vitka, runes were far more than mere letters, more than mere marks drawn on a page to represent sounds.

Each rune was believed to be a link to one of the 25 cosmic forces or energies that are the fundamental building blocks of the universe. Among them were energy, sharpness, movement, burning (consumption), constraint, abundance, duality, renewal, and the unknown in which our future, wishes, and fate lie.

Naming of the Runes

The people of those days lived amidst nature, and they discovered the 25 forces by observing the world around them. They understood that most things—like sheep and rocks—were mixtures of these forces, the way we today understand that most things are mixtures of different atoms.

But some things the ancients saw as composed of a single one of the forces. Just as we see iron as all one type of atom, they saw the wild ox as almost pure untamed force, ice as pure static force (stasis), and water as pure flowing force. That is how the runes got their names: Uruz (wild ox), Isa (ice), Lagu (water), and so on.

Cosmic Microchips?

To the Vitka, the shape of a rune was like a printed circuit on a microchip, channeling a specific cosmic force into a specific path to perform a specific task. Fehu (abundance) was for attracting prosperity, and Gebo (connection) was for bringing new opportunities into your life. When you work with a rune, you switch on its link to the cosmic force that it directs and release its energy to perform that task.

Take, for example, the first rune, Fehu. It looks like the English letter "F" with the two bars of the F directed upward at a 45° angle—a lot like an old-fashioned television antenna. Fehu's circuitry is for drawing down the cosmic force that fertilizes whatever it touches, creating prosperity, abundance, and wisdom.

However, what's important isn't *how* runes work, but that they indisputably *do* work. And, that you can learn to use runes to empower your own life.

Three Paths to Rune Power

Threes predominate in mystical systems. The goddess has three faces—girl, woman, and elder; I-Ching is read with three coins; words of power are often repeated three times; and the triangle, which has three points, plays a central role in astrological and rune readings. The magical significance of three comes down to us in folk sayings such as, "Three is a lucky number!" and "Good things come in threes."

Good things certainly come in threes where runes are concerned. For the ways of connecting with and channeling the power of the runes are also three. This trio of paths to rune power is:

- Rune reading
- Rune magic
- Rune meditation

Let's take a closer look at each of these.

Rune Reading

Readings are usually the first thing that comes to mind when people think of runes. Here, the power of the runes serves as a means of divination, for generating wisdom and insight. Rune stones answer questions (such as "Should I change jobs?" and "Why do all my romantic relationships end in disaster?"), or they shed light on difficult problems (like long-standing family feuds or how to surmount a business downturn).

Rune readings are also known as "rune castings" because the runes are cast or thrown. In a typical reading, someone with a dilemma gently tosses rune stones on the ground or a cloth. How the stones fall—which lie near and which lie far from each other, small groupings, and even geometric figures (several stones forming a cross or triangle, say)—provides a snapshot of the problem and clues to resolving it.

This might sound complicated, but anyone can learn rune reading with only a little practice—and, like riding a bicycle, once you acquire the knack, you never lose it.

Rune Magic

Stones, crystals, and rocks are traditional implements for channeling magical forces. So are talismans, charms, and amulets bearing mystical symbols. Rune stones by their very nature partake of the qualities of both, and so are especially suited to focusing the power of the runes to enhance your life and the lives of those you love.

Whether or not you've ever worked with magic, whether or not you even believe in magic, whether or not you think you have a single psychic or magical ability—with rune stones to aid you, you can quickly become a powerful practitioner of magic. Wield the forces embodied in the runes to help ailing friends, heal a lovers' quarrel, seal the success of a new business venture, draw money like a magnet, and more.

Rune Meditation

Meditation is a way of stilling the mind, to liberate it from inner and outer distractions. In the internal quiet this creates, tensions dissipate, a sense of well-being arises, and the "still, small voice of within" can be heard. Meditation can pave the way to physical vitality, professional success, and personal fulfillment. No wonder millions of people around the world take 15 minutes to a half-hour every day to practice some form of meditation.

Meditating on runes develops your rapport with the cosmic force linked to the runes. It furthers your understanding of the ideas and qualities each rune embodies. Finally, rune meditation opens the gateway to the secret wisdom of which runes are only the outward symbol.

Meet the Runes

Now that you know a bit more about them, it's time to get acquainted with the individual runes and their meanings. In each chapter, you'll find sections profiling one of the 25 runes. Each begins with the rune's image or symbol, along with its name and pronunciation. Beneath the name, you will find the portion of an Old English Rune Poem that peoples of medieval times used to help them remember the meaning of the rune. Next comes a description of the force in nature or human society that led to the naming of the rune, how the runic symbol or image relates to the meaning of the rune, and the larger symbolism of the rune. After this introduction you'll find further information on the meaning and use of the rune:

- *Rune Image* explains how the rune's shape is related to the object it symbolizes (the upward slanting lines of Fehu, for instance, represents the horns of cattle).

- *In Rune Reading* gives a thumbnail sketch of how to interpret the rune in divination when it lands faceup (indicating its energies are flowing freely) or lands facedown (indicating its energies are "occluded" or blocked); as well as comparing the rune to the Tarot card and astrological symbol it most closely approximates.

- *In Rune Magic* and *In Rune Meditation* suggest ways to use the rune to help yourself and others lead better, healthier, happier lives.

- *Rune Gods* tells you the name of the rune's guardian deity (or deities), who unlocks its forces for you during magical rituals and will provide further insights into their rune, if you but ask.

- *Rune Totems* lists the totem animals associated with the rune, which is particularly important when consulting or working with runes on issues of illness and health.

◢ *Rune Herb* and *Rune Color* list the herb to be burned as incense and the color of candle to be lit when working magic with the rune.

The following table tells which runes are profiled in which chapter.

Rune(s)	Profiled in Chapter ...
Wyrd (blank)	Introduction
Fehu, Uruz	1
Thurisaz, Ansuz	2
Raidho, Kenaz	3
Gebo, Wunjo	4
Hagalaz, Naudhiz	5
Isa, Jera	6
Eihwaz, Perdhro	7
Algiz, Sowilo	8
Tiwaz, Berkana	9
Ehwaz, Mannaz	10
Lagaz, Ingwaz	11
Dagaz, Othala	12

Rune #1: Fehu or Feoh

Prosperity is a blessing/to everyone/but share it freely/that God may continue/blessing you.

—*The Old English Rune Poem*

Fehu

Fehu (pronounced fay-who) is your rune of wealth—of inner and outward riches. It signifies both wisdom and prosperity. Fehu means "cattle"; to ancient peoples, cattle meant wealth. To these people, civilization began with cattle. In Norse mythology, the primal cow liberates the first human by licking them free from a prison of salt. So Fehu also symbolizes the primal creative force needed to bring anything into being.

Rune Image: Cattle tossing their horns high

In Rune Reading

Faceup meanings: Money, earned or inherited, fulfillment, abundance, prosperity, possessions, having enough (to share), luck, social success, foresight, wisdom, fertility, creative fire. *Tarot comparison:* The Tower. *Astrological comparison:* Aries.

Occluded (facedown) meanings: Loss of something important—unless you change your ways; the negative side of prosperity: waste, greed, jealousy, discord, poverty, stupidity. *Tarot comparison:* The Tower reversed. *Astrological comparison:* Aries afflicted.

In Rune Magic

Use to: Increase prosperity; boost your personal and professional success; move a project or relationship to the next stage; direct the runes' power for projecting energy and blessings during magical work

In Rune Meditation

Use to: Strengthen your natural psychic powers

Rune Gods: The Aesir, Nordic gods and goddesses who rule over the human realm

Rune Totems: Cattle, sheep, boars, horses, rabbits, bees, goats, chickens, geese, pigeons

Rune Herb: Nettle

Rune Color: Light red

Making or Buying Rune Stones

You'll receive many benefits from making your own rune stones. All that's really involved is drawing the runes on small rocks (as I'll discuss in a moment). But, if for some reason this is impractical, don't let it stop you from purchasing a set of rune stones. Buying them from a store or over the Internet is fine—over the long run you will establish the same connection and get just as much out of stones you purchase as stones you make. However, you'll learn the names and significance of each rune much more quickly if you fashion the stones with your own hands.

You'll also discover that in the process certain runes or the ideas associated with them may pique your interest or be easier to understand than others. Pay attention to these runes; the forces they represent play an important role in your life and will appear frequently in your future readings.

Making your own rune stones establishes a strong affinity between you and the stones. Everyone is born with natural psychic abilities, though few of us develop them in any way. Have you ever felt the phone was going to ring just before a friend called you? Or been on your way to work with a difficult decision to make against a deadline, and decided to blow it off and not decide—then arrived at the office to discover your instincts had been right and something unexpected had come up to render the decision unnecessary? When people who don't think they have any psychic abilities pause to reflect like this, they usually discover they have always had a definite psychic link to the things they are most involved with.

Finally, creating your own rune stones is fun. If it feels like a chore, don't do it. Buy yourself a set. Any object intended as a focus for mystical forces should only be made with an ungrudging heart that finds joy in the task—or not at all.

Stone lends itself well to use as an oracle because it is of the Earth herself. Stones have been forming their shapes for millions of years. It is said that earth currents, captured in the vibrations of the stones, stimulate the feminine-intuitive or right side of the brain.

—Deon Dolphin, *Rune Magic*

Finding Your Own Stones

The rune makers of antiquity lived in nature and were on watch for likely looking stones wherever they went. Today, many of us live in cities, away from the countryside. Getting out in the fresh air and sunshine is one advantage of looking for stones yourself.

Riverbeds and rocky hillsides are the places to begin your search. The ideal rune stone is flat enough that there are two distinct sides (so it will always fall on one side or the other in a reading), about one inch across, and roundish or oval shaped. Look for the kind of rocks kids like to skim across the water.

Although these stones are different shapes, each is ideal for carving or drawing runes.

Buying Blank Stones

Journeying to some idyllic spot in search of just the right stones isn't an option for everyone. You don't have to go any further than the local mall or the Internet to locate a perfect set of blank, unmarked stones. Trays heaped with smooth, polished rocks, crystals, and semiprecious gems of just the right size and shape await you at rock shops, new age emporiums, magic stores, and even some home and garden stores (and their Internet websites). After all, it's the rapport established by your personally drawing the runes on the stones that's important. To create it, all you really need are 25 blank stones.

Making Rune Stones from Clay

Clay is another wonderful natural substance for making rune stones, and working with it also creates a psychic link between you and the stones, because when you fashion the stones by hand it deepens your connection to them. Almost any crafts shop will have fast drying clay. It's a very inexpensive way to create your own stones and inscribing the runes on clay with a stylus is, literally, child's play—you probably learned how in kindergarten.

Adapt Game Tiles

Small flat wooden or plastic tiles with letters or numbers on them are standard equipment in children's and party games such as Scrabble. Just paint out the letter or number with white correction fluid, and draw your rune over it. Or turn the tile over and place the rune on the opposite side.

Buying Rune Stone Sets

By all means, buy a set of pre-made rune stones—if that's what fits your lifestyle. Internet shoppers can begin pricing rune stone sets right away. If you are the touchy-feely type who prefers to personally inspect the merchandise before purchasing it, locate the new age, magic, or women's bookstore nearest you.

There's a tempting variety to choose from. Handmade stones, with a rune lovingly carved into each, come in every conceivable hue—even striped and tiger's eye. Your choice of stone is just as broad—quartz, obsidian, moonstone, amethyst, and even beautifully polished river stone. Average prices range from $20 to $40, depending on where and what you buy. Through use, you will develop as strong a link with your stones as if you made them yourself.

How to Make Rune Stones

You don't need any artistic ability. Runes are composed of only a few straight lines and are easy to copy. If you can draw a capital "F" and "X" in English, you already have all the skills necessary to make your own rune stones. (See Appendix A for a look at all the rune designs and their key meanings.)

Rune stones are also cheap to make. There's nothing complicated or fancy to purchase. Besides the stones, all you need is an indelible marker and some shellac or clear nail polish. If you acquired your stones free in the wild, the total cost for a set other people charge $20 to $40 for will be under $5!

Odin and Freja, look upon my making with favor.
Let the marking and symbol empower it,
Let this rune faithfully guide the one who makes it.
   —Rune-maker's Hymn (trad.)

There are only two steps involved in making rune stones. What could be simpler?

1. Pick a stone and draw the first rune on it. Set it aside to dry while you draw the remaining runes on the other 23 stones (remember, one stone, the Wishing Stone, is left blank).

2. Coat the rune with a clear sealant to protect it from wear and tear (or coat the whole stone, if you like).

You now have your own personal set of rune stones. There, that was easy, wasn't it?

If you are really ambitious and artistically inclined, you can engrave the runes in your stones, and fill in the rune with a marker or paint. This gives them a more elegant appearance, and ensures that even if the ink wears off, the rune can still be read. Flecks of paint found in ancient runic inscriptions show that originally the stones were engraved and painted in exactly this way. Carving the runes isn't very difficult if you have a Dremel tool, or any other tool that can engrave a small straight line on a rock.

Consecrating Your Rune Stones

Consecrating any item you use for magic or meditation helps ensure its powers can only be directed toward good. On the night of the full moon, stand alone by a window where the moonlight can reach you if you are indoors, or directly in the open under its beams if you are out-side. Hold your rune stones cupped in your two hands and raise them toward the lunar orb. Chant the following:

Divine Freya, Goddess of the Moon and all Life,
In the name of the Aesir, Vanir, and the Norns,
In the name of the Ancestors and the Kin-Fetch,
May these runes be made sacred.
Consecrate and hallow these runes,
Fill them with your radiance and power.
May I use the sacred stones rightly,
May they bring me wisdom and well-being,
May I deserve the Gods' blessing.
In the name of the Aesir, Vanir, and the Norns,
Let the Goddess' will be done.

Storing Your Rune Stones

Practitioners who are learned in rune lore caution never to leave your stones loose where anyone can pick them up and handle them. This interferes with the psychic link between you and your stones. Of course, the situation is different when you are doing a reading for someone else; then you want that person to hold the runes for casting. But, otherwise it's a good rule to store your stones somewhere safe and out of sight when they are not in use.

Many people who work with rune stones keep them in a small cloth bag. (Most commercial sets come with one.) You can find drawstring bags or purses ready-made at Renaissance fairs, crafts shows, and new age shops. Or, should your tastes run a bit fancier, some people store their stones in those small wooden boxes with the intricately carved lids that you often see at import stores.

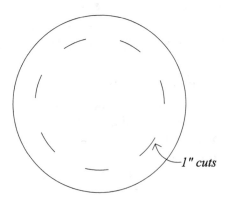

1" cuts

Pattern for Rune Pouch

Completed Pouch

Follow these guidelines to make a bag for your runes.

It's even easier to make a drawstring bag for your set than to make the stones. Select a piece of cloth you like and cut out a circle 12 inches in diameter. Go around the rim of the circle, and about every 3 inches make a small ¼-inch incision 1 inch in from the edge. Thread a piece of string through the incisions and draw it tight. Voilà! You have the perfect drawstring sack for your rune stones.

Rune Meditation: Experiencing the Power of Runes

This meditation in rune consciousness will give you the first real taste of the powers that lie within your rune stones. Ideally, you would do this meditation alone, outside in the heart of nature. When that's impractical, find a quiet, restful room, and arrange not to be interrupted for at least 20 minutes. Kneel or sit on the floor if possible, if not settle in a comfortable chair.

Hold all 25 rune stones in your cupped hands. Close your eyes (and keep them closed throughout this meditation). Take several long deep breaths to calm your mind and relax your body.

Mentally picture yourself sitting on a soft, grassy plain of deep emerald green. Not far to your right imagine a mighty forest, brown trunks shooting up to unfold in white blossoms against a vivid blue sky. To your left, visualize a clear, babbling stream rushing past. In the distance, a gray-skinned doe shyly nibbles the grass. The profound silence is broken only by the sibilant sigh of wind through the trees and the tinkling of the water.

When you have this picture as clear as you can get it, shift your attention to the runes in your hands. Feel their weight. How heavy are they? Become aware of their bulk. Do they fill your hands comfortably or do they threaten to spill over the sides?

How do they feel to the touch? Can you sense their round smoothness, if they are polished stones? Or their roughness, if they are of clay? Or their corners, if they were made from game tiles?

Now, go deeper. Open yourself to sensing the forces contained in your stones. The power of divination, the power of healing, the power of magic, the power of success and, greatest of all, the power of self-understanding are held in your two hands.

Can you feel the warmth this power radiates? Can you sense its tingling or vibration? Can you feel a warmth or buzzing moving up your hands into your arms and chest? When it reaches your head is there a slight shifting of awareness or perception?

If so, you have now tuned in a little way to the universe inhabited by runes and the cosmic forces they embody.

Open your eyes and look down at your rune stones. Do they seem to glow? Is their color more vivid? Do you see a faint aura around the edges of each stone? Do the runes seem to pulse?

This is the world as seen by Vitka when working with runes. Entering into this state before working with runes makes the reading, magic, or meditation that much easier and more effective.

While you still feel the power tingling in your body and still see a glow around the stones, picture whatever it is you most want runes to help you with—passing that real estate exam you have been cramming for, getting that promotion, keeping a friend in recovery, rekindling the intimacy you once had with your partner or spouse.

Now, say out loud the following prayer:

May the power granted by these runes,
pass out of my hands
and aid in [state your problem].

Visualize the energy that is buzzing through you, and radiating in the rune stones, streaming from your hands and entering your mental picture of what you want to happen. See that picture glow brightly and sparkle as the rune power leaves you and suffuses it. As you visualize this, you should sense the power of the rune stones draining away, though your palms and fingers might continue tingling for a while.

You have now experienced the power of the runes for yourself. Pay attention to how the situation you were concerned with turns out. The results may surprise you!

Your Radar Through the Seas of Life

Sailors crossing the ocean must keep informed of what the weather is like ahead, so that they can avoid storms in their path, or "batten down the hatches" and prepare to sail through those that can't be avoided. By night, they require some means of warning them when other ships and dangerous marine objects are nearby and threaten collision. At all times, they must be able to sound the depth of the ocean to within a few fathoms—so they know if it is safe to proceed or not.

Radar does all these for ships and their sailors. A radar screen displays a picture of everything around a ship within a circle dozens of miles wide—with the ship in the exact center. Those who know how can look at the white ghostly images on the radar screen and accurately estimate what they are, where they are, and what should be done about them.

Working with runes—particularly rune readings—is like having your own personal radar system to guide you through life's storms, treacherous currents, dangerous collisions, and shallows where you can no longer proceed on your original course.

Just like radar, runes are read on a circular "screen." Traditionally, three concentric circles, one inside another inside another, are drawn on the ground—or woven in a special "rune cloth." This screen captures a picture of your surroundings—past, present, and future—with you at the center.

The patterns runes make when they are cast speak volumes to an accomplished rune reader. Once you learn how, you can interpret the stones the same way radar experts interpret the ghostly images on a radar screen. Where the rune stones fall shows where each of the 25 cosmic forces is at work in your life at that moment.

In this sense, the popular conception of rune readings foretelling or predicting the future is wrong. A rune reading doesn't snap a picture of some predestined event—one that's fated to happen and cannot be changed or prevented. Rather, it presents an image of the forces—positive and negative—at work around you, showing how they are likely to interact if left to operate on their own, and the best path through them for you.

A rune reading, for instance, picturing a serious business reversal doesn't automatically condemn you to failure. The reading will also offer indications on how you can minimize and even prevent disaster. Fehu occluded (the image side is face down) might suggest you will need to put far more creative energy into it, if the business is to survive the coming months. Uruz in a key position—as part of a line of stones or triangle, for example—might indicate that far greater organization is needed.

Likewise, a reading that indicates you are about to meet your soul mate doesn't guarantee romance and marriage. How you react and the role you play in the relationship will determine the outcome. Ponder the reading closely enough and the rune patterns will reveal missteps you should avoid (like rushing headlong into the relationship) and self-defeating character traits you should beware of (like jealousy)—as well as desirable qualities (like humor and understanding) you would do well to capitalize on *before* Mr. or Ms. Right enters your life.

What to Ask the Stones

When should you turn to runes for guidance? Rune readings can help when …

- You have a specific problem or issue you can't seem to solve on your own.
- You have a general sense of unease or something being wrong, but aren't certain what is going on and need help formulating a question.
- You are certain you already know the answer, but others disagree and you want to double-check who is right.
- You want a quick picture of where you are, where you are headed, and the forces at work in your immediate surroundings.

Rune #2: Uruz or Ur

The wild ox is fearless/with great sharp horns/a savage beast/the horns are for fighting/as it roams the savage moorland/bravest of beasts.
—*The Old English Rune Poem*

Uruz

Uruz (pronounced ooo-ruze) is your rune of health and vitality—physical and mental. The wild ox of antiquity (the auroch) was a powerful creature so strong and hardy it thrived in the deadly moorlands—the perfect symbol of tenacity and health. Unlike domesticated cattle, the ox ran wild. So Uruz also represented untamed forces. When harnessed to the plow, the ox pulled left patterns in the soil and gave birth to agriculture.

Rune Image: The square horn of the wild ox

In Rune Reading

Faceup meanings: Strength, healing, courage, tenacity, strong emotions; untamed potential to organize, create, and make things happen; overcoming obstacles, improvement through effort, natural changes that should not be resisted (and are usually for the better). *Tarot comparison:* The High Priestess. *Astrological comparison:* Taurus.

Occluded (facedown) meanings: Illness, weakness, misdirected strength, brutality, violence, violent emotions, over-control or over-defensiveness, the untamed self, lack of will power, being led by others. *Tarot comparison:* The Tower reversed. *Astrological comparison:* Taurus afflicted.

In Rune Magic

Use to: Shape events into the pattern you desire; draw new personal and professional opportunities; promote healing of body and spirit

In Rune Meditation

Use to: Deepen self-knowledge and understanding

Rune Gods: The Vanir, Nordic gods and goddesses who rule over nature

Rune Totems: Oxen, bison, buffalo, bears, gorillas, dinosaurs, alligators, whales, dolphins

Rune Herb: Moss (sphagnum)

Rune Color: Dark green

Rune Reading: Choosing a Personal Rune of Guidance

Each of us has a personal Rune of Guidance. Out of the marked runes, there is one that best represents who you are. The meaning and symbolism of this rune reflect you with all your flaws and virtues, and points out the wisest course for you to sail in life. (You will probably find that this rune plays a prominent role in many of your readings.) Wherever your Rune of Guidance appears in a reading, play close attention to it. This stone represents your position in the situation and the key to its resolution.

The affinity between you and your Rune of Guidance is so strong that it will practically select you. In a quiet space where you won't be disturbed, stand or sit comfortably. Remove the blank rune stone, Wyrd, and set it aside. Cast the remaining runes by throwing them or spilling them from your rune stone bag.

Now visualize a circle drawn around the scattered stones before you, with one side at your feet and its farthest point directly opposite you. Picture a line drawn straight from where you are to the opposite side bisecting the circle. This line represents you going forward into the future, and your Rune of Guidance will be on it. Because it lies opposite you, this rune is said to act as a mirror and reflects your most essential characteristics as a person. For this reason, it is sometimes called the Mirror Stone.

To locate your Rune of Guidance, look straight down that imaginary line. One or more stones will lie on or close to that line. The rune stone that lies farthest from you—opposite you—on or near that line is your Rune of Guidance.

Sometimes the Rune of Guidance might lie quite close to you. There might be stones much farther away, across the circle, but off to the sides of the imaginary line. Sometimes, it may be in a cluster of several stones, all near the line, and you may have to look a moment to be certain which one is your Rune of Guidance. The two examples in the following illustration should help make it easy to locate this rune stone when you first perform this rune reading.

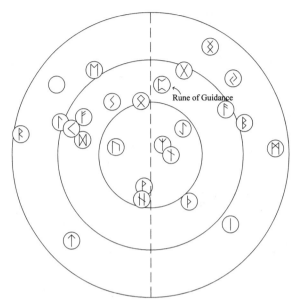

Two examples of how to locate your Rune of Guidance.

Study Your Rune of Guidance

Look in the Index and find the chapter where your rune is described (you can also see all the runes at a glance in Appendix A). Read the meanings carefully and consider how they apply to you. Most likely you will be struck by how uncomfortably close the fit is. Your pluses as a person will be represented by the description of the rune; your minuses by the description of the rune's characteristics when they are occluded.

If Uruz were your Rune of Guidance, your positive qualities would probably be physical or mental strength and drive, that you aren't easily daunted, and are a good organizer and leader who makes things happen. Your failings would likely be a tendency to heedlessly override the interests of others when they conflict with your own, or perhaps a lack of will power altogether, so much so that you are often the puppet of others.

When Your Rune of Guidance Doesn't Seem to Apply

When your Rune of Guidance doesn't seem to apply to you, don't dismiss it out of hand. My friend Sophia made that mistake. She didn't see any correspondences between her character and life and Naudhiz, Rune of Guidance she picked. Naudhiz, among other qualities, represents restraint, patience, and timely deliverance from distress. Sophia was impatient, mercurial, and always seemed to be in more trouble than she could get out of. Patience, restraint, and other qualities typically associated with Naudhiz were not among her more apparent character traits.

Years later, after smoothing out her life with meditation and therapy, Sophia became interested in runes again. She signed up for a course under a famous rune master. The first time they met, the modern-day vitki reached into his bag, and handed a stone to Sophia. "Here," he said, "this rune is you." It was Naudhiz.

By that time, Sophia had grown sufficiently to see that Naudhiz repre-sented not, as it often does, qualities she possessed when she first drew it—but those she had most needed to develop if she wanted to enjoy a rich, fulfilling life. Sophia would laughingly tell friends what a fool she had been and just how accurate her Rune of Guidance's assessment of her character had turned out to be.

The lesson? Trust your Rune of Guidance's evaluation of your person-ality. Look for similarities. The characteristics you are denying might be ones you don't want to admit you have. When this happens, meditate on your Rune of Guidance. There is always a positive side of any character-istic or quality, and this most personal of runes will show you how to transform negative aspects of your character and personality into positives.

The Negative Side

The Rune of Guidance also illuminates aspects of your character and behavior that are in need of work or transformation. Every positive qual-ity has its negative aspect. A sense of humor can be out of place; sticking up for yourself can end in bullying others; and patience can lead to action taken too late.

This is also true of the characteristics you share with your Rune of Guidance. The negative side of Fehu includes loss, poverty, ignorance, waste, greed, and discord. That of Kenaz includes creative energies out of control, destruction, and spiritual blindness. Where do you see the negative forms of the qualities embodied in your Rune of Guidance at work in your life? Be certain they are there. Recognizing them is the first step toward changing them. Later chapters will show you how you can use rune readings, magic, and ritual to transform your negative qualities into positive ones.

Rune Magic: Releasing the Power of Your Personal Rune

Because your Rune of Guidance embodies many of the same qualities you do, there is a natural resonance between you and it. Strengthen that channel and the result is clearer, easier-to-interpret readings, more powerful magical workings, and more profound and illuminating meditations. The following magical ceremony, adapted for modern rune workers from traditional sources, brings you and your Rune of Guidance into even greater rapport.

This ritual requires at least two candles. Four are better, set at the four points of a square large enough for you to kneel in comfortably. If you only have two candles, set one at least two feet away on each side of you. The candles should be the same color as the mystic color of your Rune of Guidance. Dark green candles, if it's Uruz, for instance.

First, light the candles. Then, in a small incense burner, burn a bit of the herb associated with your rune. Holding your Rune of Guidance in your cupped palms, kneel or sit in the middle of the square formed by your candles. For several minutes, concentrate on the rune, on its shape, on its name, on whatever positive and negative qualities you believe you share with it.

You gained experience getting in touch with the power of all the runes in the earlier rune meditation. This time the object is to tune in on the power of one rune—your Rune of Guidance. Rub it gently between your palms. Holding an image of the rune in your mind's eye, focus on its texture, temperature, and shape. Let this fill your senses until you are aware of nothing else.

By this point, you ought to be experiencing a warmth or tingling in your palms, just as you did in the previous rune meditation. Keep concentrating on your Rune of Guidance and rolling it between your hands until you feel the tingling move up your arms to your chest and head. When you sense the slight shift of consciousness (you may sense it as a feeling of light-headedness), you are in rapport with your rune and ready to commence the ceremony.

Raise your Rune of Guidance heavenward and chant:

By the powers of [say name of rune's Ruling God],
By the powers of Earth and Sky
Make of this rune
Breath of my breath
Bone of my bone.
Bind me to this rune
And bind this rune to me.
Let it guide my way
Wherever I go.
Let it shower upon me
Wisdom, and may I have
The wisdom to listen.
By the powers of Fire and Ice,
By the powers of [say name of rune's Ruling God],
Let the binding be done!

Bring your attention back to your rune stone. Typically, after this ceremony, people report their Rune of Guidance seems to shine more brightly or radiate with unusual warmth. Is there a strange sensation in your heart or chest area? Do you actually feel some emotion toward your rune? All these are signs that you have achieved your goal and established a deep-rooted connection with it.

When you are ready to conclude the ritual, snuff out the candle. If it is safe to so, allow the incense to burn itself out.

Rune Meditation: Getting in Tune with Your Rune

This meditation deepens your understanding of yourself through deepening your understanding of your Rune of Guidance and the qualities and connection you share. It also provides a taste of the transformative potential of the Rune of Guidance as a meditation device.

Quickly review the page in this book describing the rune that is your
Rune of Guidance. Take that rune stone and sit down in a place conducive to meditation. Hold the rune stone in your left hand as this is the
hand closest to your heart. Take a few deep slow breaths to unwind and
center yourself for meditation.

Gaze at the Rune of Guidance for a moment. Impress its shape into
your mind. Next, close your eyes and let the image of the rune come
back before your mind's eye.

Each rune is a pictorial representation or image of one of the embodi-
ments of 25 natural forces. Fehu's "F" shape with the two arms pointed
upward, the horns of a cow, for instance; the triangular point of Kenaz,
the upward dart of a flame. Whatever your Rune of Guidance, visualize
the object the rune represents superimposed over the rune's basic shape.
Picture the tossing horns of a cow in the same position as the arms of
Fehu; the dancing flame when Kenaz points upward.

When you have that image clearly before your closed eyes, try to see
the how the cosmic force or energy the object symbolizes permeates and
radiates from it. If you are visualizing Fehu, try to see, within the cow,
the blazing red of primal creative energy, the energy that gave birth to
the physical universe and that is necessary to the creation of anything—
from a fertile field to a new invention to a giant corporation, a love affair,
or a work of art. For Kenaz, visualize the golden, controlled glow of a
forge fire into which iron is being thrust for the making, the fire that
illuminates and consumes on both the material and spiritual planes.

Redirect your focus inward and seek this energy within you. Because
it is one of the forces out of which everything—including you—is made,
you will find this force vibrating within you, infusing your thoughts,
actions, and memories. You might see the primal creative energy in the
way you have created a home for your family, or in your music, or business or hobby or ceaseless flow of ideas. You might see the controlled
fire of Kenaz that creates and consumes in a fast-moving lifestyle, in a
personal spiritual quest, in an avocation that calls for creativity but also
constantly uses up or abandons old modes and models in favor of the
new (such as the computer technologies). When you are in contact with
that energy at work in your inner being and outward life, take a few
moments to feel it permeating you and radiating from you.

Now deepen your meditation on your Rune of Guidance. Call to mind some of the qualities and phrases associated with it. Fehu might bring to mind abundance, money, wisdom, and possessions. For Kenaz, you might remember creative energy put to use, inward or spiritual illumination, ability, regeneration, and creativity. Again, look for those qualities within you. When you find them, pause to meditate on ways in which they are reflected in your outward life.

By this point, you should be far more aware of some of the essential qualities that make you *you*. And, you should understand why that particular rune stone is your personal Rune of Guidance.

In the future, when you have a need for guidance, take this rune out, hold it in your hand, and repeat the preceding meditation. Before the meditation is over, you will have received the guidance you need.

Chapter 2

Runes of Self and Wholeness

Are you the person you want to be? Right now, in this moment of your life? Do you have everything you want to have? Have you done all that you would like to accomplish? Or are there parts of yourself you would like to change? Are there self-defeating, even self-destructive, attitudes and behaviors you'd like to change—drinking, spending, anger? Are there healthier qualities and abilities you would like to have—assertiveness, calm, freedom from substance abuse—but don't?

Can you honestly say you feel whole, healthy, happy, successful? Satisfied with who you are, who you know, and what you are doing?

If not, runes can change all that. Runes can help you erase destructive habits, germinate healthy behaviors, move from where you are as a person to where you would like to be. Whatever you lack—wealth, wisdom, the career of your dreams—runes can help you gain.

You can accomplish all this and more—when you begin to use runes as a tool for self-understanding. For self-understanding is the key to self-change, accomplishment, and becoming the person you have always pictured yourself being.

The Runic Path to Self-Understanding

Runes are almost without peer as a path to self-insight and self-transformation. That's because the runes are about you. Runes are linked to the 25 energies that make up the universe—and you are part of the universe. At any moment, runes can give you an accurate picture of how and where those energies are at work in you and your life.

"Know thy self!" is an old folk admonition that goes back to ancient Rome, at least. Even then, people realized the paramount importance of understanding yourself if you ever hope to direct the course of your life. You can't tune-up or repair a car if you don't know what's inside the engine and what forces are driving it, and you can't get your life on the track you want it on if you don't know what's inside you and what forces are driving you.

Another folk saying that applies to this situation is "Easier said than done!" The three-pound universe inside your skull is so vast, has so many corridors and chambers, so much of it remains buried out of sight, that it is impossible to explore or know it all without hours of expensive psychotherapy—or through rune readings.

> Runes reconnect you with your inner resources and wisdom. When you use runes, you increase your self-awareness, relieve stress, heal, and clear out blockages in your life.
>
> —Sirona Knight, *The Little Giant Encyclopedia of Runes*

Our Many Selves

One obstacle to knowing ourselves fully is that we actually have many selves. Psychotherapists tell us we all have an inner child, an inner parent, and an inner adult. Others add a happy self (the way you typically perceive and respond to the world when happy) and an unhappy self (a way you typically perceive and respond when unhappy). Still others add a critical self, a creative self, a spiritual self, a sexual self, a practical self, a conscious self, an unconscious self ... the list goes on.

So Much to Do

Another obstacle to self-knowledge is that we are all involved in so many activities so much of the time—appointments, work, family life, long commutes, social and charitable activities, friends, recreation. Naturally, our thoughts are scattered over such a wide area of our lives that it is difficult to find the time to focus on the big picture. When was the last time you paused to reflect on the whole pattern of your life and all the myriad elements in it? "Never!" is the typical answer.

What You'd Rather Not Know About You

There are some things we would just rather not know about ourselves. Things we dislike—aspects of ourselves we don't think are so attractive, are ashamed of, don't want others to find out about. Our mortifying secrets can encompass something we've done or failed to do: times when we were dishonest, hurt someone we loved, transgressed some shameful boundary, made a ghastly mistake, or surrendered to a self-destructive habit.

Flushed with embarrassment, we try not to think about these parts of our selves at all and shove them down out of sight anytime they begin to surface in our thoughts. We "put out of mind," "don't think about it," "bury it down deep," and "deny." We have many words for the way we put mental blinders on to our less desirable qualities and behaviors, because we do it so often.

It's natural not to want to dwell on what is hurtful to us, and often who we are and what we do are hurtful to us. But this reluctance to face our darker side keeps us from knowing ourselves—and thus from seeing how we got where we are and how we can move to where we want to be.

Discovering Your Strengths and Best Qualities

It's not merely our negative side that all these factors keep us from knowing. They keep us unaware of many of our best qualities, as well. Ignorant that we have attitudes and behaviors that could help us make more of our own lives, reach out more fully to others, and move closer to the person we dream of being, we stumble along, accomplishing only a fraction of what we might accomplish, if only we understood how strong the assets we do possess really are.

A rune reading captures the picture of your self that you don't have time to see, don't want to see, or may be overlooking. It paints a fully rounded portrait of you, in all your many aspects. It allows you to know yourself in a profound and meaningful way that generates the insights you need to begin the process of change and self-transformation.

Three Steps to Rune Reading

If you can remember three simple rules you can do rune readings. Interpreting the runes is just that easy. Once you learn this trio of rules, your mastery of rune readings is only minutes away.

To interpret a rune reading, look for stones that ...

1. Make patterns or shapes with other stones.
2. Lie close or far from others.
3. Land faceup or facedown ("occluded").

There are a few other frills and flourishes you'll learn later in this book. But these three are the basics. With them in mind, even if you never read that far, even if they are the only thing you learn about rune reading, you'd be able to glean all the essentials of a reading, every time.

During your initial readings, you will probably have to look up the meanings of the individual runes several times until you learn them all. But looking runes up this way, in conjunction with a reading, will impress them more quickly and deeply on your mind. So it won't be long before you've memorized the whole 25—often in no more than two or three readings.

Stones That Make Patterns

What does looking for patterns mean? The best answer is that you will know when you see them. Even if the pattern seems vague to you, if your intuition suggests a shape, don't block it out. You don't need to be psychic to read the runes, but you do need to use your intuition.

Typically, when you look at the way the stones have fallen in a reading, you will notice that some of them form patterns. Lines, triangles, and clusters are common patterns. Certain patterns symbolize relationships between forces in your life that interact harmoniously. Other configurations indicate runes whose energies interact inharmoniously.

Sometimes these are called positive and negative configurations, but this is a misnomer. There are no negative aspects in rune readings, only inharmonious ones. But what is inharmonious can be harmonized. In short, such patterns are not truly negative because each apparent difficulty also holds an opportunity—if you look for it—as symbolized by the rune Thurisaz.

The forces represented by runes in certain patterns work harmoniously together. These runes reinforce each other and blend their energies well— just like notes in music. Runes that touch, lines, and triangles are among the more harmonious configurations:

- *Stones that touch.* The forces symbolized by these runes are so harmonious they act together almost as one. The powers of runes that touch are said to be multiplied by the number of runes touching. When two runes touch, their effect is doubled; when three touch their power is tripled, and so forth.

- *Straight or curved lines.* These are also called "lines of power." Runes that are part of such a line indicate the special strengths of the person being read for. Such lines should be read like a sentence or paragraph that begins, "These are _____'s best qualities."

- *Triangles.* The triangle has been recognized as a symbol of wholeness and well-being since ancient times. Sacred and mystical designs frequently incorporate triangular shapes and configurations. A triangle is the least number of lines that can enclose a space and is one of the most inherently stable of structures. (Unlike a square or rectangle, they cannot easily be made to collapse.)

As I've said, some configurations are inharmonious. Like certain notes in music, they are dissonant and jarring. Rather than working together to further your life, these runes disrupt each other's forces—so that their effectiveness is undercut or paralyzed. Energies of runes that form patterns such as squares and rectangles, or rune stones that lie at the opposite sides of a reading, always conflict:

- *Squares.* Squares have four corners formed by lines that form 90° angles. When forces intersect at this angle, they cross each other. Runes at the corners of squares are therefore said to work at cross-purposes—each undercutting the other's energies.

- *Rectangles.* A rectangle is one of the least stable shapes in geometry. One side is already over-balanced and a rectangle will easily collapse unless it is well braced. The energies embodied in runes that form rectangles tend to collapse in a heap and remain inert.

- *Stones at opposite ends.* When two runes lie on the opposing sides of a reading, the forces they symbolize oppose—and so block or neutralize—each other. Such runes represent key parts of the life or self that are in conflict.

Stones That Lie Close to or Far from Others

How near or distant stones land from each other also sheds important light on a rune reading. Frequently several stones will land together in a cluster; likewise, in many readings, one or more stones will land far from the others, isolated and alone:

- *Clusters.* Runes that form a small grouping when they land are a sign of a strong area of energy or activity in your life. Clusters are generally harmonious and the forces embodied in the runes work together. However, look for other rune stones outside the cluster that may form inharmonious, disruptive patterns with the runes in the cluster.

- *Isolated runes.* Sometimes runes land alone, in areas bare of other stones. Generally, the energy of the rune will also be isolated and shed very little influence on the others in the reading. But because the rune is the only one in the region, its influence will reign supreme throughout. Isolated though it is, such a rune might also form patterns with other runes much farther away and through them have a significant effect on the overall reading.

Stones Land Faceup or Facedown

When you throw the rune stones, some land faceup, with the image side showing; and some facedown, with the blank side showing. When the latter happens, the facedown stone is said to be "occluded." When runes are occluded, the energies they are linked to are either blocked entirely or working outside your conscious awareness.

In some readings, stones that are faceup represent the conscious mind, while those that fall facedown represent the unconscious. In other readings, a faceup stone indicates that the energy embodied in the rune is active in the conscious areas of your life, while a facedown stone suggests its energy is active in areas and ways of which you are unaware. In both cases, when you turn a facedown rune faceup to read it, you become aware of those forces, which is the first step toward making the best use of them.

This is one of the most important ways in which runes promote growth, transformation, and healing. In leaving no stone unturned, you bring to consciousness elements of your life that otherwise would lie in shadow. Having uncovered these previously unsuspected aspects of yourself, you are in a far better position to accept, harmonize, and harness them—making you a saner, healthier individual in the long run.

Interpreting Rune Readings

When you take your first look at the way runes have fallen in a reading, they may appear to be nothing more than a random scattering of stones. But keep focusing on them. No matter how jumbled the reading seems, you will soon begin to notice patterns.

To interpret or understand a reading, simply read each configuration of runes as if it were a sentence in a letter. In fact, that is precisely what a reading is—a letter from some higher or inner realm with an important message meant for you. Begin reading a pattern by phrasing it in a sentence. You might begin something like this:

These runes touch, they work together as one, and their power is multiplied by ...

These runes form a line, they are harmonious and suggest [name of person being read for]'s best qualities are [insert qualities associated with these runes].

These runes are opposite each other, they are inharmonious and suggest [insert qualities associated with these runes] oppose and neutralize each other in [name of person being read for]'s life or personality.

Rune #3: Thurisaz or Thorn

The Thorn cuts sharply/into everyone who grasps it/and is an agony to anyone/who lies amidst it.

—*The Old English Rune Poem*

Thurisaz

Thurisaz (pronounced thur-ee-saws) is your rune of defense and of opportunities found in troubles. Thorny bushes (thurisaz), cut down and tied together (later cultivated and grown in rows) were the first fences, penning livestock safely in so they did not stray, while keeping wolves and enemies out. Plants with thorns often have beautiful flowers, just as in life there are problems and in every problem an opportunity. To the people of ancient times, thorns symbolized both the power of defense and the silver lining in every cloud.

Rune Image: The sharp point of a thorn

In Rune Reading

Faceup meanings: Protection against unfriendly forces, defense, organization, opportunities in difficulties. *Tarot comparison:* The Emperor. *Astrological comparison:* Mars.

Occluded (facedown) meanings: Obstacles, problems, destruction, barriers, enmity. *Tarot comparison:* The Emperor reversed. *Astrological comparison:* Mars afflicted.

In Rune Magic

Use to: Ward off harm from adverse events, emotion, people; work male sex magic; move a negative situation to a positive outcome

In Rune Meditation

Use to: Deepen awareness of your strength and resiliency; find opportunities in setbacks; lower emotional barriers and become less defensive; further your awareness of the separateness and unity of the cosmos

Rune Gods: Thor, God of Thunder; Thrud, daughter of Thor
Rune Totems: Dogs, geese, pigs, cats, elephants, wolves, lions, tigers
Rune Herb: Leek
Rune Color: Red

Sample Reading

The following sample rune reading has been slightly adapted from one I did a few years ago for a woman I will call Marcia. She was interested in runes and wanted a general reading to see what insights they might offer about her self. (In this reading and all other sample readings presented in this book, stones that landed facedown are shaded in the artwork to distinguish them from stones that landed faceup.)

I knew very little about her other than her name when the reading began. Everything I learned came from the runes. Take a few minutes and try to read Marcia's runes yourself. Just remember the guidelines for interpreting runes. Watch for stones that:

1. Make patterns or shapes with other stones.
2. Lie near or far from others.
3. Land faceup or facedown (occluded).

And read the runes like the words and sentences in a book.

Go with your intuition, and you may be surprised by how just how good the result is. My interpretation follows the illustration.

The runes are not a fortune-telling device but rather a way of reading the present time patterns in a person's life, although both past and future may be seen in the context of the reading. Through casting and interpreting the runes, we discover new ways of viewing the forces within ourselves and new ways of using these energies to resolve the problems in our lives.

—Camden Benares, *An Essay on Runes*

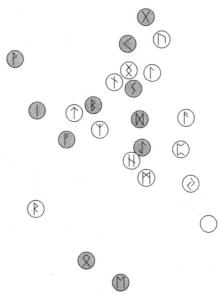

Marcia's reading.

Just taking an overall look, you can see that the stones are widely scattered. In a reading about the self, this shows that Marcia is a person with a diverse range of interests and activities, and is not narrowly focused on one facet of life to the exclusion of all else.

The next thing that really stands out visually is the line of three occluded stones rising up from Eihwaz (which lies roughly near the center) through Dagaz to Sowilo. When your eye gets that far, it is easy to see that this line of facedown stones skips over one faceup rune and extends on through Kenaz and with a slight turn to Gebo. Once you see this arrangement of occluded stones you will probably notice that it extends downward from Eihwaz (skipping over another faceup rune) to Thurisaz and Mannaz.

In fact, this line of occluded runes roughly bisects the reading from bottom to top. Having seen it, you might notice another line of facedown stones that almost bisects the reading. This one runs from right to left beginning with Ansuz and extending through Dagaz and Beork. Nor does it take much imagination to see this line of occluded runes dipping slightly to pass through Fehu and then running up to include Isa and Wunjo.

Remember, lines of runes like this, straight or curved, are lines of power, and represent a person's strengths. As the stones lie facedown, it suggests that Marcia is not aware of many of her best qualities and that they are almost instinctive with her.

What are Marcia's strengths as a person? Beginning with the most pronounced line, the vertical one, read it as if it were a sentence from bottom to top. The runes say Marcia's best qualities are Mannaz (social skills, liking for other people), Thurisaz (ability to transform defeat into victory), Eihwaz (ability to manage and direct), Dagaz (taking it easy gives ability to harmoniously balance differing or opposing forces and people), Sowilo (vitality to overcome difficulty), Kenaz (positive attitude and a strong connection with the still small voice within), and Gebo (ability to work with others, to make connections between others).

The horizontal line, reading from left to right, as if you were reading a book, says Marcia's other key strengths are Wunjo (joy, inwardly and the ability to create it), Isa (caution, slow expansion), Fehu (material and spiritual riches), Berkana (nurturing, giving), Dagaz (taking it easy gives ability to harmoniously balance differing or opposing forces and people), and Ansuz (wisdom, the ability to communicate it and receive it).

You've probably noticed several recurring themes in this runic description of many of Marcia's best traits. The most frequently reiterated suggests she possesses exceptional people skills: Mannaz (social skills, liking for other people), Eihwaz (ability to manage and direct), Dagaz (taking it easy gives ability to harmoniously balance differing or opposing forces and people), Gebo (ability to work with others, to make connections between others), Wunjo (joy, inwardly and the ability to create it), Berkana (nurturing, giving), and Ansuz (wisdom, the ability to communicate it and receive it).

Another related theme in these two intersecting lines of runes relates to what we would today call managerial ability. In addition to people skills, which are essential to being a good manager, Marcia's runes are strong in several other areas essential to managerial excellence: Thurisaz (ability to transform defeat into victory), and the allied Wunjo (ability to turn things around), plus Isa (caution, slow expansion), Fehu (material and spiritual riches), Sowilo (vitality to overcome difficulty), and Kenaz (positive attitude and a strong connection with the still small voice within).

Significantly, both lines cross at Dagaz, rune of balanced polarities. This is a clue that harmony and balance are the axis around which Marcia's world revolves. Furthermore, here, at the very symbol of two forces intersecting harmoniously, two lines of unconscious traits meet. Surely, a personality represented by such a configuration of runes will be almost instinctively well-balanced, and her or his most prominent characteristics will work together harmoniously.

There's one last configuration that leaps out at you once you start to see the stones this way. Near the middle of the reading, two runes, Eihwaz and Hagalaz, touch each other. Physical contact between stones means the forces embodied in the two runes will work together as one and each will be doubly powerful. Because Hagalaz often stands for the organized direction and management of energies and Eihwaz symbolizes problems that have opportunities concealed within them, these runes suggest someone who will be a good manager in large part because of her talent for seeing solutions where others only see problems.

At this point in the reading, I told Marcia that, taken together, these two lines suggested she would be a people-oriented person, with highly developed social skills and critical managerial assets. I would expect such a person would have a responsible job working with others, probably at a supervisory level, would enjoy spending her free time with friends and family, and to be valued for her knack for getting along well with others, even in the most trying of circumstances.

Marcia was surprised at how accurate her runic portrait was. She explained that she was the office manager for a large, prestigious law firm. Every day she had to interact with the firm's exacting partners, its worried clients, hostile opposing attorneys, and a staff of more than two dozen secretaries, office aids, and paralegals. It was an environment of constant crisis and personality conflict, yet Marcia handled it all with such unflappable aplomb and kept the office running so smoothly that twice when she had tried to quit, the firm had made her an offer she couldn't refuse in the form of a very significant raise in pay.

Furthermore, Marcia was deeply involved with her family. She made a four-hour drive every Friday night to spend the weekend at her parent's home, with them and her youngest sister who was attending a local college. As might be expected of someone with a reading like hers, Marcia never missed a family celebration, and was present at both her brothers' graduations and weddings, and at the christening of all three of her nephews.

The two crossing lines of stones and the two runes that touch are the most significant patterns dominating Marcia's reading. There are a few smaller configurations, and you should pat yourself on the back if you noticed them. You have the kind of eye it takes to become an expert rune reader.

No reading is complete, however, until you have considered both the Rune of Guidance and the blank Wishing Stone or Rune of Fate. In Marcia's reading, the blank rune has fallen far to the side of the rest of her stones. Its position indicates that her deepest wishes, and perhaps the sphere she will ultimately come to occupy in life, lie far outside her current sphere of interests and activities.

Marcia confirmed this. Though she loved her work, and loved being around people, her longtime dream was to buy a small house in the country and start a new career making pottery. At the moment this seemed an impossible dream, because her job and the need to finish paying off her college loans kept her chained to the city.

I might have guessed Marcia's dreams centered on creativity, as the Wishing Stone is also a symbol of pure creativity. For, what is creativity if not our deepest dreams made manifest. Because the rune was isolated, creativity would naturally extend a strong influence over the unfulfilled part of her life.

Though I said nothing about it at the time, Marcia's Rune of Guidance, Thurisaz, seemed to point the way toward a future solution to her problem. Note that Thurisaz can be seen as the center stone in a line running from left to right connecting Marcia's Wishing Stone with Othala (family support, inheritance). Three years later, a family inheritance made it possible for Marcia to realize her dream. Today she is a successful, prize-winning potter.

If you didn't notice all these aspects of Marcia's reading, don't be discouraged. Keep working at rune interpretation. You will find you acquire the knack easily enough after only a few tries.

Rune Reading: Instant Self-Assessment

Now it's your turn to take a runic self-portrait. Runes will reveal your strongest assets as a person, even those you are unaware of, as well as your deepest wishes and how you can make them a reality. This reading will also give you your first opportunity to read the runes on your own.

Don't begin this exercise until you can settle down alone and be alone with your thoughts for at least 20 minutes. You'll get much more out of the reading, in terms of insight and self-understanding, if you are not interrupted. You also need to have already discovered your Rune of Guidance—as described in the previous chapter.

Take all the rune stones in your hand and toss them onto a table or a rug. Look them over carefully after they land, keeping the basic guidelines you've learned in mind. As you study the runes, ask yourself: Do I see any patterns? Are they positive or negative? Do I see runes that lie near to or far from other runes? Which stones are faceup and which facedown?

Take your time and make your first rune reading (and for that matter, every rune reading) a meditation. Rune readings are not meant to be rushed through. You are being gifted with insight and wisdom not normally accessible to you—and you should show proper appreciation by taking the time to glean all you can from the stones.

Understanding the Three Circles of Self

There's more to you than just the conscious part of you that is reading this book and thinking about what you are reading. There are all your memories, feelings, attitudes, interests, habits, and reactions that aren't in play at the moment. This part of you that lies outside your conscious awareness is sometimes called the "unconscious."

There is also more to you than just yourself; you're not a solitary, isolated individual. Nearly every minute of every day, you are interacting with other people. Unless you have a very unusual occupation and lifestyle, you spend the majority of your waking hours surrounded by and relating to others—from the workplace to the store, from the gym to home, on the subway or shopping at the supermarket. And, some of these people—family, friends, lovers—probably mean as much to you as yourself (maybe more).

While a general rune casting can give you a remarkably accurate portrait of who you are, it is in a sense a one-dimensional picture. For complete self-understanding you also need to be able to see what is going on with all three selves—your inner self, conscious self, and outward self. There's no point in attempting to transform yourself into a $5 million a year sales executive if what you really yearn for deep down inside is to spend your life on a deserted shore, alone, painting the waves. Nor are you likely to succeed in a blockbuster sales career if you are someone who loathes being around people.

Traditional rune reading, as practiced by the Vitka, provides something more like a three-dimensional video of this trio of selves in action. Vitka read the runes on three concentric rings drawn on the ground with their staffs, or on a cloth with three concentric white circles woven into the fabric. The inner circle symbolized the inner self, the middle circle the conscious self, and the outer circle the outward self that interacts with other people.

This traditional Celtic design is an artistic representation of the three rings of self. Although few are now aware of it, this design was originally created for use with rune readings.

Circle of Inner Self

The center circle represents your inner self in all its aspects—the unconscious, the spiritual, the shadow side, vulnerabilities, fears, the dreams you fear to dream, and more. This circle, like your inner being, lies hidden beneath your conscious self and outward self. It contains the fundamental building blocks of your character, the basic dynamics of your life, the very essence of your being.

Circle of Conscious Self

The middle circle represents your conscious self in all its aspects—your thoughts and feelings, aspirations, awareness of self, ego, hatreds, and more. This circle, like your consciousness, rests on the surface of the inner self and looks out toward the world and people around you. It contains the fundamental building blocks of your personality, the way you act and react, the person that you think you are.

Circle of Outward Self

The outer circle represents your outward self in all its aspects—you as a social animal, the face you put on for the world, your feelings for and about others, the different selves you are with different people, and more. This circle, like your outward self, is an outer layer that rests on and partially obscures your conscious self, and almost completely obscures your inner self. It contains the fundamental building blocks of your image, the way you react to others and others react to you, the persona others perceive as yours.

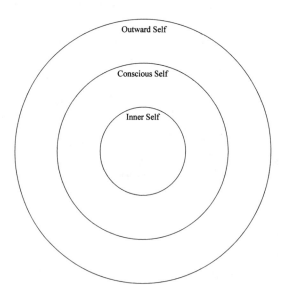

The three concentric circles as typically used in rune readings today.

Interpreting the Three Circles of Self

Now that you have absorbed the basics of reading the runes, you won't experience any difficulty in interpreting a reading using the Three Circles of Self. In addition to the guidelines you have already learned about general rune interpretation, look for the following:

- *Patterns of stones continued from one circle to another.* These indicate that the qualities of the self (represented by the runes) play an important role in all the levels of the self (represented by the circles the runes cross). A triangle formed by a rune in the outer circle and two in the middle circle would mean the energies represented by those stones would work at cross-purposes in both the conscious and outward self. A straight line of rune stones running from the inner circle to the middle one might suggest that the runes involved worked together harmoniously in the inner and conscious selves.

- *Times when most stones end up in a single ring.* An introverted or inward-directed person will tend to cast their rune stones so the majority land in or near the inner circle, which represents the inner self. An extroverted person will tend to cast them so that more fall in or near the outer ring, which represents the outward self. Those who are reasonably well balanced between introversion and extraversion will tend to throw stones so that they land in or near the middle circle—or spread out evenly over all three.

- *Stones that have landed in the exact center.* Runes don't always land there—but when one (or more) does, it has great significance. The energy symbolized by that rune is the hub of the wheel of your life at the moment, and everything in it revolves around that particular energy and how you handle it.

- *In which circle individual stones have fallen.* Which rune falls inside which circle indicates which area of your life the force embodied in the rune is operating in. Apply what you know about patterns and groupings to the stones within that circle—and your reading is complete.

- *Stones that fall outside the rings.* Sometimes runes will scatter beyond the third ring. These indicate vital elements that for some reason are missing from your life at present. When this happens, examine the reading for any relationship between these runes and the stones that landed within the three circles. These will offer clues to how you can bring these energies into your life.

Begin interpreting the rune stones with those that have fallen in the Circle of Inner Self, then proceed to the middle ring, and so forth. This way you read the runes from the inside out—which is the only way anyone can be truly understood.

The stones in the center circle reveal the forces at play below the threshold of consciousness. Runes that land there manifest their energies in your inner realm of memory, the unconscious, spirituality, and your shadow side. They shine a light on what is transpiring deep inside the part of you that is otherwise difficult to get in touch with or see.

On those rare occasions when no runes land in the inner circle, it points toward two possibilities. The first, and most common, is that the person being read for is currently cut off from her or his inner self. The second, and less likely, is that little or nothing significant is manifesting through the person's inner life at the moment—leaving it lacking in both creativity and conflict.

Second, examine the runes in the Circle of Conscious Self. Stones in the middle ring reveal the forces at work in your conscious mind and personality at the time of the reading. Runes that land there manifest their energies in your realm of awareness—thoughts, feelings, goals, daydreams, personality. They show you all that goes on in your conscious, which you are ordinarily too busy mentally to be fully aware of.

Finally, turn your attention to whatever stones lie in the Circle of Outward Self. Runes in the outer circle reveal the forces at work in your relations with other people. They manifest their energies through your interactions with those in your life or about to enter your life—family, friends, lovers, co-workers, strangers you encounter along the way. These stones offer a clear look into what is otherwise a complex dance of self with others that moves too quickly and intricately to be clearly seen.

Rune Cloths

Unless you live by a park, drawing three circles in the dirt, like the Vitka of ancient times, may not be practical. For this reason many Vitka began carrying handmade rune cloths with the three circles woven (or sometimes painted) into the fabric. They merely had to spread out the cloth and they were ready to read runes or work rune magic.

Rune cloths aren't nearly as personal as rune stones, so you don't need to make one unless you really want to. Any scarf or square piece of fabric with three concentric rings or bands of color on it will do. Or the traditional Celtic design shown earlier, like rune stones, is available at many new age type stores and over the Internet.

If you don't have a scarf or piece of fabric, you can use paper instead. Get a pad about two feet long and two feet wide at an art or crafts store. With a compass draw three equally spaced concentric circles. Tear the sheet out, lay it on a table or the floor, and you have a set of rune casting circles as good as any a vitki ever drew in the earth with a staff.

If you're making your own cloth, select a light, solid color. That will be less visually distracting and make your circles stand out more vividly. Scarves of this type are easy to find, or pick out a color and texture you like at a fabric store. Look for square cloths. A circle will fit more snugly in a square. Your cloth will take up less space and won't have useless ends sticking out on two sides of the circle.

For your circles, use a waterproof, indelible marker, just like you did for making your rune stones. Be sure to fasten your cloth down at all four corners with tacks or tape before you begin, so the fabric remains steady while you draw the circles—otherwise, they will come out misshapen. One way to make the circle is with a compass, just like on paper. Another is to use three kitchen canisters that come in sets, each slightly larger than the next, and trace around the bottoms.

Making the rune cloth is simpler than making stones or a rune pouch and only takes a few minutes. When you have your rune cloth, you are ready to begin your first advanced rune reading.

A Second Sample Reading

Again, to take the fear out of the process, here's a sample reading that will give you a sense of what interpreting runes with the Three Circles of Self is like. To make it even easier, we'll use the arrangement of runes stones you are already familiar with from the first sample reading earlier in this chapter. These were the runes Marcia cast. I originally had her throw them on a rune cloth with three circles. So here you see them as I saw them, lying inside the three circles.

With the experience you've gained during the Instant Self-Assessment reading you will probably find that insights into the meaning of the runes in a three-circle reading come to you readily.

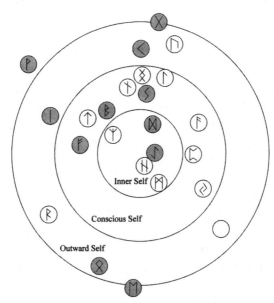

Marcia's original reading showing where her rune stones fell on the Three Circles of Self.

The first thing you are likely to notice is that the vertical line of occluded stones running all the way from Mannaz at the bottom to Gebo at the top literally runs through and connects every circle of the self. And, so does the horizontal line extending from Ansuz on the right to Wunjo on the extreme left. This signifies that unlike many people, Marcia is in touch with all three aspects of herself, as these runes show strong linkages or channels of communication between them.

Through Algiz the double triangle formed by that rune with Berkana and Tiwaz and by Algiz and Tiwaz with Fehu, extends through the inner and middle circles. Here is another hint as to why Marcia puts others and her job before her own dreams and things that would nurture her. The conflicts between her need to nurture, her sense of self-protection, her motivation, and her desire for spiritual as well as material success encompass both her inner self and her conscious self—making them very difficult to resolve.

A slight majority of the stones ended up in the Circle of Conscious Self, showing Marcia is neither an introvert nor an extrovert. Instead, she is a well-balanced personality that is a happy blend of the two.

You can also see what a bull's-eye Hagalaz made, landing in the exact center of the Circle of Inner Self. This reinforces the theme of the two lines of stones: that people are the hub around which Marcia's world revolves.

Wynn has landed completely outside the three circles implying that joy is missing from Marcia's life. Considering the challenges of her job and her secret desire to move to the country and become a designer and maker of pottery, this is not surprising.

Rune Reading: Discovering Your Three Circles of Self

At a suitable time and place, when you are alone, lay out your rune cloth. Relax and quiet your mind. Then invoke the gods' guidance. Say:

Great Odin, who brought
these runes
from the darkness
to light our way
guide my hands
direct my mind
that I might sup
of their wisdom.

Cast the stones onto the cloth. Try not to cast them from too high a level, or they will bounce and scatter in all directions. Don't drop them from too low a level, or most of them will land in a heap. It might take some experimentation to make all the stones fall right and stay on the cloth, but you'll soon get a feel for it. As late runeologist Deon Dolphin used say, "Above all, do whatever feels right to you and they will land in the most perfect way."

Keeping in mind what you have learned about a Three Circles of Self reading, ponder the way the stones have landed. Ask yourself if there are patterns of stones that involve more than one circle. What do those patterns say about the runes in relation to the circles they extend across?

Look for a circle that has more stones in it than the others. Ask yourself what that says about introversion versus extroversion. Look for stones that fell in the exact center. Ask yourself what this rune says about the forces on which your life turns. Look for stones that fall outside the rings. Ask yourself what this says about elements missing from your life. Finally, consider in which circles individual stones have landed.

When you have gleaned all you feel you can from the reading, express your gratitude to Odin for whatever insights you have gained. Say:

Thank you, Great Odin,
for the blessing
of runes
and the gift
of this wisdom.

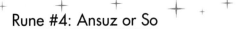

Rune #4: Ansuz or So

The mouth is the source of speech/the foundation of wisdom/provides comfort to the wise/bestows happiness and consolation for everyone.

—*The Old English Rune Poem*

Ansuz

Ansuz (pronounced awn-sooz) is your rune of communication and the wisdom it bestows. The mouth (Ansuz) symbolized the discovery of speech and the ability to communicate with each other, a breakthrough that still held great significance for the peoples of antiquity. It made working together, the passing on of knowledge, and the sharing of wisdom—and therefore logic, science, and civilization—possible. Because speech is two-way, the mouth represents both the imparting and reception of knowledge, spiritual as well as material.

Rune Image: Lips on a mouth

In Rune Reading

Faceup meanings: An important communication or piece of advice, spiritual illumination, literary arts, the use of knowledge or reason, the learning process, inspired mental activity and genius, verbal assistance from others, an impending test, exam, or interview. *Tarot comparison:* Death. *Astrological comparison:* Pluto.

Occluded (facedown) meanings: Missed communication, spiritual blindness, being tongue-tied or stuck for the right words, lies, trickery, deceit, bad advice, verbal interference by others, refusal to learn. *Tarot comparison:* Death reversed. *Astrological comparison:* Pluto afflicted.

In Rune Magic

Use to: Strengthen rituals, send energy, help or healing, charms, and other magical powers; shape-shifting to transform yourself mentally, emotionally, spiritually, physically; develop clairvoyance; convince others and win them to your viewpoint

In Rune Meditation

Use to: Stir creative inspiration in the literary and verbal arts; discover the best way to communicate your ideas to others; receive divine wisdom and guidance

Rune Gods: Odin, the All-father, as father of wisdom who brought the gift of communication (runes); Frigga, the All-mother, who put runes to use for teaching and learning

Rune Totems: Hounds, wolves, tigers, lions, elephants, chimpanzees, hyenas, owls, song birds

Rune Herb: Fly agric

Rune Color: Dark blue

Rune Magic: Attuning Your Three Selves

Often our lives are out of kilter because our three selves are not attuned. Sometimes all three may be out of harmony with each other. Sometimes two may be aligned while one is out of tune. Like a car engine needing a tune-up, until all three selves are in harmony and working together, your life will be full of false starts, stalls, and run slowly and fitfully, if at all.

Your inner self might be blocked off from your interactions with the outside world, like when you feel miserable all the time, but put on a happy face to everyone else (or when it is inharmonious with the direction your conscious self has taken as a career, like when you have an office job but your inner self is nourished by outdoor activity). Your outward self might respond to one particular kind of potential lover (someone exciting and dangerous), while your inner self and conscious self know this is the wrong kind of relationship for you and always turns out badly.

In this magical ceremony you will learn how to use the power of the runes to attune your three selves. As always, you will want to be in a quiet place where no one will disturb you. In addition to your runes, you will need a cloth or large sheet of paper with the Three Circles of Self clearly marked, an incense burner, a bit of the herb heartsease, and a dark blue candle.

Darken the room. Light the candle, place the heartsease in the incense burner, and light it, too. Sit down before the three circles.

You will be placing Gebo in the center of the Circle of Inner Self because it is the rune of connecting, of the intersection of things and forces. Positioning it at the center of all three circles creates a place where the energies represented by the three circles can meet and be harmonized. The arms of the "X" act like a circuit, along which the energies of inner self can move outward to the other selves and along which their energies can move inward.

In rune magic, Gebo's powers can be focused to increase harmony in relationships. In this ceremony, it will become a vehicle for increasing harmony between all three of your selves, bringing them into greater alignment. Gebo's unique potential is also used for connecting streams of runic energy. Here, it will conduct runic energy in a stream along the axis made by Gebo, your Rune of Guidance, and the Wishing Rune, and it will open the channels of communication between all three levels of your self.

You will put the Rune of Guidance in the Circle of Conscious Self because it is your conscious self that needs to be guided to greater knowledge of your inner and outward selves. In addition, laying it there in this ceremony creates a magical bridge that enables energies to pass back and forth from Gebo to Wyrd, linking all three selves.

Finally, you will lay Wyrd in the Circle of Outward Self because your hopes, dreams, and fate are inextricably bound up with other people. In this ceremony, it joins with the Rune of Guidance and Gebo in establishing a channel along which the three levels of self can communicate.

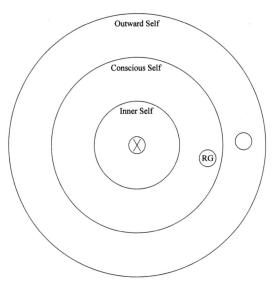

Arrangement of runes in Attunement of Three Selves ceremony.

Take several deep breaths to center yourself and bring your mind and will into focus. Try to sense or picture your three levels of self: inner, conscious, and outward. Then say:

Odin, Gefn (gay-fun),
hold these sacred runes
in your hands,
may they work my will.

Take out the rune Gebo and lay it in the center of the inner circle. Say:

May this rune light the darkness of my inner self.

As you say this, sense or picture the connecting power of the rune, with energies passing back and forth along its arms, lighting up within your inner self.

Place your personal Rune of Guidance in the middle circle. Say:

May this rune light the darkness of my conscious self.

When you say this, sense or picture the Rune of Guidance in you working as a channel through the energies of your inner self flows from Gebo to Wyrd and your outward self.

Finally, lay Wyrd in the outermost circle. Say:

May this rune light the darkness of my outward self.

Try to sense or picture this rune as one point in a round-trip circuit of energy constantly flowing to and fro from one circle to another via the three runes. Hold this image in your mind. You will probably begin to feel a greater inner strength, a sense of clarity, well-being, and harmony. This is the result of your three selves coming into greater connection and attunement.

If you want to know what is going on with any of your three selves, just ask. The answer will probably come in loud and clear.

Enjoy this sensation for a moment. To end the ceremony, turn your face heavenward and say:

The rune's magic
has been worked;
with thanks to
Odin and Gefn!
Honor to them
and these runes.

Snuff out the candle and put the runes away. Let the incense burn itself out.

Rune Meditation: Achieving Harmony and Wholeness

Mindfulness of the three selves and bringing them into harmony are the goals of this meditation. You will need a quiet spot and this book, opened to the page with the Celtic circle design shown earlier in this chapter. (Some people like to photocopy and color it first. Feel free to do this if you find the idea appealing.)

You will use the Celtic circle as a mandala. A mandala is a sacred diagram used to focus concentration and open awareness in meditation. Usually, mandalas are circular, often a circle within a square. Almost every culture current or past has used mandalas to represent and promote psychic wholeness.

Mind-Runes must thou know to have good and wise thoughts.
—*The Elder Edda*

Place your Rune of Guidance in the center of the design and take several deep, relaxing breaths. Bring your gaze and attention to the center, which symbolizes the inner self. It is blank, just as our inner self is often blank and unknown to us. Because it is an empty void, it is full of infinite possibilities. Just like your inner self.

The inner portion of the design is also a twelve-pointed star. Twelve is an important number with runes just as it is with astrology tarot. In astrology, it is the number of houses, and in tarot, the number of the "Hanged Man." As you'll recall from Chapter 1, Odin hung suspended by one foot upside down staring into the void to discern the wisdom represented by runes.

Let your eyes rest on your Rune of Guidance in the center of the three circles. Gaze at it in a relaxed fashion until you sense the rune expanding to fill your vision, and lose awareness of the all the rest of the design except the blank circle representing the inner self that surrounds it. At this point you should sense the Rune of Guidance trying to tell you something about the nature of your inner self. What is it trying to say to you? What is the message? Straining to receive the message will only block it. Remain relaxed and in a few minutes it will come to you.

Shift your gaze to the middle ring of the circle—the one that looks like an Islamic arabesque. It is also a twelve-pointed star. Pick a spot on one of the big lines that arcs around the middle circle and follow it with your eye. You will discover that, though it looks as if there were three or four separate lines, there is actually only one line or strand. This strand has been so cunningly interwoven that it passes through all 12 points of the star before it reaches the spot where you began. This braid symbolizes the conscious self, a single strand woven so complexly that it appears to be a maze of different selves in which we often find ourselves lost, seeking a way out.

Let your eyes dwell on the braid of the middle ring. Don't try to follow the maze again. Instead, just let the whole pattern absorb itself into your eyes. You might even feel your eyes, or need to allow them, to go a bit out of focus. You will find that you are still aware of the Rune of Guidance in the center. This is because the rune is again trying to communicate with you about your conscious self. Remain relaxed and with your awareness on the twelve-pointed maze, until the message comes through.

Next, widen your gaze a bit farther and try to let your visual awareness absorb the outer circle. This ring is exactly what it seems like—three separate strands braided in a intricate design. Like 12 (which is 3 times 4), 3 is a number of great mystical and magical significance. 3 times 3 equals 9 (the number of nights Odin hung on the Yggdrasil); 3 is also the number of faces of the goddess and of the holy trinity.

The complex triple weaving of the outer circle in the Celtic rune cloth design has several meanings. Your own existence, for instance, is so intricately interwoven with those of other, individual human beings that it is nearly impossible to separate your life from theirs. On another level, the three strands that weave the outer circle represent the intricate interrelationship of your three selves: inner, conscious, and outward.

Allow the outer circle to fill your vision until you are aware only of it and of your Rune of Guidance sitting in the center. This is when the rune will attempt to communicate with you. Open yourself to the message. What is it trying to say about your relationship with others and with the world around you?

Now you are at the culmination of this meditation. Refocus on the Rune of Guidance. At the same time, try to let your vision take in all three circles around it. Listen for your Rune of Guidance. What does it tell you about the relationships of these three aspects of your self? Where are they aligned? Where do they need to be harmonized? What steps does it say you need to take to bring all three into harmony?

If you don't receive answers right away, don't be concerned. Sometimes when the insights you need are buried deeply enough, it takes a few days for them to manifest. Look for them to appear in your dreams, or during a random moment of daydreaming.

Chapter 3

Runes of Solution and Insight

Everyone has them. Questions. Concerns. Worries. Dilemmas. Difficult choices. Impossible problems. Times when you are uncertain. Times when you are stuck for an answer. Times when there doesn't seem to be an answer. It might be work related: How to develop a blockbuster sales strategy to win a dream vacation. It might be romantic: Will a new relationship develop into something more? It might be personal: A seemingly unsolvable financial crisis caused by simultaneous illness, loss of a job, and a balloon payment on a mortgage. It might be family: How to handle a rebellious child. It might be creative: The need for a theme for the next school prom, or an ending to that new song or book. It could be business: What to do if a new chain store has opened in direct competition against you and is stealing customers away. Or even something as simple as whether you'd be better off spending your vacation with family in the Rockies or with friends in Jamaica.

Whatever your question, runes can answer it; and whatever your difficulty, runes can outline a path to its solution. The 25 universal forces embodied in runes are embodied in your problem. This link between them works to produce just the right runes to provide the insight or decision you need.

In short, whether you are perplexed, worried, or overwhelmed—don't just sit there. Let the runes guide you to the answers you've been seeking!

The runes as described here are healing, merciful runes; they will do you no harm. Learn their language and let them speak to you. ... they can provide a mirror for the magic of our knowing selves, a means of communication with the knowledge of our subconscious mind.

—Ralph Blum, *The Book of Runes*

Generating Insight with Runes

Is there a major problem in your life right now that you don't know how to resolve successfully? A pressing decision you can't seem to get a grip on? Perhaps you are stuck for a new idea when you are badly in need of one?

Cast the runes for a reading and the solution will literally stare you in the face. In fact, one of the main purposes of runes is to provide people with answers and insight. Just as runes can provide you with an accurate picture of yourself at any given moment, they can capture an accurate picture of any situation that concerns you. A rune reading lays out all the factors, personalities, and interrelationships involved so clearly that the solution becomes easy to see.

Problem Solving

Runes are your haven when you are faced with any important problem, large or small, you can't seem to get a handle on. No problem is unsolvable. Every challenge, crisis, setback, or decision has an answer. Often it's just hard to find the answer because you are in a crisis, the problem is complicated, or the alternatives seem almost equally balanced. A rune reading helps clarify the issues by pointing you toward the key elements that tip the balance. Read the runes for insight when you are faced with the following:

- *A daunting challenge.* For example, your boss has asked you to recommend ways your mail-order company can streamline the process for getting items into customers' hands so that it goes faster, and study the problem though you might, you can't see how it can be done.

- *A personal or professional crisis.* For example, a breakup with a lover has left you so torn up inside with grief and anger that you just don't know how to get over it and get on with your life.

- *An obstacle or setback.* For example, your plan to quit work and return to college for an advanced degree is blocked because the investments you depended on to carry your family through suddenly fell to an all time low and you can't see any other way to finance it.

- *A difficult decision.* For example, you have to choose between a new relationship that seems to have real potential and the wonderful new job you've just been offered two thousand miles away, and you're at a loss about what to do.

Creative Inspiration

Stuck for an idea, just when you need one most? Hate all the ideas you have come up with? Runes draw the lightning bolt of creative energy from the heavens and channel inspiration to you.

Artists aren't the only people who need creative inspiration. Everyone needs a new idea now and then. Ask any at-home mom who has to find a new way to keep the kids entertained indoors on a rainy day. Or any manager who must dream up a method for getting the same volume of work done with half the staff after a company downsizing. Or someone whose job suddenly challenges him or her to do the impossible—or the improbable.

Of course, artists require an almost constant stream of fresh insights, ideas, and creative notions. To a chef, musician, painter, writer, teacher, architect, or publicist, creativity isn't just a help—it's their stock in trade. They depend on inspirations the way the rest of us depend on food and air.

You may be familiar with the concept of writer's block. That's when an author's fund of ideas unexpectedly dries up and he or she can't write a word until the creative juices start flowing again. You've probably experienced the same phenomenon but didn't realize it. Just when inspiration is most essential, it fails you. You do your utmost to cook up something novel, captivating, different, and draw a blank. You end up doing less than your best—or even failing—and it stings. Frustratingly, the solution comes to you afterward, when it's too late—and often seems so obvious in hindsight you want to kick yourself for having missed it at the time.

Instead of drawing a blank, draw on runes for inspiration. As symbols, they will stir your creative unconscious. As channels for cosmic energy, they will convey the lightning flash of inspiration you need.

Reading Runes in an Instant

Frequently, you don't even have to throw the 25 rune stones and take time analyzing them to answer your questions. In many instances, you can find the solution with one stone—in less than a minute. That's because most of our questions can be answered simply "yes" or "no."

Often the answers we seek aren't complicated. It's the questions that are complicated. In some cases, whether there are three or three thousand factors involved, the answer comes down simply to whether or not to do something.

For example, you might be wondering whether this is a propitious moment to ask for a greater commitment from a longtime girlfriend or boyfriend. Doubtless there are many factors involved that you might ponder at length. But, in the final analysis, what you really need to know is if now's the time to bring up the issue of commitment. What you want to know might be much simpler: perhaps something as off-hand as whether to rent a comedy or thriller at the video store, or whether to accept a date with a new acquaintance.

Each of these problems is about possible action and its outcome. All will result in either a favorable or unfavorable consequence. In short, the basic question is one that can be framed so that it can be answered "yes" or "no."

You are about to be introduced to an effortless, time-honored technique for reading runes in an instant. It was devised by those masters of rune lore, the Vitka, for using rune stones for questions that could be answered in the affirmative or negative. Before you try it, however, here are a few guidelines to help you frame your question so you get the most accurate answer.

How Not to Word Your Question

It's critical to phrase your question so it can be answered either "yes" or "no." If you don't word it this way, you will get a confusing or meaningless answer. Here are some examples of how *not* to word your question:

- Don't word it as just a general statement of the situation. For example, "I want to know about the problem I am having with that new supervisor."

- Don't word it as a question requiring an expository answer. For example, "What should I do about the problem I am having with that new supervisor?"

- Don't word it as an "either or." For instance, "Should I discuss the problem with that new supervisor or wait to see if the situation works itself out in time?"

How to Word Your Question

Frame your question in terms of "should" and "shouldn't," "does" and "doesn't," "is" or "isn't," or "will" or "won't." Notice how all of these examples can be answered with a "yes" or "no":

- "Should I ignore the problem for a while and see if things improve?"

- "Is it a good tactic to discuss the issue with the new supervisor?"

- "Does the new supervisor have some personal animosity for me?"

- "Will pressing the issue make things worse?"

Rune #5: Raidho or Rad

Travel broadens everyone/and wisdom visits those who journey/down the road on wagons/to places far from home.
—*The Old English Rune Poem*

Raidho

Raidho (pronounced rye-though) is your rune of travel, negotiation, and cyclic change. The wheel transformed human society. In good and bad weather farmers could travel (raidho) further to markets, merchants could transport greater amounts and varieties of goods greater distances, and wars of conquest were carried to more distant lands. Turning wheels were seen as symbols for motion and for cosmic cycles, like the turning of the seasons.

Rune Image: The wheel of a wagon

In Rune Reading

Faceup meanings: Pleasant journey (physical or spiritual), differences where happy compromise is possible, change, motion, progression, rhythm, natural cosmic cycles. *Tarot comparison:* The Chariot. *Astrological comparison:* Sagittarius.

Occluded (facedown) meanings: Unexpected, unsettling journey, impasses, ruptures, difficulty and delay in transit, accidents, and rituals upset plans, stasis, interrupted rhythms and cycles. *Tarot comparison:* The Chariot reversed. *Astrological comparison:* Sagittarius afflicted.

In Rune Magic

Use to: Strengthen powers during rituals, empower rituals on sacred days, move runic streams of energy, journey astrally, resolve conflicts, further all cycles

In Rune Meditation

Use to: Deepen connection with cyclic flow of life, expand conscious thought processes, access inner wisdom

Rune Gods: Forseti, God of Justice and Law

Rune Totems: Horses, donkeys, mules, llamas, elephants, pigeons, antelopes, ostriches

Rune Herb: Mugwort

Rune Color: Ruby

Rune Reading: Determining Favorable Outcomes

This is the simplest and easiest of all rune reading methods. It is the reading to use when your question can be answered "yes" or "no." Choose it anytime you want to find out if an action, decision, or assumption will have a positive or negative consequence. One great advantage to this reading is its simplicity. You can use it any time, anywhere. Noise, people, and other distractions don't matter.

If the question is urgent, there is no need to wait. You don't have to locate a room where you are ensured of remaining undisturbed for

20 minutes or half an hour. The whole reading takes just one minute. A busy office is fine, if you can shut your door for 60 seconds or so. At home you only need to step into a room away from everyone for a minute. Actually, anyplace where you can steal a moment to yourself will work.

Of course, if you are comfortable reading runes in a more public setting, you don't have to be alone. This reading is so simple you can do it at a mall, restaurant, lecture, or ballgame. There is nothing to ponder, no complicated readings or interpretation involved. The sole prerequisite is a question that can be answered in "yes" or "no." The only items required are a pouch full of runes and a question. If you have these, you are ready to begin.

With your question firmly in mind, begin by saying silently (or out loud if you are alone), "Runar radh rett radh." (Which loosely translated means, "Runes bless me with good guidance.") Shake a single stone out of the pouch. If it falls faceup so that the sunlight (or whatever light there is) falls on the rune, the prognosis is positive. If, when the stone lands facedown, the rune is turned away from the light so that it is in darkness, the outcome will be unfavorable.

Unraveling Difficult or Complex Problems

Of course, not every quandary can be resolved by a simple thumbs up or thumbs down. It may be that you don't have a clue about how to solve your problem in the first place. There may be so many issues, aspects, and elements involved—or the possible solutions may be so equally balanced—that you hardly even know where to start looking for answers. Or earnest days of effort may have only left you frustrated and depressed over your inability to discover a remedy.

When this happens, its time for a full-scale rune reading. Use the 25 rune stones and the three circles of self. It will be like opening a book with an expert's analysis that maps out every factor causing your difficulty so that you can see and understand where it began and how you can put it to an end.

With runes to guide you through the complexities and the unessential aspects straight to a successful solution, there is no reason to ever again feel you can't handle a challenge, crisis, setback, decision, or creative hurdle.

The runes are there to guide you through your problems by showing what is likely to happen, given your variables, and suggesting how you ought to behave.
—Lisa Peschel, *A Practical Guide to the Runes*

Principles of Reading Unchanged

You learned how to interpret a self reading in Chapter 2. When looking for solutions and insight, you read the stones the exact same way. Just watch for runes that ...

1. Make patterns or shapes with other stones.
2. Lie near or far from others.
3. Land faceup or facedown (occluded).

There is one more guideline. When you are seeking insight into a problem, keep an eye out for runes that indicate the source of your troubles and runes that offer clues to its resolution. These are sometimes called Runes of Difficulty and Runes of Solution.

Runes of Difficulty

Inharmonious configurations and the blocked energy embodied in facedown runes point to the cause of your problem. For instance, if you were doing poorly at school, and Uruz, rune of health and resiliency were occluded, it might remind you that you haven't been getting enough sleep. Or, if you are having trouble getting two colleagues to work together, and find Dagaz, rune of balancing differing viewpoints, in an inharmonious relationship with Fehu, rune of prosperity and jealousy, also occluded, it might suggest a financial jealousy at the root of the conflict.

Runes of Solution

Harmonious patterns and faceup runes in configurations with facedown runes point to a way out of your difficulties. Say you have launched a home-based business but you aren't attracting clients fast enough. Your personal Rune of Guidance might be laying next to Mannaz, the rune symbolizing interdependence with other people, conveying a strong hint that you needed to network more and seek the aid of friends who could provide tips or perhaps send a few prospects your way.

Sample Reading

This reading was done for a client I will call Reba. She was the owner of a women's clothing boutique on Melrose Avenue in Los Angeles. Reba had built the store up with a series of clever promotions.

However, a dip in the economy was cutting into her bottom line, just as her silent partner who had provided the boutique's line of credit was experiencing his own difficulties and was forced to withdraw his backing at the bank. This made it nearly impossible for Reba to pay her suppliers during the downturn, and at the same time she seemed to run out of inspirations for the promotions that might have given a shot in the arm to sales and carried her through the crisis.

Reba reported she was depressed and discouraged—and little wonder! It was a scenario that would have discouraged far more experienced business people, with probable bankruptcy just around the corner. Unable to discover a solution to her problems herself, Reba hoped the runes might provide a life-saving insight.

Here, too, as in the other readings in this book, the facedown stones are shown slightly shaded in the illustrations. As always, you will get more out of this sample reading if you study the way the runes fell in the following illustration and take a few minutes to study and interpret them on your own before going on to see how I read them.

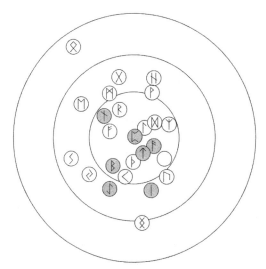

Reba's reading.

Strong Lines Lead to Success

This reading revealed both the pluses and minuses of Reba's situation at the time. The strong organizational skills that enabled her to pull together the original financing needed to launch her boutique and then keep it running smoothly on a day to day level are shown in the way so many of her runes were lined up across the Circle of Inner Self. The clear consciousness (thinking ability) that allowed her to operate profitably in the highly competitive and trend-based business can be seen in the way so many of the runes in the reading landed faceup.

Lines of stones, especially in the center circle, point toward an individual's key qualities or characteristics. Here, the two lines in the center circle are composed of rune stones touching each other. Runes that touch each other indicate forces so harmonious they work as one, and their power is multiplied by the number of runes touching. This means that these two complexes of stones will be the strongest and most dynamic aspects of Reba's character and have much to do with any success she enjoys in life. The biggest, four stones, moves upward to the right from the rune in the precise center of the circle, Perdhro (the laughter of the playful, creative inner child), and includes Lagaz (intuition from the unconscious), Dagaz (taking it easy gives ability to harmoniously balance differing or opposing forces and people), and Algiz (protection by a guiding spirit).

Read as a sentence the line pointed to one of Reba's most important characteristics. She has a very strong creative streak that contributed to her success so strongly, and her powers are derived from both her playful inner child (her imagination) bolstered by intuitions from her unconscious. These are wedded to powerful managerial skills—as indicated by Dagaz and Algiz.

The second line consists of three touching stones beginning just below the first line. It begins with Ansuz (wisdom, the ability to communicate it and receive it), followed by Tiwaz (guiding beacon of success), and Thurisaz (ability to transform defeat into victory). Read as a sentence, they add to the theme of managerial skills, pointing toward exceptional abilities to know the right thing to do and how to communicate it to others, powered by instinctive success skills and a native talent for overcoming any difficulties that might crop up in her path.

Put all this together and it is no surprise that Reba was able to create and successfully run a business.

Facedown Stones at Root of Troubles

On the other hand, Reba's Runes of Difficulty, the trio of stones in the very center of the Circle of Inner Self (Perdhro, Ansuz, and Tiwaz), offered clues to the cause and the cure of a situation that lead to Reba's current crisis. All three were occluded. Given their location, this meant that the central qualities behind Reba's success—creativity, knowing what to do and how to communicate it to others, and even her almost instinctive success skill—were being blocked for some reason.

I soon saw two Runes of Difficulty that seemed to be interfering with this trio. They form one tip of a triangle of occluded stones that lies within the inner circle. Another tip is Naudhiz, up to the left, just touching the rim of the circle. The last tip is Berkana, down to the left near the bottom of the circle. And runes that form triangles, recall, are always inharmonious.

The nature of Naudhiz might be summarized as a learning situation involving constraint, which one has to evolve beyond. Berkana usually symbolizes nurturing of some kind, and in the inner circle is always self-nurturing. That the pair were facedown and in a nonharmonious rela-tionship with each other and the three central occluded stones pointed directly toward the cause of her two big concerns.

The shrinkage of her store's cash flow and credit appeared to be part of a natural process with some greater lesson to teach. As for her sudden inability to dream up the kind of promotional ideas and gimmicks that had carried the boutique to success, it appeared to stem from a lack of self-nurturing. Worried about her business' financial crisis, Reba was forgetting to rest, meditate, eat wisely, and take time out for herself. No wonder her creative energies were blocked.

Reba's Runes of Solution

As for Runes of Solution, Naudhiz and Berkana hinted at possible steps Reba could take to end her problems. If there was a lesson for her to learn, it appeared to be for Reba to start taking better care of herself and not let her concerns get in the way of proper rest and nutrition—and to do the things that nurtured her spirit. This would surely revitalize her and give her creative faculties the healthy energy they needed to pro-vide the inspirations she needed. Should she act on that advice in time, there seemed no reason she could not apply it and save her business.

The Rune of Guidance also often acts as a Rune of Solution. In this reading, Reba's Rune of Guidance, Kenaz (energy under control shaping things to creative ends) lies next to the occluded Berkana stone. Her Rune of Guidance was reinforcing the point that the flow of ideas that had helped her start and grow her business was closely related to good self-nurturing. Reba's creative energies would become unblocked as soon as she began putting herself first over her financial worries.

Reba could see the sense of this. What the runes told her was what she had known all along. But, she had been so caught up in the crisis she had not fully realized just how much her frazzled state was contributing to her failure to dream up promotions to boost her cash flow or to find solutions to the boutique's other financial problems. She swore she would begin to eat right, resume the meditation class she had dropped, and even take time to window shop at the mall with friends, which always revitalized her.

The location of the Wishing Stone (the blank stone) suggested an additional approach to extricating Reba from her business difficulties. Looking left, you realize it is one end of a longer line that incorporates the three facedown runes of Perdhro, Ansuz, and Tiwaz as its middle and extends to Eihwaz in the Circle of Conscious Self. Even though these runes form part of a vast, triangle of occluded, inharmonious stones, the fact that they are also part of a larger straight line anchored by two faceup runes (the blank rune is always read as faceup) suggests that the solution to their blocked or inharmonious energies is to be found in the faceup runes.

Ehwaz, the faceup rune at the opposite end of the line from the Wishing Stone, is a rune of travel and partnership. Because Reba's troubles began when her silent partner was forced to withdraw his support, the notion of partnership suggested a replacement might be lurking in the wings. The rune's presence in the Circle of Conscious Self seemed to be saying that she needed to make a conscious effort to locate a new financial backer for the store. Ehwaz' secondary meaning of travel seemed to hint that this person would not be discovered close to home, but farther away.

At the time, Reba did not have a clue about where she might travel to locate a replacement for her former partner. However, a few weeks later some friends invited her to join them for a weekend house party at their condo in Hawaii. Reba felt she couldn't afford to take the time away from trying to resolve her business problems. But she remembered this reading and reluctantly accepted. Later, she would say attending that party was the best decision she ever made. Not only did she meet the man who became her new silent partner—but two years later, she married him as well.

Rune #6: Kenaz or Cen

The torch is to all living things/known by its flame/clear and bright/it sheds radiance protectively/in the dark night/while all sleep safe in their beds.

—*The Old English Rune Poem*

Kenaz

Kenaz (pronounced kane-awz) is your rune of controlled strength, energy, and power. The control of fire was an epic event for early humans. Torches (kenaz) gave them light at night, hearth fires warmed homes and cooked meals, and forge fires made tools and utensils for living. Little wonder the torch became a symbol for energy under control shaping things to creative ends.

Rune Image: The torch

In Rune Reading

Faceup meanings: The guiding, ever-present, spiritual light, controlled energy, inspiration, truth, skill, transformation and regeneration, beginnings, creativity, sexual desire. *Tarot comparison:* The High Priestess. *Astrological comparison:* Venus.

Occluded (facedown) meanings: Prolonged spiritual darkness, lack of energy to accomplish or energy out of control, falsity, endings, poor judgment, creative emptiness, waning of sexual passion. *Tarot comparison:* The High Priestess reversed. *Astrological comparison:* Venus afflicted.

In Rune Magic

Use for: Healing, regeneration, guide and protect creative projects, sex magic, and intensify passion

In Rune Meditation

Use to: Further personal transformation, increase insight and creative inspiration, access divine wisdom

Rune Gods: Freyja or Valfreya, Goddess of fertility and physical love

Rune Totems: Cats, tigers, pumas, mountain lions, hawks, falcons, eagles, dogs, monkeys

Rune Herb: Cowslip

Rune Color: Reddish gold

Rune Reading: Seeing the Keys to Your Solution

This reading is exactly like the Three Circles of Self reading in the previous chapter, except that you will also be looking for Runes of Difficulty and Solution. As always, pick a suitable place and time, lay out your rune cloth, and relax for a few minutes to quiet your mind so you can concentrate.

Start with the invocation:

Great Odin, who brought
these runes
from the darkness
to light our way
guide my hands
direct my mind
that I might sup
of their wisdom.

With your problem clearly in mind, cast the rune stones. Remember to watch for ...

- Patterns and shapes.
- Nearness and distance from other stones.
- Whether runes are faceup or facedown (occluded).
- Runes of Difficulty.
- Runes of Solution.

Don't rush your interpretation. If it is important enough that you want to consult runes, it is important enough for you to take the time to work out all the details of the reading and whatever counsel it offers.

If you don't understand right away how a certain rune that seems significant relates to your issue and your question, ponder it a moment; if nothing comes to mind immediately, proceed with the rest of the reading. Usually before you have gone very much further, the relevance of the rune will pop up out of your subconscious. (This phenomenon might continue for several days, with additional ideas and meanings relating to the whole reading coming to you at odd moments.)

At the end of the reading, remember to say:

Thank you, Great Odin,
for the blessing
of runes
and the gift
of this wisdom.

Rune Magic: Germinating Genius

It seems like everyone is in need of a dash of genius now then. There are problems and challenges where ordinary brainpower just doesn't seem to get you anywhere. How often have you found yourself mentally stuck when you really needed to be able to come up with a solution and thought that if you were only as smart as [fill the blank] you would have easily been able to find an answer?

This rune ritual will draw that genius right down out of the heavens and empower you to arrive at perceptions into things and thoughts about them that only geniuses have. Even if you are convinced you are not a genius and can never be one, this ceremony will make you a believer. In it, you use the Ansuz or mouth rune stone as a magical focus or talisman to bring down what the Norse called "odhr" (inspired mental activity, or genius).

Odin bestowed the gift of odhr on Ask and Embla (the ash and yew trees that became the first man and woman) when he brought them to life. The All-father communicated it to them in a bolt of lightning that bestowed the gift of genius on them. Here, Odin will bestow the gift of genius on you, in the same way, when you invoke Ask and Embla, beseeching them to intercede with the All-father in your behalf.

You can use this ritual when you need assistance with a specific issue or problem or if you just need a general boost in all-around genius. You will need a rune cloth, or drawing of the three circles, a dark blue candle, and the herb, fly agaric. Dim the lights, set the herb smoldering in an incense burner, and light your candle. Place the rune cloth before you, and the rune Ansuz in the center of the inner ring to represent you.

Relax and empty your mind of all distracting thoughts. Then say:

Ask and Embla,
share the gift of All-father
when he gave you life.
Let me quaff anda,
the mead of genius,
as you did,
from the holy cup Othroerir,
"the exciter of inspiration."
First man, first woman,
speak in my behalf
to the one Most High.
Grant me this boon
that I, too,
may know the gift
of Ansuz
and drink the mead
of genius.

Stand and raise both your arms out from your body at about a 45° angle. One should be slightly higher than the other. So that seen in outline you would look very much like the ash tree shape of the rune itself, with your body the trunk and your arms its downward slanting branches.

Say:

May holy rune Ansuz
draw to me odhr.

As a tree, you are the natural target of lightning. You will probably sense energy beginning to tingle at the top of your head. It might come slowly or all at once in a rush. As soon as you feel it begin, affirm:

The wisdom of Odin streams in me!

If you came to this ritual with a specific need, you will probably receive your answer quickly. Either way, over the next few days you should notice a boost in your overall intelligence; your senses and perceptions will seem more acute, and you will be thinking better and more clearly than ever before.

Rune Meditation: Drawing in Cosmic Creativity

Looking for a theme to raise money for church repairs? Looking for the idea for a Grammy-winning song? Looking for a new invention or service that can make you rich even in an economy where other businesses are failing?

This meditation, built around Eihwaz, will help channel the primal creative forces represented by the rune directly to your conscious mind. Eihwaz' vertical line represents the trunk of a tree—in specific, Yggdrasil, the World Tree. The slanting line at bottom represents its roots, the one at the top, its branches.

> Thought-runes you should know if you would be thought by all the wisest of mortal men.
> —*The Elder Edda*

When you are in search of a creative jump-start, short of ideas, and desperately in need of one, try this runic meditation. It sparks your creative abilities by facilitating communication between different levels of awareness. This meditation on Eihwaz will draw in the inspiration you seek.

In Norse mythology, Yggdrasil pierced, supported, and united the triple worlds: heaven, the earthly plane, and the underworld. It is from the dwarves of the underworld that we received tools, technology, all forms of mechanical inspiration, and it is from the gods of the heavens that we receive wisdom, inspiration, and new ideas. Both forms of creativity were carried to us via Yggdrasil. This cosmic tree is knotted through everything in the universe—including you—uniting all three worlds. At any time you have access to cosmic inspiration from each realm through Yggdrasil. And you can access Yggdrasil by meditating on the rune that embodies its powers—Eihwaz.

Go to a place where you can meditate. Sit comfortably. Draw Eihwaz from your rune pouch and place it before you. Take several deep breaths and relax. Focus on the rune symbol on the stone, and just stare at its shape while you relax for a minute or two. Let the vertical line that stands for the trunk and the angled lines at bottom and top that stand for roots and branches sink into your vision.

75

Now close your eyes. The image of Eihwaz will probably still be vivid in your mind's eye against the darkness. Without straining, try to see the tree in the symbol: Yggdrasil, the mighty World Tree. Yggdrasil's vast and leafy crown supports the roof of heaven. Its immense girth is the pillar supporting our world. The billion, knotted roots are the soil of the underworld. Allow this image of the World Tree to fill your mind and vision.

Look deeper into the tree. Picture its capillaries, running up and down the trunk, circulating nourishment from roots to branches and back through all three worlds. This nourishment is the creative knowledge and energy that maintains heaven, earth, and the underworld.

Open your eyes and allow them to rest for a few minutes again on Eihwaz.

Close your eyes again. Visualize the Eihwaz symbol moving upward off the stone toward you and growing larger. See and feel it merge with you and continue to expand upward and downward until it reaches infinity in each direction. Now, see and feel the Eihwaz symbol that has merged with, and extends through, you becoming the World Tree it represents.

Experience the trunk that is Yggdrasil extending upward through your head and downward through your feet. The roots sink far into the underworld below; the branches soar far above. Buried within it, the capillaries circulate the creative forces of both worlds—and bring them to you.

There is a blank space in your mind where the inspiration you need—the solution, idea, insight—should be. Continue to sit quietly and picture the World Tree sprouting through you, creativity and inspiration flowing from above to below and back again through you. Very slowly the idea you need should begin to take form in your mind.

When this happens, don't hurry the process—it's the cosmic creative power of Eihwaz in action. Don't interrupt it by trying to think about it prematurely. Instead, let the thoughts come to you. Be a passive receptor for at least a few minutes more. Only when you are sure the whole idea is fully formed should you finally open your eyes and break the connection.

Close your hand over Eihwaz. Mentally thank the rune and the gods for what you have received. If you don't get the creative insight you've been seeking during the meditation, don't be concerned. Sometimes it takes just a bit longer for the inspiration to surface. In many cases it will come to you that night either just prior to falling asleep or in a dream. On rare occasions, it might wait until the following day—and then pop out just when you least expect it.

Chapter 4

Runes of Career and Destiny

It's what we all want to do. The more materially oriented call it finding "the right job." Those with a more psychological bent refer to it as finding "your calling in life." The more spiritually minded term it "fulfilling your destiny." Buddhists speak of "right work." Terminology isn't important; it's what you want and what it means to you that's important. Unless you already have the ideal (for you) job in the ideal (for you) working environment, or unless your interests lie elsewhere and you don't care what you do for a living, you probably have a concept of your dream job and the type of work you'd like to end up doing.

For some people the ideal career involves significant remuneration. Others want the opportunity to use their unique talents and abilities. Still others feel they were put on Earth for some special purpose and seek work that enables them to fulfill it. Yet others simply seek fulfilling work.

Of course, your career issue may not be finding the ideal job or determining your destiny. At the moment, those might be on the backburner while you worry about obtaining a raise or promotion, a better job, or a job with different hours that's closer to home. Or, with the uncertain economy, you might be tied up in a knot over whether the timing is right to look for another job or stick with your present one—despite all its drawbacks.

Career Runes, Career Readings

Do you wonder if you are on the right career path? Do you know you are in the wrong job, but don't know what the right job would be? Did you once think you had chosen the right career, but now realize you blundered? Or are you just starting out in life, and wondering what the right path is for you? Perhaps you are a college student or someone older just entering the workforce for first time. Should you opt for the first job you are offered? The highest paying job? Or should you hold out for a job that offers exciting possibilities?

It can be hard to decide what course to pursue. In a world where people earn their livings in such a wide variety of jobs and professions, where there are hundreds of thousands of different kinds of work, there are a bewildering number of possibilities. Plus, everyone has their own agenda and attempts to convince you that following the path they chose is the best.

People in ancient times were also very much concerned with questions regarding their work and destined calling in life. Certain runes specifically reflect this universal human concern and could be called career runes, so great is their focus on career and work—especially Perdhro and Ehwaz. Several traditional approaches to rune reading also acknowledge this concern, among them the Three Norns reading (which you will learn later in this chapter) and the Success Mirror reading in Chapter 8.

Used correctly, runes can show you how to …

- Get a raise.
- Earn a promotion.
- Reactivate a stalled career.
- Improve your current job.
- Determine if the time is right to change jobs.
- Plot the best path to success in your career.
- Locate a better job.
- Decide if you are on the right career track.
- Find the right job.
- Discover your calling in life.
- Identify your destiny.

Your Destined Calling in Life

Choosing what's wisest for your long-term future comes down to knowing who you are supposed to be. Or, to put it another way, who you can best be. In short, it helps you learn more about your destiny.

Guidance counselors, career placement services, and aptitude and preference tests only go so far. They can give you guesses and probabilities, because their knowledge of you is incomplete. Even if they knew everything about you, they still would not be able to predict how you might change in the future.

Because they are attuned to the cosmic forces from which you are constituted, runes reflect who you were, who you are—and most important, who you *could* be. Runes don't foretell your destiny, they point out possible destinies that depend on the courses you take. They also point out the most fulfilling course—the person you are supposed to be.

> Destiny as used in rune readings means your ideal passage through life, your ideal possibility. There is no such thing as a bad Destiny … An energy exists that ceaselessly moves to change for good rather than ill … Your Destiny is your spiritual destination.
>
> —Lisa Peschel, *A Practical Guide to the Runes*

Rune Reading: Finding Your Calling in Life

By now, you have acquired the basics of interpreting a rune reading from the earlier chapters. Reading the runes to help find your ideal job is no different. Here, you focus on your career-related concern or question. Then, as you examine each configuration and rune, you make connections between runes and the various aspects of your problem, just as I did with Cory in the following sample reading.

Remember to pay particular attention to rune stones that …

- Make patterns or shapes with other stones.
- Lie near or far from others.
- Land faceup or facedown (occluded).
- Indicate the source of troubles.
- Offer clues to its resolution.

Now it's time to sit down with your rune cloth before you, and cast the runes to help discover your calling in life.

Sample Reading

Cory lived in an apartment in an upscale neighborhood and had a well-paying position with a company that performed job evaluations. But after 10 years with the company and as many promotions, she was beginning to experience a vague sense of restlessness and dissatisfaction. As she put it to me, "The work I do is very beneficial, but I keep wondering if there isn't something more I could be doing. A higher calling. I mean is this all I was put here on Earth for?"

When Cory cast the runes, they assumed such unusual configurations that it was apparent they were giving her a very definite answer. One of the most conspicuous was the fact that only two runes fell within the Circle of Inner Self. And no rune fell in the very center, indicating that something was missing at the core of her being. This was doubtless the cause of the inner hunger for something more that had sent Cory to me. (Runes that landed facedown are shown shaded.)

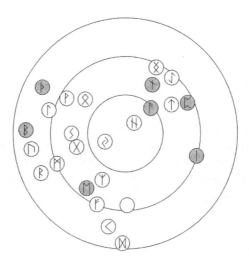

Cory's reading.

Another very conspicuous arrangement is the way Isa (delay, vision) is facedown on the border between the Rings of Conscious Self and Outward Self. This reflected the difficulty Cory was experiencing in consciously identifying the cause of her hunger for something more in life.

Another pronounced feature of Cory's reading is the large triangle of six rune stones on the upper right. One bridges the border between the Rings of Inner Self and Conscious Self, while three bridge the border between the Rings of Conscious Self and Outward Self. This triangle points toward a way of overcoming the blocked vision represented by Isa by opening up the alternative channels of communication radiating out from the bottom tip of the triangle along its sides and connecting all three layers of the self.

Because triangles are harmonious, and the energies of all runes involved work together, creating a powerful complex of personal qualities and possibilities, this one was clearly the key to her current situation and future destiny. Though there are several facedown runes in this triangle, which generally means the energies of those runes are blocked, the powerful harmony embodied in the triangle suggests those blockages could be overcome with very little effort.

This triangle begins with a occluded Ansuz (wisdom, the ability to communicate it and receive it), acting as a bridge from the Circles of Inner Self to the Circle of Conscious Self. Ansuz's energy spreads out in two divergent directions (the sides of the triangle). But, significantly, they both converge at the same place, rune Sowilo (vitality to overcome difficulty)—directly opposite Ansuz, suggesting they are twin powers.

On the lower or right side of the triangle, the energy embodied in Ansuz spreads to Tiwaz (guiding beacon of success), and then Perdhro (the laughter of the playful, creative inner child) occluded. On the other side of the triangle, it moves from Ansuz to Naudhiz (a lesson, involving constraint, that must be evolved beyond) occluded and Ingwaz (the person being read for as hero bringing a successful conclusion). Joining the two flows of energy is Sowilo, which bridges and brings into contact the Circles of Conscious and Outward Self.

Cory's reading showed she had the ability to communicate wisdom both to others and herself, but like her vision, it was blocked. When unblocked it would lead her to success, but the pathway there was blocked by repressing her inner child. Unblocked, Ansuz's energies would flow through

Naudhiz, but as it is facedown, there was a lesson she must first learn, and when she did Cory would become her own hero. Both paths led her to success through a vastly increased ability to overcome difficulty.

The other notable pattern in Cory's reading is the line of four stones slanting upward to the right from the bottom of the reading. Because lines are very powerful configurations, I told Cory we might hope to find some indication of the lesson she was supposed to learn there. We did, but it was Cory who recognized it because only the person being read for is in a position to fully grasp all the implications of what runes have to say to them.

This line begins with Dagaz (taking it easy gives ability to harmoniously balance differing or opposing forces and people), and moves through Algiz (protection by a guiding spirit) to Kenaz (energy under control shaping things to creative ends), then Fehu (possession leads to abundance and prosperity), and finally Ehwaz (working in harness and tandem with others) facedown.

As the energy in lines always moves upward, Dagaz was a very significant rune in this reading. The line, read as a sentence, seemed to say that somehow through using an ability to take it easy, which would harmonize energies and people, Cory would release the energy of the line which would lead to some worthwhile accomplishment, which in turn would result in prosperity, either with or through working with others. But, as Ehwaz was facedown, something was preventing her from working with them.

It seemed that if Cory could find a way to work with or through some group, it would free all the energies in the reading, perhaps open up the blocked forces of Ansuz and release the forces embodied in the upper triangle creating communication and harmony throughout all levels of her being. That sounded like fulfilling work in her future to me. The only problem was that I did not quite know what it all meant. I needn't have worried; as usually happens, the subject did know, and the reading would clearly reveal Cory's destined field of work to her.

When Cory heard the words, taking it easy and harmoniously balancing energies, she connected it with the meditation classes she had begun taking a few months earlier. When I described one key to her inability to identify her calling in life seemed to lie in something that held her back from working with others, Cory connected it with the fact that several people at her office had begged her to conduct a lunchtime meditation session for them. Cory had declined, feeling she was no authority, and didn't have the right to teach meditation on her own.

Now, Cory saw the runes as telling her she should overcome her reluctance and hold the meditational gathering her work mates asked for. Even as she thought about it, Cory's whole face and body seemed to light up and change. She saw that what she wanted to do was to transition out of her present job and become a teacher of meditation and holistic healing. This, she knew, was something she could spend her life doing without regret. It would release her inner child and allow her to share (communicate) the wisdom she had developed over many years of studying yoga, I-Ching, astrology, macrobiotics, and other related subjects. Thus she would become the hero of her own story.

Rune #7: Gebo or Gyfu

When two people meet/generosity is an act worthy of praise/To those who know hunger/to those with no shelter/to those who lack love/it is a support and sustenance.

—*The Old English Rune Poem*

Gebo

Gebo (pronounced gay-bow) is your rune of interrelationships and generosity. Places where two paths crossed (gebo) became natural meeting places for the men and women of old. Markets flourished, goods were exchanged, and towns grew up—leading to divisions between rich and poor. Thus the "X" symbol came to represent meetings, generosity from the high to the low, even marriage and sexual union.

Rune Image: Two paths crossing

In Rune Reading

Faceup meanings: A favorable meeting, connections, exchange, harmonious intersection of forces, relationships, people working to achieve a common goal, good fortune in any undertaking, gift, giving, giver, given to, generosity, charity, sacrifice, gratitude, marriage, sexual union. *Tarot comparison:* The Lovers. *Astrological comparison:* Pisces.

Occluded (facedown) meanings: Missed connections, unharmonious relationships, greed, miserliness, hunger, want, need, divorce, sexual incompatibility. *Tarot comparison:* The Lovers reversed. *Astrological comparison:* Pisces afflicted.

In Rune Magic

Use to: Bring about meetings, safely cross and blend runic forces, stimulate generosity, initiation ceremonies, love magic, the union of the god and goddess

In Rune Meditation

Use to: Understand relationships, harmonize with a group, develop compassion and empathy

Rune Gods: Odin, as giver of life; Gefn, Goddess of the Virgin Dead

Rune Totems: Serpents, crocodiles, wolves, deer, bear, birds, flying insects

Rune Herb: Heartsease

Rune Color: Deep blue

Eliminating False Starts

A friend, let's call him Fred, dropped out of college during his sophomore year, convinced he was on the wrong track with the management degree he was pursuing. After dropping out he took a low-paying job as telephone customer support for a small mail order catalog company. Although he hated the job and constantly thought about going back to college, Fred seemed unable to decide what kind of degree he wanted and what kind of career path he wanted to pursue. He thought about music, teaching, computers, journalism, even becoming a crew member on a yacht and sailing around the world. But he never acted on any of these ideas, and remained stuck in his demoralizing, dead-end job.

One day I asked Fred why he was having so much difficulty in choosing a career. He then related one of the saddest stories I have ever heard.

Toward the end of his second year at the university, Fred had lunch with an older cousin who held a high-level management position with a major banking firm. Fred quickly discovered his cousin loathed his job;

he felt trapped, doomed to a lifetime of boredom and drudgery. His cousin toyed with the idea of looking for a new career more suited to his temperament, but gave it up because it would mean returning to college for several years to obtain a new degree in a new field. As a result, Fred became obsessed with the thought of making the same kind of disastrous career choice. He was overwhelmed by the fear of earning a degree in the wrong field, and being stuck for life with a job he hated. The result was complete career paralysis. Even the most attractive opportunities looked like potential lifetime traps to him.

Fred and his cousin are not alone. Many people get off on the wrong career path. False starts like this are common. It's easy at 20 to think that what you are passionate about now, or have been convinced is the wisest thing to do, is something you will enjoy doing 10 or even 20 years later. If you discover you have made a mistake several years down the line, your only choices are to continue putting your time in until retirement in a job you'd rather not be doing or to start all over again, building a life in a field you find more congenial.

Changing careers is no small thing. It is well worth it, of course, when it satisfies your deepest yearnings and brings you far greater fulfillment and satisfaction. But even so, it can mean a return to school for a supplementary degree, beginning all over again at the bottom or as an unknown in a new field, and slowly building a new career.

Runes show you how to bypass these kinds of false starts and career dead ends. Like a compass needle, some rune readings are designed to point straight past all the blind alleys to your true calling in life.

The Three Norns Reading

The Three Norns reading is one of the most powerful runic methods used by rune masters (such as the Vitka) for helping people zero in on the right job in the right field. This deceptively simple approach to utilizing runes is a powerful tool for discovering your destiny. The three Norns—Urd, Verdandi, and Skuld—ruled over past, present, and future fate, respectively. You will encounter them again in the rune meditation at the end of this chapter.

You may have heard of the Norns, even if you aren't familiar with Norse mythology. These are the three female deities who weave the web of existence and snip off the threads of life when your time on Earth is done. In Greek mythology they are known as the three Fates, and they were shown as the three witches in productions of *Macbeth*.

For this reading, all you need to know about the Norns is that they are the beings who weave the pattern of your destiny from conception to life through your final passage from this earthly realm. If you are uncertain about your proper calling in life, or if you are pretty sure that you already know what it should be but want to be positive so you don't invest time and effort on the wrong life path, this reading will help point you in the proper direction.

The Three Norns reading is deceptively simple. Instead of 23 rune stones, you only use 3. You shuffle the stones around facedown to mix them up and then choose three: one to represent elements in your past that offer clues to your calling in life, one to represent elements in your present that point toward that career, and one to represent elements in your future bearing on your destined field of work.

You lay the stones out and then turn them faceup one at a time as you read them. As you interpret each rune, ask yourself ...

- What are the forces and qualities associated with the rune?
- How do they seem to relate to my past experiences?
- Is there anything about them that points toward one or more potential callings in my life?

Sample Reading

Roberto was the friend of a friend who came to me for a rune reading. Roberto was a second-generation Latino. After coming to this country, his father had worked for years at a series of menial jobs, until he had saved enough money to purchase a small, local convenience store. Through hard work and dedication, he developed the business into a regional chain of eight stores serving the Latino community in three different cities. And his only son, Roberto, was expected to go into the business and eventually assume its management when his father finally retired.

Roberto, however, had his own notion about his future and career, and it did not include managing a chain of convenience stores. He wasn't completely certain about what he did want to do—though he did have

86

several ideas—but he was certain about how he *didn't* want to spend his life. Rather than making money from his community, he wanted to give something back.

Among the potential careers he felt drawn to were teaching, journalism, and mental health. This already said a good deal about Roberto, as was confirmed in his reading. Because his concerns were concentrated on one narrow focus—selecting the right career—rather than a more complicated reading, I had Roberto use the Three Norns reading, traditionally used by Vitka for unraveling just these kinds of questions.

Roberto drew the following runes:

- On the left, Ansuz, in the Place of Urd, Norn of Past Destiny
- In the middle, Othala, in the Place of Verdandi, Norn of Present Destiny
- On the right, Ingwaz, in the Place of Skuld, Norn of Future Destiny

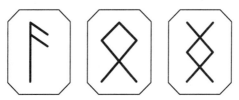

Roberto's Three Norns reading.

We began with Ansuz. I described to Roberto some of the meanings and associations of the rune—mouth, communication. Then I asked him if he felt it might relate to any past experiences bearing on his calling in life. Roberto, it turned out, had always been verbally gifted—an inveterate reader, a good writer, and a good speaker almost from his earliest days in school. He was strong in just those qualities represented by Ansuz.

I inquired if what he had learned suggested one or more potential callings in life. Roberto said that it seemed to point toward work that involved communicating with people. He noted that this also seemed true of all the potential jobs that interested him.

We discussed Othala next. I summarized its associations with family and inheritance. Roberto didn't need to be asked what he thought Othala might indicate about present experiences and influences on his search for a calling in life. He immediately recognized that the rune symbolized the enormous pressure he was feeling from his father to go into the family business.

Last, we considered Ingwaz, in the position of Future Destiny. This rune, I told Roberto, often signified teacher and hero. I really had to go no further. Roberto burst out with the fact that what he really wanted to do was be a teacher. He loved working with young people, and because the money people had spent at his father's stores had put him through college, it felt like a good way to pay back the community.

It turned out Roberto had always had teaching in mind, but his father was always putting teachers down because they made so little money and seemed to get so little respect. This had made it difficult for Roberto to find the strength to defy his father and consciously choose teaching as a career.

To Roberto, the reading had confirmed everything: his natural talents for teaching, that the only block was his fear of openly opposing his father's wishes, and that his true future destiny was in teaching. He decided to apply for admission to a university where he could seek an additional degree in teaching.

Although Roberto's father was initially furious, he eventually came around, and five years later was bragging to everyone about his son the teacher, who was doing so much for the youth of their community.

Rune Reading: Finding Your Calling in Life

In a location and time where you can open yourself to the message of the runes, relax by taking several deep breaths to clear and still your mind. Take out your rune stones and set Wyrd (the blank one) aside. Turn the other 24 stones facedown, and shuffle them around until you lose track of which are which.

Invoke the aid of the Norns by saying, "Urd, Verdandi, Skuld, guide me in choosing these runes that I may know my destined work in life."

Hold your hand over the runes for a moment, listening for the guidance of the Norns. It is likely to manifest as a tingling or heaviness in your hand. Pick up whatever stone your hand is drawn to. Without looking at the rune, lay that stone facedown on your left. This position is called the Place of Urd, Norn of Past Destiny.

Repeat this procedure with a second stone, selecting the one to which your hand feels guided. Again, keeping the image hidden from your view, set the stone facedown directly before you. This position is called the Place of Verdandi, Norn of Present Destiny.

Repeat the process a final time, laying the stone you are drawn to pick facedown unseen to your right. This position is called the Place of Skuld, Norn of Future Destiny.

Begin this reading by turning the rune on the left faceup. The rune, in the Place of Urd, represents everything in your past that contributes to— and moves you toward—your destiny. This includes the character you have formed, the people you've known, the knowledge you've acquired, innate talents you were born with, skills you developed, choices you have made, things that have fulfilled you, and jobs you've held, as well as personal interests and inner aspirations.

Reflect on the rune you found in the Place of Urd, Norn of Past Destiny. Ask yourself these questions, and take your time answering each. Don't hurry through them—after all, this is your destiny we are talking about.

- What are the forces and qualities associated with the rune?
- How do they seem to relate to my past experiences?
- Is there anything about them that points toward one or more potential callings in my life?

When you feel you have learned all there is to learn from this first rune, turn the rune in the center faceup. This rune lies in the Place of Verdandi, and represents everything in your present that contributes to your destiny. Among them will be your current interests and desires, your current awareness both of your own potentials and of the possible destinies you could fulfill, your current thoughts and feelings, your current job or field of study, choices you are making, the people you know right now, what fulfills you now, what you now hope to accomplish and what you now want to accomplish, and much more.

Consider the rune you find in the Place of Verdandi, Norn of Present Destiny. Ask yourself the same three questions:

- What are the forces and qualities associated with the rune?
- How do they seem to relate to my past experiences?

🖋 Is there anything about them that points toward one or more potential callings in my life?

Again, take time to give some thought to each, these are very important questions. And, don't be surprised if the number of potential callings you can see has shrunk a bit.

When you are through, turn the last stone faceup. The rune occupies the Place of Skuld, and represents everything in your future that will contribute to your destiny. It tells of the things you will learn, the skills you will develop, the jobs you will have, the choices you will make, the people you will meet, the dreams and aspirations you will develop, and the things that will fulfill you.

Again, ask yourself the same three questions and devote a few minutes to each answer:

🖋 What are the forces and qualities associated with the rune?

🖋 How do they seem to relate to my past experiences?

🖋 Is there anything about them that points toward one or more potential callings in my life?

Typically, by this point in a Three Norns reading, people either see exactly what their true calling in life is or have narrowed it down to a small cluster of possibilities centered around a common theme—such as public service, the arts, banking, entrepreneurship, teaching, spiritual issues, the outdoors, or fitness.

However, if you are still having trouble getting a clear picture of the right destiny for you, or if you want to further refine the results, this quick review usually brings your calling into focus. Go back to the first rune and ask yourself: In light of what you have just learned from the runes is there anything else of significance in this specific rune being in the Place of Urd, Norn of Past Destiny, that I see now that I didn't see before? Repeat this process with the second and third runes in the reading. Usually, before you reach the third rune, you are clear about what career you should pursue in the future—and why.

Rune #8: Wunjo or Wynn

Joyful is the person/who knows few troubles/afflictions or sorrows/and who has prosperity/the blessing of happiness/and a stout roof overhead.

—*The Old English Rune Poem*

Wunjo

Wunjo (pronounced woon-yo) is your rune of happiness and harmony with self and the world. To Nordic peoples, fair weather and sunshine was a cause of joy (Wunjo). It meant bountiful harvests, thriving markets, and celebrations. Thus the weathervane came to represent overflowing happiness, fellowship, and harmony.

Rune Image: The weathervane

In Rune Reading

Faceup meanings: End to troubles, occasion for joyfulness, hopes fulfilled, winds shifting in your favor, turning things around, fellowship, harmony among groups. *Tarot comparison:* The Sun. *Astrological comparison:* Leo.

Occluded (facedown) meanings: Continuing difficulties, sorrow, hope deferred, unfavorable circumstances, dissent, disagreement, fragmentation in groups. *Tarot comparison:* The Sun reversed. *Astrological comparison:* Leo afflicted.

In Rune Magic

Use to: Shift the winds of fortune in your favor, strengthen social bonds and promote harmony within a group, send out or increase your own happiness and well-being

In Rune Meditation

Use to: End feelings of alienation, increase a sense of connection and fellowship with others

Rune Gods: Frey, God of Sunshine; Uller, God of Winter

Rune Totems: House cats, dogs, horses, bovines, pigs, bees, dolphins

Rune Herb: Flax

Rune Color: Yellowish gold

Rune Magic: Smoothing the Bumps in the Road

Every career hits bumps along the path, goes astray down a side branch for a while, or encounters major obstacles. A company might downsize, sending you on a long search for new work in the same field. You might leave a good job because you got a much better offer, only to find things aren't the way they were presented to you. You might find almost your entire field out of work, in an economic downturn.

You can eliminate and minimize many of those career bumps *before* they happen. The following ritual releases runic energies into your future life's work to help smooth the path. Your career might not run trouble-free, but after using this ritual you will find yourself encountering far fewer difficulties.

> In Viking times … instead of a helpless predestination, "fate" meant a destiny created by one's earlier actions. Wyrd [fate] was pictured as a web, like that of a spider. The symbology is excellent. When the spider steps onto a thread (a path) the vibrations affect the entire web and that which is contained within the web, just as our actions affect our immediate world and those around us, and the actions of others affect our lives.
>
> —Ingrid Halvorsen, *Runes: Alphabet of Mystery*

This magical ceremony allows you to direct the energy of Perdhro, rune of fate, past, present, and future, the rune that reveals where your patterns will lead. Perdhro gives you power over cause and effect and draws down the power to make things work for you. In this ceremony, Perdhro is sent into your future to act like a computer virus program and erase potential career difficulties from your path.

You will need the herb aconite and one or more dark silver candles. Light your candle and set the herb smoldering in an incense burner. Then lay out your rune cloth and place the rune Perdhro in the center.

Take a few relaxing breaths and let your cares and thoughts float away with them. Now, sit on the ground, back straight, knees together, feet flat on the ground before you. Place your elbows on your knees with your forearms slanting forward from your knees at about a 45° angle. In this position, seen from the side you will look exactly like rune Perdhro. You are now in the perfect posture for accumulating the energy of this rune. Invoke the gods who rule over Perdhro, and ask them to aid, strengthen, and bless your magical powers during the ceremony. Say:

Frigga, Mother Goddess,
Mimir, God of Wisdom,
bestow your blessing
on this worthy work.
Release to me
the power of Perdhro,
grant me sway
over cause and effect.
Let the way
to my calling in life
be made smooth.
May the power of Perdhro
guide me to my destiny.
Release the power
of Perdhro now!

Consciously open yourself to that energy. Feel the energy of fate, past, present, and future, the power of cause and effect, to make things come out your way, flow down to you. Perdhro's energy typically begins to manifest in the head or hands. People have described it as deep vibration or buzzing.

When the energy has suffused your whole body and you can feel it in your toes, stand up very slowly. As your body unfolds, you should feel the energy rushing out from your middle, through the opening made as your arms come off your knees. While you still have the power to direct it, say:

Let the way
to my calling in life
be made smooth.
May the power of Perdhro
guide me to my destiny.

Put the force of your imagination behind projecting the energy down the timeline of your future life's work and smoothing out all the bumps it encounters long the way. When you feel the energy has reached the infinite future and its work is done, say:

Thank you
Frigga, Mother Goddess.
Thank you
Mimir, God of Wisdom.

Thank you again
for bestowing your blessing
on this worthy work.

Now snuff out the candle. The ritual is complete.

Rune Meditation: Paving Your Path to Destiny

This meditation paves the path to the right job or your life's work by aligning your energies of past, present, and future. In it, you use runes Hagalaz, Isa, and Naudhiz as channels for drawing down the energies of the three Norns: Urd, Verdandi, and Skuld.

In a quiet place conducive to meditation, take a few relaxing breaths to calm your mind. Place the three runes facedown before you: Rune Hagalaz on the left, Isa in the middle, and rune Naudhiz to the right.

Urd

Turn Hagalaz faceup. Hagalaz is the rune of Urd, Norn of the Past and Fate. Her word is "was." Urd sits at a spinning wheel, spinning out the threads of destiny or Life. Urd is often depicted as an aged woman, staring backward into the past. Her name is related to the Anglo-Saxon "Wyrd," which means the unseen influences behind events.

Notice the rune symbol, so much like an "H" with the crossbar tilted down to the right. If you allow your eyes to rest on it for a few moments, you will see that its shape somewhat resembles that of a woman seated at a spinning wheel. Picture Urd, her seamed, ancient face bent over her wheel, one hand twisting the flax of possibility and feeding it to the wheel, the other passing on the thread of Fate as it is spun.

Urd is spinning the thread of your fate. Visualize yourself leaning forward and calling her name (say it out loud). Picture her eyes turning to you, infinitely wise, looking out from her many wrinkles.

Now, while you have Urd's attention, visualize yourself telling her everything about your past that relates to your destiny (it's okay to say it out loud). Tell it all to her: the source nature of your desire for this destiny, relevant experiences (if you have none yet, that's okay), your hopes and dreams—whatever else you consider relevant.

When you have nothing more to say on the topic, visualize yourself thanking Urd for listening and having already worked these elements into the threads of your fate she is spinning (do so out loud). See her turn her withered face back to the wheel and return her attention to her spinning. You will probably find yourself making connections, and discover strong feelings on the subject you were unaware of before.

Verdandi

Reach out and turn rune Isa face up. Isa is the rune of Verdandi, Norn of the Present and Necessity. Her word is "is." Verdandi takes the threads of fate as they come off Urd's spinning wheel, and weaves them into the pattern of current existence or life. She is usually portrayed as a young woman staring straight forward.

The symbol on the Isa stone is a vertical line. Like Verdandi, the rune stands straight and tall. Let your eye rest on it for a moment and you will see the resemblance.

In your mind's eye, see the line metamorphose into Verdandi standing by her sister, looking straight forward, eyes focused somewhere far beyond you, as she takes the spun thread and weaves it into the fabric of the present. Picture yourself calling her name (say it out loud). Her eyes focus on you.

While you have Verdandi's ear, tell her all you can think of in your present life that points toward your destiny and makes it so important to you. Tell her what else you feel you need in your present life to reach that calling—additional schooling, financial backing, connections. Picture her young face listening to you intently.

When you have nothing more to say on the topic, visualize yourself thanking Verdandi for her time and for weaving these elements into the pattern of your present life (do so out loud).

Skuld

Next, turn rune Naudhiz faceup. Naudhiz is the rune of Skuld, Norn of the Future and Death. Her word is "should be." Skuld stands beside Verdandi and severs the threads with scissors when an individual's fated lifespan is concluded. She is shown veiled and holds the scroll or Book of Death, which is always unopened to symbolize her reluctance to reveal the future.

The runic symbol for Naudhiz is a shorter line crossing a longer line at an angle. Look at it for a few moments, and it isn't hard to see how much Naudhiz resembles a pair of scissors. Skuld holds scissors with which to cut the thread of life when your appointed time on Earth is done.

Picture the crossed lines of the rune becoming the scissors in Skuld's hand. See her standing there, scissors in one hand, the Book of Death in the other, face veiled, staring off into the future as she waits to cut a thread in the web Verdandi is weaving. Visualize yourself calling her name (say it out loud), and her veiled face turning to you.

While you have Skuld's attention, describe the destiny you desire, how you want to get there, why you feel it will be so important to you. Skuld's unseen eyes seem to glow from behind her veil; such is the strength of her interest.

When you are finished, visualize yourself thanking Skuld for the gift of her attention and for weaving these elements into the pattern of your future life (do so out loud). Picture her eyes dimming behind her veil as her thoughts return to the work without which, the world would soon be overrun with all the generations of the earth.

As you continue to sit quietly for a while, you may discover you are having a rush of insights into your future career path. These could include ways of putting past experiences to better use, solutions to current concerns, and potential difficulties along the way. This is a sign the Norns are already at work paving the path toward your destined career.

Chapter 5

Runes of Health and Healing

Can runes really influence health and healing? It's a natural question, one people ask all the time. Think of it this way: Even if you don't believe runes have any mystical powers, you can't deny the power of symbols to influence the unconscious. And there is a vast body of medical evidence proving the unconscious plays a vital role in health and healing.

Rune masters like the Vitka used runes to diagnose illness, reinforce health, and speed healing from the very beginning. Vitki applied the powers of runes to both physical and mental-spiritual ailments. Ancient records show them working with everything from depression to problem pregnancies, from colds to mood swings, from cancer to obsession and addiction.

Bringing back the gift of health and healing was one of Odin's main reasons for the ordeal he endured during the nine days and nights he hung upside-down over the abyss to win the runes. The Norse sagas remind us that the runes' two principal benefits are wisdom and well-being. Well-being (wellness, health, and vitality) has been a gift of runes ever since.

In fact, 8 of the 25 runes (or nearly a full third) have connotations related to wellness, recuperation, vitality, and regeneration. These runes of health and healing are Uruz, Kenaz, Jera, Perdhro, Sowilo, Tiwaz, Laguz, and Ingwaz. Meditate on any of these runes when you are suffering from any kind of illness and you will experience a new surge of energy and vitality almost immediately.

With the aid of runes, you can reduce the frequency and severity of illness, cut recovery time in half, and more. Runes can point out your individual health weaknesses that leave you vulnerable to sickness and disease. They can guide you to a healthier, more energetic life and lifestyle.

Runes will empower you to ...

- Get (and stay) healthy.
- Boost your immune system.
- Gain insight into cause of illness.
- Discover a cure or remedy when physicians and therapists fail.
- Identify personal health weaknesses.
- Develop your own, personalized path to maximum health.
- Recover from illness and heal from operations faster.
- Generate an instant charge of energy and vitality.

With rune readings, magic, and meditation, you can help yourself and others live longer, remain healthier longer, and become far less vulnerable to illness. However, runes and rune readings should not be substituted for a physician or therapist's advice. They are meant to supplement the efforts of medical and mental health professionals—not replace them.

> Runes you should know if a physician you would be, who can properly heal illness.
> —The Elder Edda

Creating Maximum Health

One aspect of runic philosophy holds that each individual is born with his or her individual health strengths and weaknesses. The best way to get healthy and stay healthy, according to this philosophy, is to let runes identify where your vulnerabilities in the health arena lie and point out ways they can be strengthened. This produces a condition of maximum health and resistance.

Mirroring today's cutting-edge health-care practitioners, Vitki looked beyond merely fighting disease. They looked toward runes as a means of mapping your personal path to creating and maintaining wellness. Using the same techniques they did, you can discover your own physical and mental health perils—and what you can do to end or alleviate them.

What are these health vulnerabilities? They include inborn tendencies like asthma, stroke, cancer, mood swings, or obsessive-compulsive disorder. They also include dietary and lifestyle choices that can weaken your constitution while they compromise your immune system: cigarette use, heavy drinking, hard-core drug abuse, poor nutritional habits, lack of exercise, frequent anger, or a generally negative attitude toward life.

Do what you can to counteract your inborn health weaknesses and eliminate health sabotaging lifestyle choices, and you can easily see that you will be on the road to maximum health. You can do this with what has been called the Health Perils reading.

Rune Reading: Spotting Your Health Perils

The Health Perils reading is a modified form of the Three Circles of Self reading you are already familiar with from Chapter 2. In this reading, the inner circle stands for Inner (mental and spiritual) Health and matters related to it. The middle ring signifies Bodily Health and matters concerning it. The outer ring represents Health in the Outer World and factors that impinge on it.

The main difference is that in this reading the focus is on health. Patterns like lines and triangles are ignored; and so is the Wishing Stone and the runes that land faceup. Only the facedown rune stones are read. In this reading, the facedown runes indicate your health vulnerabilities and weakness. These stones will also show what to do about your health perils.

There is one other difference. In the Health Perils reading, you look up the totem animals linked to the rune. If the list includes any animals that human beings typically eat, it can be a signal that it is unhealthy for the person being read to consume those meats—especially if more than one rune in the reading reiterates the warning.

Most people who throw the stones for this reading wind up with about an equal portion landing faceup and facedown. This is a typical reading, as most of us have an equal number of problem areas in regard to health and an equal number of areas of health strength. A majority of faceup runes suggests the person has few health vulnerabilities and is exceptionally vital and resistant to illness; a majority of facedown runes indicates the individual has many health vulnerabilities and will need to exercise care to keep his or her vitality high and ward off sicknesses.

Sample Reading

Julie's health was generally good, but she had always had the sense she didn't have enough energy, certainly not as much as others she knew. She had gone hiking with friends a few weeks earlier, and had to give up halfway to their destination and wait for the rest of her party to return. Her doctor said she seemed in overall good health, and because she had gotten beneficial advice from runes before on personal relationships and intimacy issues, Julie decided to see if runes could shed any light on her tendency to poop out.

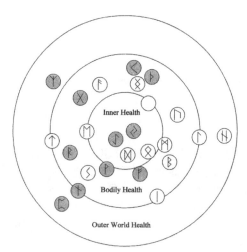

Julie's reading.

When Julie threw the rune stones, about the same number ended up faceup and facedown, a normal reading indicating normal health. What is interesting about it is that most of the facedown stones, 7 out of 11, landed in the Circle of Bodily Health. This suggested that most of her problems arise from her physical body as opposed to stresses and strains from the outer world (only two facedown stones), or inner health issues (only two facedown stones). (Runes that landed facedown are shown shaded.)

We began studying the runes with the seven facedown stones in the Circle of Bodily Health for clues to Julie's lack of pep. We started with Raidho, because it was nearest the bottom of the reading.

What Raidho Said

Facedown Raidho points to an important area of health, the circular flow or recirculation of energy within the body. By singling it out as a concern, the rune suggested that Julie has some serious vulnerabilities, possibly blockages, around this flow within which could partially account for her own lack of physical energy. In addition, its facedown condition, taken with the animals associated with Raidho, hints that she could alleviate this problem somewhat by avoiding the flesh of the two animals associated with this rune: pork and beef.

What Naudhiz Said

When Naudhiz is considered in terms of a health concern, the association that catches most people's eye is that with a constriction of the chest. This often points to bronchial or heart problems, and when I mentioned this to Julie, she stated that she indeed suffered from asthma.

Thinking of health, there is also Naudhiz's facedown meaning of things that can't be done without. When it comes to health, the one thing we can't do without is vitamins, opening the possibility that Julie might be suffering from a mild vitamin deficiency. When the rune is studied for clues to a remedy for the problem, the image of a fertile tree linked to Naudhiz might indicate Julie could alleviate this deficiency by eating more fruit—as fruit comes from trees.

What Wunjo Said

Wunjo is the rune of happiness and harmony; facedown generally signifies its opposite—sorrow and woe. When these become a health issue, we call it depression. Julie admitted that she was often subject to bouts of depression.

Looking for solutions Wunjo might offer to the problem it delineated (Julie's depressions), two meanings stood out. The first is the rune image of a weathervane, which suggested wind or fresh air. The second is Wunjo's reigning deity, Frey, God of Sunshine. Together they indicated getting more fresh air and sunshine would help lift Julie's depressions.

Because sunshine is the principle source of Vitamin D, the rune might also have been reinforcing the idea that she suffered from a vitamin deficiency. As boars are also associated with Wunjo, the rune might also have been emphasizing her need to steer clear of eating pork.

What Fehu Said

Fehu facedown in the Circle of Bodily Health can be perplexing. However, because Fehu relates to fertility or creative energy, it does suggest at least one of the two will be blocked. This, of course, would point to another cause of Julie's general lack of energy.

Fehu is another cattle-themed rune facedown. This rune is associated with the primal cow that set the first man free by licking the prison of salt in which he was cocooned. Taken into consideration with the other facedown runes in the Circle of Bodily Health relating to cattle seems to emphasize the warning against eating beef. Because the primal cow licked salt, Fehu may also be suggesting Julie regulate her salt intake.

What Gebo Said

Because Gebo is a rune of harmoniously intersecting energies, here facedown it reiterates the fact that the cause of Julie's lack of energy is a physical problem with her body, and not job stress or spiritual-mental concerns. Gebo is another rune related to beef, suggesting an all out ban on it might perk Julie up considerably. Reviewing Gebo's associations with other animals whose flesh we commonly eat, it may also be hinting that she avoid lobster, oysters, and other shellfish.

What Thurisaz Said

The meaning of Thurisaz facedown in a health reading is a bit more obscure than the others. One of the rune's meanings is regeneration, and regeneration blocked might indicate an impaired immune system. Although no animals are associated with Thurisaz, many delicious berries grow on the thorny vines the rune image represents—blackberries, for instance. So the rune could be reiterating the earlier hint that Julie eat more fruit.

What Kenaz Said

Though Kenaz threw little new light in the reading, it seemed to sum up Julie's problem as physical, for Kenaz facedown means lack of energy to do and accomplish.

After the reading, Julie followed the reading's advice, getting more exercise, eating more fruits, and cutting out pork and beef. A year later, she reported her energy level was much improved and that long hikes were part of her daily exercise regimen.

Rune #9: Hagalaz or Haegl

Hailstone, the whitest of grains/falls from high in the heavens/gusts of strong wind/toss it violently about/then the hard stone becomes water.

—*The Old English Rune Poem*

Hagalaz

Hagalaz (pronounced haw-gaw-laws) is your rune of disruptive forces with the potential to be transformed into benign ones. The arrival of the season of hail (hagalaz) was a matter of great significance to the peoples of ancient northern Europe. Icy-hard hail could destroy crops and property, and kill livestock and people. At the same time, hail possessed the potential to transform its nature completely, melting from the iron-hard destructive form to soft water, the nurturer of nature and a new season of crops. Thus hail became a many-layered symbol for them.

Rune Image: A hailstone of many layers

In Rune Reading

Faceup meanings: Destructive forces you can direct to beneficial ends, karma, opportunity, smooth sailing, transformation, nourishment, auspicious time for a new undertaking or for taking a risk, good luck through a natural event. *Tarot comparison:* The World. *Astrological comparison:* Aquarius.

Occluded (facedown) meanings: Bad weather ahead (literal as well as symbolic), catastrophe, limitation, delay, forces outside your control, inauspicious time for new starts or risks, disruption by a natural event. *Tarot comparison:* The World reversed. *Astrological comparison:* Aquarius afflicted.

In Rune Magic

Use to: Transform destructive energies into beneficial ones, launch new projects, especially those with many layers or requiring slow evolution over time, protect from harm, assist in personal transformation, open doorway to shapeshifting

In Rune Meditation

Use to: Access deep layers of self and ancestral memory, empower personal change and transformation, increase mystical experience and knowledge

Rune Gods: Ymir, the Roarer, primeval troll whose primal vibrations gave birth to all orders of creation, even the gods

Rune Totems: Lizards, dragons, nesting birds, elephants, turtles, web spiders, penguins, cows

Rune Herb: Lily of the Valley

Rune Color: Ash gray

Runes and Healing

Why be sick when you don't have to? Since time immemorial, Vitki have turned to runes to identify the sources of sickness and suggest potential remedies. Take advantage of this runic power to alleviate and even end sudden or chronic illness. Today, runes can supplement and support the efforts of your personal physician (but should never be substituted for a clinician's care).

Science has only recently acknowledged what people of previous eras knew that ill health is not always the result of bodily malfunction alone. Instead, it can be caused by problems of body, mind, or spirit. Any one alone or in combination can trigger illness and make the body far more susceptible to disease. For example, when you are happy and everything is going right, you catch colds and flu far less often than when you are blue and everything is going wrong. Laughter has even been proven to help cancer patients reverse the progress of their illness, go into remission, and enjoy long, full lives.

Mind and spirit play a central part in many of the most common medical problems of our era: bronchial difficulties, heart disease, stress, ulcers, and cancer. The same is true of most mental illness, including depression, schizophrenia, anxiety, and others.

Runes encompass the three worlds of body, mind, and spirit, and can often shed light on where the real origin of an illness lies. One ancient method of using runes to uncover the cause and cure of sickness is called the Column of Health reading. It looks for elements in your body, mind, or spirit that might be responsible for your ailing health. This reading uses only five runes, set out one above the other in a vertical column.

Heidi, the healer, men call me when their homes I visit, a far seeing Vitki, wise in talismans. Caster of spells, cunning in magic. To women with child welcome always.
—*The Elder Edda*

The Column of Health

Anytime you have a health concern—a cold that just won't go away, or you aren't recovering from surgery fast enough, or bouts of depression that come and go, or a series of headaches that just won't quit—the Column of Health reading reveals whether the cause is bodily, mental, spiritual—or a combination of two or even all three.

In this reading, you lay out all the runes except the blank one, Wyrd, facedown, mix them up, and then draw five guided by a higher power. You set these runes out faceup before you, placing each rune just over the previous rune like the rungs in a ladder. When you have finished the runes should look like this:

5. Rune of Remedy
4. Rune of Cause

3. Rune of Spirit

2. Rune of Mind

1. Rune of Body

The bottom rune, the first one you drew, illuminates the current condition of your body as it relates to your illness or concern. The rune above it, the second you drew, represents the condition of your mind as it relates to the problem. The third rune indicates the current state of your spirit as it reflects on your concern. Often, because you are dealing with ill health, which is health upside-down, you will want to consider the meaning of the rune when facedown.

In the majority of Column of Health readings, studying the lower three runes alone is enough to supply the necessary clues to the root causes of a sickness. When for some reason the source of the illness still isn't clear, a look at the fourth rune will provide the answer. This rune always reveals where your health problem lies. The fifth, and topmost, rune points you toward potential remedies and cures.

The Column of Health reading may have been inspired by the spinal column. The people of those times believed vital life energies that maintain bodily health flowed upward and downward through the spinal column.

Sample Reading

Ernest worked as a senior computer designer for a company whose name still remains synonymous with cutting-edge computers. He was a senior member of the team responsible for designing the next generation of the company's product. For the past several years, Ernest had been plagued with a constant succession of illnesses. As soon as he would get over a cold, he would catch the flu. Once over the flu, he would get gastritis. After that, he would have an asthmatic attack. Cured of it, he would develop cluster headaches, whose ending would be followed by a cold. And on and on. These had cost him so much time off work that even his highly liberal employers were beginning to lose their patience with the situation, and his job was on the line.

In an attempt to "get well and stop being sick all the time," Ernest had tried physicians and the specialists they recommended. He had been tested dozens of times for a multitude of suspected condition with negative or inclusive results. Ernest had consulted specialists in qui gong, the Chinese medical system, as well as naturopathy, acupuncture, and macrobiotics—all without result.

Finally, in desperation, Ernest acted on the advice of a friend and decided to see my rune teacher. After a short consultation, she suggested that, rather than the more typical three circles reading, Ernest seek any enlightenment the runes might bestow on his problem through the Column of Health. My teacher explained the reading and then asked Ernest to shuffle the rune stones. After he had finished, he felt called to choose five runes. He arranged them in order as he drew them, and then my teacher described the meaning and associations of each stone, with special emphasis on their meanings when occluded.

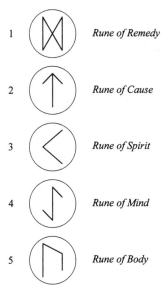

1	Rune of Remedy
2	Rune of Cause
3	Rune of Spirit
4	Rune of Mind
5	Rune of Body

Ernest's Column of Health reading.

The appearance of Uruz (health) as Rune of Body indicated that his illnesses were all genuine—Ernest was not imagining them. Eihwaz as Rune of Mind pointed to his work being very much in his thoughts. Ernest responded that this was true. He was part of a team that had been working for several years to develop a much more powerful computer of a radical design, and all had not been going well. So his job was very much on his mind.

Ernest had drawn Kenaz third, and it occupied the position of his Rune of Spirit. Because these runes typically indicate any malign influences on health, Kenaz here acts to block progress, causing loss or delay, generating internal trauma and anxiety. Ernest admitted that things had not been progressing satisfactorily on the designing of the new computer. In fact, they were more than 18 months behind schedule. Their jobs were all on the line, the company's stock was falling, and as a senior member of the team, Ernest took the delay personally and was sick at heart about it, as Kenaz and Eihwaz indicated.

In the fourth position, the Rune of Cause, was Tiwaz, normally a rune of victory and success. But occluded, it often represents a negative situation which has reached its darkest point—because it is the darkness before the dawn. Ernest felt that if he could believe his problems were the result of being in the darkness before the dawn and that his team was close to a breakthrough on the computer that would allow them to move forward rapidly in the near future, he would be the happiest man in the world.

At the top, representing the Rune of Remedy, was Dagaz, which because it is the solution can be read straight up. Dagaz often relates to meditation. Here, it seemed to be telling Ernest that until the breakthrough his team was searching for, he could reduce his health problems by reducing the stress of his job through meditation.

Rune Reading: Locating the Source of Your Health Concern

In a place where you can read the runes without interruption, relax for a few moments. Set the blank stone or Wyrd, the Stone of Fate, aside, and lay the 24 rune stones facedown before you. Shuffle them around until they are thoroughly mixed up.

Hold your hand over the runes and say:

Runar radh rett radh. (Runes bless me with good guidance.)

When you feel an impulse to reach for a specific rune, take it, turn it right side up, and place it before you at what will be the bottom of the column. Repeat this process with each of the four other runes needed for this reading. Place them one above another until you have set the fifth stone at the top.

To interpret your Column of Health reading, begin with the Rune of Body. Consider the various meanings associated with it—both when it is faceup and when it is facedown—and how they might relate to what you know of the current influences on your body and your illness. Continue this with the Rune of Mind and the Rune of Body.

Take more time when you reach the Rune of Cause. Ask yourself if it in any way relates to or is similar to any of the first three runes. If so, this is like an arrow pointing toward the origin of your problem.

Use a similar approach to the Rune of Remedy. Devote some thought to what the rune you have drawn might be saying about potential cures. Examine its meanings for any resonances or linkages it might have with the other four stones. Sometimes this stone might suggest that you see a physician, seek family medical history from a relative, look for a specific course of treatment a physician might have recommended, or change your diet or lifestyle.

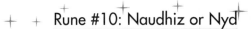

Rune #10: Naudhiz or Nyd

Need constricts all those/who feel its pinch./Yet if people heed/its warning signs in time/need can point the way/to salvation.
—*The Old English Rune Poem*

Naudhiz

Naudhiz (pronounced now-these) is your rune of deliverance from distress. The cross has been a symbol for need (naudhiz) and deliverance from time immemorial in almost every culture and land. Little wonder that it echoes the same meaning among runes.

Rune Image: A cross

In Rune Reading

Faceup meanings: Sign of coming difficulty that can be averted, need, affliction, friction that leads to conflict, disagreement, importance of thinking twice before taking any step, legal proceedings, constraint, emotional needs, love and the heat of passion, a difficult lesson that must be learned. *Tarot comparison:* The Devil. *Astrological comparison:* Capricorn.

Occluded (facedown) meanings: A course of action that should be abandoned, failure and despair, hasty judgment leading to disaster, karma as retribution. *Tarot comparison:* The Devil reversed. *Astrological comparison:* Capricorn afflicted.

In Rune Magic

Use to: Ensure deliverance from distress, protect your goals, find the lover you need, dampen the fires of anger and conflict, increase clairvoyance, overcome bad habits, invoke spirit guides and power animals

In Rune Meditation

Use to: Make wiser choices, understand your needs and desires, overcome psychological constraints like bad habits or behavior patterns, develop greater spirituality

Rune Gods: Nott, Goddess of Night; Skuld, Norn ruler over future and death, first rune mistress

Rune Totems: Wolves, jackals, vultures, bobcats, crows, fleas, donkeys, mules, spiders, squirrels, packrats

Rune Herb: Bisort

Rune Color: Black

Rune Magic: Supercharging Your Immune System

Try this ritual for boosting health or healing. Its power to aid you and others will astonish you. The ceremony it is based on has been used since antiquity, and is still in use today. It will boost your immune system so that your body is more resistant to illness. You will be healthier more of the time because you will ward off sickness when others are succumbing all around you, and if you do get sick your recovery periods will be shorter.

In this ritual, you will release and direct the powerful energies of three runes long associated with healing: Uruz, the rune of health and vitality; Jera, with its strong connection to the healing powers of the annual cycles of Earth, Sun, and Moon; and Sowilo, embodiment of the solar energy that ultimately lies behind life, growth, and wellness.

To fully access the immune supercharging power of the runes, you will invoke the deity who rules over each rune: Thor, God of fertility and vitality to the common people; Iduna, Goddess who tends the Golden Apples of Rejuvenation; and Eir, Goddess of Healing.

Ideally, this ceremony calls for three candles, one for each of the runes: dark green for Uruz, grass green for Jera, and sunlight gold for Sowilo. But if you can't find all three, or lighting three candles would create a potential fire hazard where you perform your rituals, then just use one candle, a gold one. As the embodiment of the primal fire that sustains life, Sowilo is the ultimate source of the energy behind the other two runes as well—so it can stand in for all three.

The ritual also calls for a mixture of herbs. If possible, take a pinch of each of the herbs that aids in unlocking your access to the three runes in question: sphagnum moss (Uruz), rosemary (Jera), and mistletoe (Sowilo). Blend them together and then put them in an incense burner. If obtaining all three is impractical for some reason, use the mistletoe because of its resonance with Sowilo.

There are many ways of healing the body and mind. I use runes in healings. The easiest way is to draw the rune on the body with your finger. While drawing it tell the rune what you want it to do (i.e., relieve headache). I also combine runes with a form of astral projection into a body. Projecting the runes also around the outside of a body or portion thereof.
—Heidyth/Linda Crowfoot, *Healing with Runes*

At a time and location you deem suitable for magical work (you should feel comfortable performing a ritual there, you should be undisturbed, and it should be quiet so you can focus your mind and spirit), light your specially blended incense. Next, lay the three runes stones out before you, in order from left to right: Uruz first, Jera second, and Sowilo third. Then, set each of the candles just beyond (at the top of) the rune its color represents, and light it.

Breath deeply and relax for a few moments, clearing your mind and being so that it will be a better conduit for the healing energies you are about to receive and channel.

When you are prepared, pick up rune Uruz in your left hand (as this is closest to the heart) and say:

In the name of Thor,
I invoke Uruz!

In no more than a minute or two, you should feel the rune stone becoming unnaturally warm in your hand. This signifies that Thor has opened the energies of Uruz to you. Lay the rune back down where it came from and repeat the process with Jera in your left hand. Say:

In the name of Iduna,
I invoke Jera!

When you feel Jera grow unnaturally warm or begin to send vibrations up your arm, place the rune stone back in its original position and say:

In the name of Eir,
I invoke Sowilo!

Once more, continue holding the rune stone in your left hand until you feel some physical change in the stone, signaling that Sowilo's energies have been activated for you by Eir. Return the rune to its place. Now say:

Thank you, Thor.
Thank you, Iduna.
Thank you, Eir.

Pick up the three rune stones. Cup them in your hands and raise them above your head. Visualize their energy streaming from your hands to the person whose immune system you wish to fortify (yourself or another). Say:

Let the energy
of these runes
flow through [name of person].
May it make [name]
strong, healthy, well.
May it ward off
disease, ill health, infirmity.
May it heal [name]
quickly of all ills.
May it preserve [name]
hale and vital

'til their years
on Earth are many.
Thor bids you obey me. Jera bids you obey me.
Eir bids you obey me.
Uruz! Jera! Eir!

By now any warmth or tingling should have left the stones. They will feel normal. This means the healing magic of the runes has done its work and has begun the process of energizing the immune system of the person you want to help.

Repeat:

Thank you, Thor,
thank you, Iduna,
thank you, Eir,
for this blessing.

Blow out the candles, but let the incense burn itself out.

Repeat whenever you feel your vitality or immune system are down below par—or to ward off potential illnesses you have been exposed to, like colds or the flu.

Rune Meditation: Strengthening Health and Healing

Medical science has long acknowledged the proven health benefits of meditation. Pausing for just a few minutes every day to relax and clear your mind has been shown to help people reduce stress, recover from cancer, heal from surgery, and significantly reduce the number and length of illnesses. It has also helped them stay vital and healthy when others were succumbing to heat, viral infections, and exhaustion. You multiply those benefits when your meditation focuses on one of the runes of health and healing.

Laguz, a rune associated with water, might seem an odd choice at first to benefit health and vitality. But don't forget, life came out of the sea. Everything that lives, from plants to animals to people, is 90 percent or more water. Indeed, we are supported and nourished from within by a mighty torrent of salt water—with a few additives—the blood stream. Your blood, your cells, just about everything but your bones and teeth and nails are mostly water.

We often speak of life, especially human life, metaphorically as "a mighty river." We unconsciously acknowledge this essential connection in the many metaphors that link life with water. Some reflect the positive sides of life, such as "going with the flow" or "riding the wave"; some negative like "going down for the third time" or "running against the tide."

Physicians recommend everyone drink at least eight glasses of water each day to maintain health. When you are sick, they advise drinking plenty of fluids. It should come as no surprise, then, that sickness and health are intimately associated with water.

In earlier ages, physicians pictured disease as storms and disruptions of the life fluids, and saw health as being like an undisturbed ocean of vitality in the body. To them, Lagaz was the embodiment of the life essence. Looking deep into Lagaz opened a channel to an endless ocean of vitality, and through vitality, health.

To begin this meditation, you will, as usual, want to be in a quiet place where you can dim the lights and be comfortable. You will want to either sit at a table or on the floor so that you can place rune Laguz faceup before you. When you have done that, breath in and out deeply several times to allow your body and mind to become calm and centered.

Shift your attention to the rune stone and the image on it. Notice how the downward angle of the arm at the top of the figure looks like a wave rising to a crest and then collapsing. Let that image fill your eyes for a moment, then close them.

Visualize how the wave comes into view, rises to a point at the crest, and then collapses as it moves out of view and another wave replaces it. Picture a succession of waves moving slowly, rhythmically, peacefully from right to left. Continue to let the waves move before your mind's eye until you begin to feel something of the calm and peace of the ocean yourself.

Now, see the ocean waves moving closer until they surround you. Feel their calm, rhythmic surge as, one after another after another after another, they move through you. Feel yourself becoming a wave, rolling endlessly across the vast expanse of the ocean, always curling upward behind, always curling sharply downward in front—but never collapsing. Instead, you are traveling peacefully forever across the face of the sea.

Feel the ocean itself rising about you. Feel yourself becoming the ocean's waters. Feel the unending vastness with which you girdle the globe. Feel the infinite power and calm of your vast depths. Feel the deep, primal energy of your surging tides. Feel the kingdom over which your liquid empire extends, as great as that of all the continents together.

Feel how nothing can harm your oceanic vastness, nothing can diminish it, nothing can limit it. Feel the latent energy that resides within that infinite liquidity: the power of tides, waterfalls, floods, rivers, and the awesome power of torrential rain.

Feel this power's resistance to change, harm, sickness, and disease. You can draw from this ocean of health forever without diminishing it by a drop. Feel this power's ability to instantly rush in to fill any hole, to return to a smooth, unblemished surface in an instant. This power infuses your body with healing energy to throw off illness and recuperate from wounds and surgery.

Feel that force surging in every cell of your body—in your blood—in your skin—in your muscles. Feel how inexhaustible this power is within you. Feel the health literally bursting from you.

Let yourself experience this supercharged state of health for a while. Then, open your eyes, shake your arms and torso to settle the energy back down. Practice this meditation when you are ill, incapacitated, or recovering from an operation to quicken the process and to keep your body at the peak of health and well-being.

Chapter 6

Runes of Conflict and Communication

Is your family being torn apart because of two relatives who fight like cats and dogs every time they meet? Are you and your spouse or partner suddenly squabbling, and you're afraid there might be something more serious concealed beneath the surface?

Are you constantly at odds with someone you work with who seems to have taken a personal dislike to you and goes out of his or her way to make life difficult for you? Have you had a violent disagreement with a colleague, each convinced of being right, and become so divisive you both feel real animosity toward each other? Did a good business venture go sour, leaving everyone bitterly blaming each other, and tempers have flared so hotly lawsuits are in the offing?

In short, are you involved in a conflict you wish you knew how to resolve? Have you tried your best to find a way out? Lain awake at night fruitlessly attempting to analyze what caused the situation in the first place? Sought in vain for points of agreement between seemingly irreconcilable points of view? Prayed you could find some line of communication that would allow all parties to put their differences aside and reach a mutually satisfactory agreement?

In most conflicts communication plays a central role. It is usually a lack of communication or miscommunication between people that leads to conflict, just as it is usually good communication that helps put an end to conflict. The runic system of philosophy implicitly recognizes this relationship. The runes of communication are also runes of conflict—and vice versa.

The runes of communication and conflict are ...

- Ansuz, the mouth, is the most archetypal, representing speech and words, our two primary means of communication. But occluded (facedown), its energies blocked, this rune also means missed or misunderstood communication, deceit, bad advice, and verbal interference by others.

- Raidho, travel, almost always involves meeting and communicating with others. But occluded it signifies impasses, ruptures, and upset plans.

- Jera, harvest, is another occasion when people come together and communicate, but occluded it signifies lawsuits and legalities.

- Mannaz is the archetypal rune of humanity, of relating to and communicating with our fellows. But occluded it indicates difficulty or obstruction by others.

- Beorc, family, symbolizes a place for communication and love, but occluded it signifies family as a center of quarrels, jealousy, and separation.

- Ehwaz, the rune of working in tandem, is all about communication, but occluded it points to strife and separations.

This idea of communication leading into and out of conflict is inherent rune lore. However, sometimes your best attempts at communicating in good will and fairness fail, are misunderstood, or are rebuffed. Sometimes, you want to find a way to open the lines of communication and turn a fight or dispute around—but don't know how. And, sometimes you aren't sure what caused the problem in the first place, and are at a complete loss as to what to say or where to begin.

This is where runes can point the way to the seeds of the conflict as well as what and how you need to communicate to resolve it satisfactorily for everyone concerned.

Transforming Personal Conflicts

Quarrels, disagreements, strife, arguments, clashes, antagonism, hostile confrontations—just thinking of the words can make you tense up. They arouse unpleasant memories. Conflict, no matter who started it, or who is in the right, or who you *think* is in the right, hurts. It hurts you, and most often, all those involved.

How often have you lain awake all night, sick at heart over an argument or legal or business clash? How often have you cringed, cut to the quick because of what someone has said or done or taken from you or threatened to do that hurt you? How often have you felt helpless because you couldn't find a way to turn the situation around?

And it's not always what's done to us. All too frequently, conflict leads us to do rash things and say rash things in the heat of anger that hurt others. Too often we say or do them to people we love, and then wish we could undo them, take them back, cut out our tongues metaphorically. Even when we know we are right and the other person is dead wrong, we regret our words. And when we realize we were a bit at fault, too, the sorrow and shame cut even deeper.

Generally arguments and antagonism aren't a matter of who's right and who's wrong. There is a bit of each on both sides. Though we might be certain at the time that the truth lies with our position and the other person is being a deliberate pain in the rear—or is even out to get us.

Being certain your position is the correct one means not being willing to compromise. That prolongs the conflict and a prolonged difference of opinion never gets better. Because it never feels good to be in a heated dispute, even when we are in the right, we are only hurting ourselves when we fail to look for some right in the other party's stance.

Less often, you really do encounter someone out to cheat you, or get the best of you—or who actively is trying to hurt you out of malice and dislike. They try to have you fired, or break up a relationship, or put you out of business, or put you down, or cheat you badly and defy you to sue—or decide to sue you over nothing at all. These are the people who can make life hell—if you don't find some way to end the conflict.

Miscommunication is at the heart of many personal imbroglios. You might have misinterpreted something the other party said, or that person might have misunderstood you. Or you may both be working out of such different frameworks that neither of you fully understands where the other is coming from.

Sadly, there are those occasions when conflict isn't the result of miscommunication. You both understand each other only too well—but there is no apparent meeting of the minds. Perhaps you disagree about how something should be done, or what the right course of action is. Sometimes, one you have something the other wants (a job, a family heirloom, a friendship), but you need it desperately, or feel the other person has no right to it whatsoever.

But when you get down to basics, it doesn't matter how or why you wound up in the contest, regardless of whether you are struggling against a friend, an enemy, or a stranger whose car bumped fenders with yours 10 minutes ago. If you are like most people, you'd probably rather not have a hassle with anybody in the first place. In fact, you'd probably prefer to nip disagreements and conflicts in the bud, before they start. In some situations, you might even sense a potential trouble between you and someone else could be brewing, and wish you had some way of knowing for certain so you could head it off.

With rune readings, you can detect the seeds of conflict developing—before they become serious—and take the proper steps to prevent the conflict from escalating. If the problem has advanced and you are so embroiled in antagonism and battle there doesn't appear to be any way out of the situation, a reading points your way toward potential areas of resolution and concrete steps you can take to restore harmony and concord. Stress and worry and negative emotions don't have to continue, runes can help transform any conflict.

In a rune reading you will learn to identify ...

- The seeds of a developing dispute.
- The cause of an advanced one.
- The miscommunications that are involved.
- What communication, made what way, leads to an amicable settlement.

Rune Reading: Identifying the Seeds of Conflict

Here is another approach to rune readings that uses the three circles discussed in Chapter 2 in an adapted form. When you read to illuminate a conflict, however, each circle has a slightly different meaning. The inner circle shows what you are doing to help create the situation and what you can do to make it better. The middle circle indicates the seeds of the conflict that lie in their character and life. The outer circle reveals elements of the struggle that originate in the outer world—specific circumstances, other people, unseen influences.

In interpreting a conflict reading, the facedown rune stones reflect the true causes underlying the struggle. When the facedown runes are evenly spread through all three circles, it means the responsibility for the situation is evenly divided. When the majority falls in one circle, it shows that the primary responsibility lies in one area.

Get out your rune cloth or draw three concentric circles. The three circles are:

- Circle of Self
- Circle of Other
- Circle of Outside World

Then throw all 25 rune stones. As you study your reading, remember ...

- Occluded runes represent the seeds of the conflict.
- A concentration of occluded stones in one circle indicates that is where the main cause of the conflict lies.
- An even scattering of occluded runes in all three circles means everyone involved is equally responsible.

Otherwise read runes as you normally would, looking for interesting patterns and their meanings.

Sample Reading

I met Gunther at a holistic health conference. He asked for a rune reading. His tone suggested it was a matter of some seriousness to him. Gunther had gone into business with his best friend. The pair lived in a small college town, both were successful professionals, and both had put away some money for a rainy day. The pair had long dreamed of opening some kind of fun, funky coffee house near the campus that would appeal to students. The town already had several upscale coffee houses operated by national and local chains. But Gunther and Jake envisioned something less pretentious: a comfortable, no-frills place, filled with secondhand chairs and tables. The low overhead would mean they could charge less for a cup of coffee, espresso, or latté, which would hopefully make them a real attraction with the budget-conscious college crowd.

Because Gunther had more time, it was their notion that both would be equal partners, though Jake would put up 65 percent of the start-up costs and Gunther only 35 percent. Gunther would make up the difference by managing the coffee house, as Jake was far too busy to be involved with the day-to-day details of running the business. It was an arrangement both men liked.

The coffee house, which they called Gunther and Jake's, was an instant success—not only with college students, but with the town's arty set and academics, who appreciated the establishment's casual, laid-back atmosphere. Gunther had a gift for getting along with people and making them feel welcome that kept customers coming back. Both partners could not have been happier—with the business and each other.

For a year all went well, then the parent firm of one of the local coffee house chains, noticing Gunther and Jake's success, decided it wanted a piece of the student action. Taking a page out of the partners' book they opened a competitive coffee house, in a similar barebones space, just down the block. But because the company enjoyed the purchasing power of the chain, they were able to undersell Gunther and Jake's. Soon, enough of Gunther and Jake's customers, attracted by the lower prices, had deserted their coffee house for the one down the block to cut into their sales. Gunther and Jake's was still turning a small profit and was in no danger of going out of business. But the cash flow had shrunk substantially. This was a real problem for Jake, who had been using his share of their profits to support a more lavish lifestyle, including vacations in the Bahamas and a spanking new cabin cruiser. It was a problem for Gunther, too, for he tried everything he could think of to win their customers back, and took his failure personally.

Forced to spend less, and feeling pinched, Jake decided to become more hands-on with the day-to-day operation of the business in an attempt to squeeze more profit from it. Among his initiatives, cutting back the portions and sizes without saying anything to their clientele while keeping the price the same. Another was to cut back on employee benefits—which lowered their enthusiasm for the job, which in turn turned off and lost them customers.

Though it created some short-term financial gains, it infuriated Gunther, who argued that in the long run their customers were sure to notice and would desert them for their competitor down the street. Jake was insistent that if Gunther knew what he was doing, their profits would never have fallen off in the first place.

The breach came when Gunther tried to over rule Jake, insisting their agreement gave him final say over the operation of the business. Jake replied that because he had put up 65 percent of the money, he was majority owner with the power to dictate policy. Gunther went to his attorney, determined to make Jake live up to his promises. Jake consulted his own attorney, determined he would be the one to make decisions about their business future. Quickly, the two became involved in a heated, acrimonious legal battle. Neither was speaking to the other and their friendship seemed a thing of the past. Finally, they were forced to hire a manager to run the coffee house, which teetered on the verge of bankruptcy.

Gunther had several questions. He wasn't certain he understood how things had gone so badly between them so fast. He also wondered if there was some way to avoid an expensive court battle, save the business, and (though this seemed unlikely to him) save his friendship with Jake, as well. We decided to throw the runes and see what a reading might reveal. (Runes that landed facedown are shown shaded.)

The Besieging Runes

This is a very unusual reading, even for one about conflict. Note the way the stones in the Circle of Other seem to curve around the rim of the Circle of Self, almost like enemy forces surrounding a town they hope to conquer. This suggests the bitterness of the dispute, particularly on the part of Gunther's partner Jake.

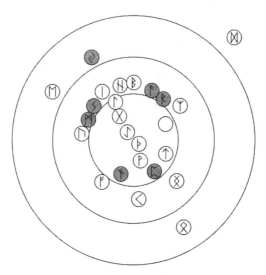

Gunther's reading.

Note, too, that there are only two facedown stones in the inner circle, whereas there are four in the Circle of Other. Because occluded runes indicate the roots of a conflict, this suggests that although Gunther is not without blame in the situation, responsibility for their conflict rests with his partner. Moreover, a single facedown rune landed in the Circle of Outside World, suggesting that while factors outside themselves may have given the impetus to their battle, most of the responsibility for beginning and maintaining it rests with them.

Runes in Circle of Self

Beginning with the Circle of Self, we find occluded Perdhro and Naudhiz. Occluded, Perdhro's associations include hopes dashed, disappointment by another, loss of money, and disillusion with a partner. Gunther's predicament could hardly be more succinctly described. Naudhiz often signifies legal proceedings, and occluded it often indicates a course of action that should be abandoned, hasty judgment leading to disaster. Considering that Gunther had begun the lawsuit, Naudhiz seems to be saying that he acted precipitously, which had made a difficult situation worse.

Runes in Circle of Other

Moving outward from the center circle representing the Gunther, we next come to the Circle of Other, representing Jake. Here we find four occluded runes: Mannaz, Sowilo, Ansuz, and Raidho. Facedown, Mannaz usually indicates the person it represents, can expect no help from others, will encounter difficulty, often involving legal matters, and is acting out of a degree of selfishness that makes him his own worst enemy. Again, this seems an amazingly accurate reading of the overall situation. As for Sowilo, occluded, it signifies a self-centered person, typically a workaholic on whom stress has begun to take a toll, an individual with a vital need to be in control, who becomes worried and nervous when they aren't. Ansuz, the supreme rune of communication, facedown can signify a person out for what's best for him; selfish, biased advice from someone; and failed communication. Finally, occluded Raidho means ruptures with others.

In part, this appeared to imply that Jake was already over-stressed from over-work when the whole situation began, which doubtless made him react to the reduction in disposable income more negatively than he might have otherwise. It also suggested that his strong impulse to be in control of everything in his life had been in abeyance, only needing the problem at their coffee house to bring it to the surface. There is also a hint that someone might be giving Jake bad advice, thus further inflaming the dispute.

Circle of Outside World

Only one occluded rune, Jera, fell here. When it lands like this, Jera represents scarcity, unrewarded effort—and lawsuits. Certainly it was a scarcity of profits, despite great efforts on both partner's parts, that led to the divisive argument between Gunther and Jake. But it is a minor influence compared with the way the two men's runes cluster around each other, indicating the actual seeds of the conflict lie in the relationship between the two men.

At this point in the reading, Gunther asked if there was any hint from the runes about how he and Jake could resolve their differences. There was. It lay in the extremely long line of rune stones running all the way across the Circle of Self.

Reading the Line

The second conspicuous aspect of Gunther's reading is the extremely long line of stones beginning with Perdhro facedown just inside and to the right of the lower arc of the Circle of Self. All the rest of the stones in this line are faceup and extend the line upward to the left across the inner circle and into the Circle of Other. There, significantly, it connects to the keystones of the arch of runes that almost surround Gunther's Circle of Self.

Perdhro, which normally symbolizes fun, laughter, and the creative inner child, is occluded, its energies blocked. From Perdhro, the line moves up to the left through Wunjo (ability to turn things around), Thurisaz (ability to transform defeat into victory), Eihwaz (ability to manage and direct), Gebo (ability to work with others, to make connections between others), and Lagaz (ability to go with flow). As lines represent a person's best qualities, it is easy to see in these runes the personality of someone who could build up a popular business in which the friendly atmosphere drew customers.

Lagaz connects the stones in the Gunther's Circle of Self with three runes in the circle representing his partner Jake. The position of these three stones, in the center of the arch of besieging runes, suggests they are the keystones of the situation, as does the fact that they separate the four occluded runes of the group. Faceup, of course, they symbolize Jake's positive qualities and characteristics.

The three runes Lagaz's energies connect with are: Isa (caution, slow expansion), Hagalaz (negative forces with the potential to be transformed into positive ones), and Berkana (nurturing, giving). Actually Lagaz only connects with Hagalaz directly, but as Hagalaz and Berkana touch, their energies act as one with twice the power. Gunther recognized the characteristics represented by Isa and Berkana (caution, nurturing) were among the things he and others like best about Jake, and which led to their partnership.

Unblocking Perdhro's Power

Stepping back to take in the overall pattern of the reading, Perdhro facedown and blocked at the start of the line truly stands out. Certainly the fun and laughter represented by Perdhro had gone out of managing the coffee house for Gunther. They had been replaced by worry over its future and the bitter feelings aroused by the conflict with his partner.

Perdhro's position at the beginning of the line seems to suggest that if the energy of the rune could be unblocked, it would travel along the line of runes, reenergizing the rest of Gunther's good qualities, like electricity along a cable. When it reached the terminus, the rune's energy would stimulate the three positive keystone runes in the Circle of Other representing his partner's good qualities. Together these positive characteristics would then be strong enough to overcome the four occluded rune stones causing the conflict.

In short, if Gunther could find some way to lighten up and get over his own guilty feelings over the profits dipping, it would free the playful, inner child part of himself that had made the business a success and that had originally been one of the foundations of his friendship with Jake. If Gunther did this, it would restore his emotional balance, bringing all his positive qualities back into play. These, in turn, would resonate well with Jake's positive qualities, and they would be strong enough to bring Jake to his senses, restore his sense of balance, and overcome the negative ones that had contributed so much to the conflict between the two men.

The reading made perfect sense to Gunther, though he doubted the situation could be rectified so easily. However, he decided to attend a week-long meditation retreat he'd heard about, hoping that would enable him to get back in touch with his playful inner child. Then he said he would call Jake up and ask him to a quiet dinner meeting where they could talk to each other face-to-face, without attorneys to get in the way, and see if they could find a way to work things out amicably between themselves.

As a result, the two men did renew their friendship, and worked together to solve the coffee house's financial problems. Within two years, Gunther and Jake's had become so successful that they had purchased the storefront next to them, torn down the wall, and expanded. Jake sold Gunther his share and now spends his retirement cruising the Bahamas, where Gunther visits him every so often for a vacation.

Rune #11: Isa or Is

Ice is bitterly cold/extremely hard./A floor of ice/is fair to see/glitters like diamonds/but is frozen solid.

—*The Old English Rune Poem*

Isa

Isa (pronounced ee-saw) is your rune of stillness, rest, and stocktaking. To early peoples living in the northlands of Europe, the coming of ice (isa) and winter was a serious matter. This was the season of waiting, when no crops grew and many normal activities, from tilling the soil to market days to social gatherings, ceased. For this reason, ice and the icicle became a symbol of immobility and a time of waiting.

Rune Image: An icicle

In Rune Reading

Faceup meanings: Stasis, frozen, static energy, gradual development, expansion, learning, concentration of force, a time for regrouping and waiting, a cooling relationship. *Tarot comparison:* The Hermit. *Astrological comparison:* The waning, crescent moon.

Occluded (facedown) meanings: Stagnation, procrastination, frustrations, delays, deadlock, a relationship from which all warmth has fled. *Tarot comparison:* The Hermit reversed. *Astrological comparison:* The waning, crescent moon afflicted.

In Rune Magic

Use to: Freeze a situation where it is, halt the progress of negative energies and affairs dead in their tracks, free constricted or frozen situations and forces

In Rune Meditation

Use to: Discover the value of periods of delay and immobility, develop greater self-control

Rune Gods: The Rime Gods, who died that Odin might create other living races; Verdandi, Norn who weaves the web of life into the pattern of present existence

Rune Totems: Reindeer, moose, penguins, polar bears, whale, snow geese, walruses, bald eagles

Rune Herb: Henbane

Rune Color: Ice white

From Antagonism to Agreement

Identifying the seeds of a conflict isn't always enough to bring it to an amicable conclusion. There are times when you know what caused it—and that is two points of view that appear to be diametrically opposite on every issue. You disagree all the way down the line.

As a person of good will, you have tried your best to find some compromise. Perhaps the other person stubbornly rebuffed all your overtures. Or maybe they made an attempt to work with you and find a way to resolve the dispute, but the two of you just couldn't come to any agreement that one or the other didn't feel was unfair.

You might have purchased an expensive item at a store and decided to return it unused, and they are willing to give you a store credit but not return your money. You might have dreamed up a new direction for your firm, only to discover your partner has dreamed up a completely different and incompatible idea—and each of you is convinced your idea will earn millions, while the other's would lead to disaster. You might have unintentionally said something that hurt a colleague or loved one, and no matter how you explain yourself, the other party remains furious, convinced you could only have meant the remark the way it was taken.

It's a familiar scenario, one we've all been stuck in at least a few times in our lives. You'd like to work things out, but every avenue seems blocked, and every one you try becomes a blind alley. Meanwhile, the hostilities between you and the other person continue—doing no one any good.

So? How do you find a way to agree when all your efforts fail? When you disagree strongly on each vital point? When you have two differing points of view—and never the twain shall meet? Often, a simple rune reading using only seven stones can point the way to unsuspected points of agreement.

Rune Reading: Finding Your Point of Agreement

When you are locked in a seemingly irresolvable conflict with someone, the Point of Agreement reading will show you a way out of the impasse. Use it anytime you are unable to find common ground with another. There may seem to be no possible point of agreement. But there is, and this reading will reveal it to you.

The Point of Agreement reading uses only seven runes, drawn from the 24 rune stones with images turned facedown and shuffled at random. The seven runes are laid out in the shape of a "V." Three rune stones on the left and three on the right form the narrowing sides of the "V." The seventh rune stone, where two sides come together at the point of the "V," reveals the key point the two parties can agree on.

The first rune drawn forms the top of the "V" on the left, and the second stone forms the top on the right. The third rune drawn becomes the middle of the "V" on the left and the fourth the middle of the "V" on the right. The fifth and sixth rune stones form the narrowest part of the "V" on the left and right, respectively. The seventh, drawn last, becomes the bottom point of the "V."

The left side of the "V" represents you, the right side represents your nemesis. The two stones at the top reveal the cause of the conflict. Stones three and four, represent two secondary points of contention. The last pair of stones pinpoints an essential miscommunication that helps perpetuate your dispute. The seventh rune reveals a key area where agreement, and a resolution you can all live with, is possible.

Once you identify a point on which the two of you can agree, it is only a short step to working things out and being able to put the whole situation behind you.

To begin, remove Wyrd, the blank rune stone, from your set and put it aside. Spread the remaining 24 runes facedown before you and swirl them around until you can't recall which are which. Let your hand be guided to pick up seven and arrange them in a "V" shape with three stones on either side and one making the point at the bottom.

Interpret them according to the previous guidelines.

Sample Reading

It had been four years now, and Andrea and her brother, Michael, had not spoken to each other since shortly after their mother's death. Mom had left her house to them equally. Andrea wanted to keep the house, both because she lived in a cramped apartment and because the place held many happy memories for her. But Michael was equally insistent that they sell it right away, as his wife had just had a new baby and he was badly strapped for cash.

Michael had offered to sell his share of the house to Andrea if she could get him the money quickly enough. But she had been between jobs, living on her savings. Though she was able to raise part of the agreed upon price by his deadline, Michael felt it wasn't enough and it would take her too long to gather the rest—so he forced the sale of the house. The two quarreled bitterly. Andrea felt Michael cared more about money than he did about her needs and feelings and their mother's memory. Michael felt that Andrea was being ghoulish for wanting to live in their parents' home, and was the one who was putting her needs above the welfare of his children.

There had been an angry split, and brother and sister were still estranged half a decade later. On the few occasions when they did meet at a family gathering, the pair immediately began to revisit the fight over the house—each convinced the other had done them great injury and injustice. These confrontations quickly escalated from angry words to raised voices, to violent arguments, shouting, and even cursing—which put a damper on family festivities.

Andrea consulted my rune teacher, who suggested the Point of Agreement reading. At first, Andrea was resistant. She was certain there was nothing she and her brother could agree on. But she eventually decided to give the reading a chance, and from among the 24 runes, which had been placed facedown, was guided to pick the following 7. As she turned each faceup to place it on the table, this is what she saw.

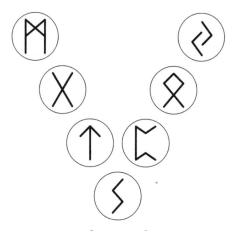

Andrea's reading.

For the stones forming the top of the "V," which embody the basis of the conflict, Andrea drew rune Mannaz first, the archetypal rune of humanity. In this position, though, the rune seems to say Andrea felt hurt by her brother because for her, people, family, and relationships were all-important, whereas he seemed to place money first. For Michael, she drew Jera, harvest. This implies that he felt hurt by Andrea because to him, the money from the house seemed a reward he had justly earned through years of devotion to his mother, whereas from Michael's point-of-view, his sister, though she claimed to put family first, seemed more interested in the house than in his welfare and that of his own family.

For the third and fourth stones, which form the neck of the "V," and point to secondary causes in a dispute, she drew Othala. This rune's association with ancestors and immovable property underscored the idea it was losing the sense of connection with the past and her parents, which the house represented, that had upset Andrea so much. For Michael, she drew rune Gebo, gift. This suggests that for him, the house had seemed a magical gift from his mother that could spell the end to all his financial problems.

For the fourth and fifth stones, which form the base of the "V," and point to misunderstandings on each person's part that prevent them from reaching a mutually acceptable resolution, Andrea drew Tiwaz. The rune suggests she saw her brother as the winner in the dispute, but that he didn't feel that way (possibly because he had lost his sister in the process). For Michael, she drew Perdhro, luck. Here, Perdhro appears to indicate that Michael is perceived as someone who was ungrateful over good luck.

The Point of Agreement

For the seventh rune, the one that serves as the point of the "V," Andrea drew Ansuz. Among this rune's meanings are an important piece of advice and verbal assistance from others. In this position, Ansuz seemed to be saying there was some individual both Andrea and Michael respected and whose advice they might heed. In fact, Andrea and Michael had such a relative, their Aunt Trish, their mother's sister. Thinking the situation over as illuminated by the reading, Andrea decided to talk the whole situation over with Trish and seek her counsel. It was a wise move; eventually, Trish was able to effect a reconciliation between the feuding siblings.

Rune #12: Jera or Ger

A bountiful harvest/is the hope of all./A year when the gods/make the earth bear fruit/is cause for rejoicing/by both the wealthy and the poor.
—*The Old English Rune Poem*

Jera

Jera (pronounced yar-awe) is your rune of abundant rewards well earned through diligent efforts. Long ago, as now, an abundant harvest (jera) spelled the difference between starvation and plenty for the people. All saw that such a harvest was the result of natural laws and hard work. Thus Jera gained the meaning of earned rewards and the repayment of deeds, often through legal means.

Rune Image: Symbolizes intertwined stalks of wheat

In Rune Reading

Faceup meanings: Fertility, gestation, abundance, harvesting, fulfillment, completion, cycles, mutual accord, natural and human law, adjudication of legal matters. *Tarot comparison:* The Fool. *Astrological comparison:* The Sun.

Occluded (facedown) meanings: Sterility, scarcity, delay, unrewarded effort, a lawsuit. *Tarot comparison:* The Fool reversed. *Astrological comparison:* The Sun afflicted.

In Rune Magic

Use to: Bring to fruition important events, bring help in legal matters, enhance seasonal rituals (especially those of harvest time), boost fertility and creativity

In Rune Meditation

Use to: Gestate projects, get in tune with natural and seasonal cycles, understand the cosmic law, increase creativity

Rune Gods: Frey, God of Sunshine

Rune Totems: Eagles, boars, horses, dogs, bears, squirrels, cattle, deer, rabbits, swallows

Rune Herb: Rosemary

Rune Color: The green of ripe cornstalks

Rune Magic: Releasing the Power of Harmony

Release the magical power of Ehwaz to turn contention into concord and hatred into harmony with this ritual. Ehwaz is the rune of partnership and cooperation. The cosmic force behind the rune works from the inside out to bring contending individuals and parties into resonance, then agreement, then harmony.

Use this ceremony when ...

- Things are going well between you and important others in your life—to keep them harmonious.
- You first sense potential discord arising—to prevent things from growing worse and keep them on an even keel.
- You find yourself in a fight, feud, or dispute, or if you're being attacked.
- The situation seems so dire you have given up hope—it will create agreement where there was only acrimony and antagonism.

To perform this magical working, arrange to have on hand the Ehwaz rune stone, a candle the white of oak wood, an incense burner, and the herb ragwort. Lower the lights, or work outside in the night air. Place the ragwort on the burner, then light it and the candle.

Next, you will need to make yourself a channel for Ehwaz' energy. Sit comfortably, relax, breathe deeply several times, and clear your mind of all distraction.

Picture the other party involved in the conflict. After you have a clear mental image of the person or people, take the Ehwaz rune stone in the hand nearest your heart (the left). Say:

In the name of Freyja and Frey,
I invoke Ehwaz!

Over the space of a few minutes, the stone will grow unusually warm. When you sense this, it is a sign that Ehwaz's energy is being sent to you via Freyja and Frey, ruling deities of the rune. Continue holding on to the stone, and you will feel the energy spread from the rune, up your arm to your heart.

Let the energy of the rune fill your heart with its warmth until you feel it begin to overflow and spill out. Focus your mind on your picture of other party in the conflict, and say:

Let the energy
of this rune
flow into [name of party].
May it fill [name]'s heart.
May it soothe [his/her] spirit.
May it bring us into harmony.
May it bring our thoughts into harmony.
May it bring our spirits into harmony.
May it bring our needs into harmony.
May it bring our wants into harmony.
May it bring our aims into harmony.
Let there be no discord between us
now or in the future.
Let the warmth of this stone
be the warmth of our feeling for each other.
Freyja and Frey bid you obey me.
Ehwaz bids you obey me.

As you recite this invocation, the warmth should flow out of your heart. At same time, however far away, whatever they are doing, the person you are directing it at will experience an unusual feeling of warmth in their heart. Over a period of days, they will find themselves rethinking some of their positions and feelings about the matter that has put the two of you at loggerheads. Very likely she or he will approach you in a different spirit than the one in which you last met.

I met a stranger yesterday.
I put food in the eating place,
Drink in the drinking place,
Music in the listening place.
In the sacred names of the Runes,
He blessed me and my house
My cattle and my dear ones.
  —Trad. Gaelic verse

Rune Meditation: Seeing Through the Other Person's Eyes

Professional conflict negotiators say that to resolve disputes and defuse hostility you must learn to understand and appreciate the other party's viewpoint. Of course, it's not always so easy to do, especially when things that really matter to you are at stake. It's even harder when angry words have already been exchanged and the other party has done something that really hurt you, or if you know you are wholly in the right and what the other side wants is not only wrong, but will actually produce disastrous results for everyone involved.

The following meditation on rune Mannaz can bridge the gap and help you see the dispute exactly the way the other person does. Even when a meeting of the minds doesn't seem possible, you will find one. Once you understand the other person's point of view, you will discover ...

- Areas you never dreamed of where they are willing to compromise.
- Unexpected points of agreement.
- Any important misunderstandings or miscommunications.
- How your case could most effectively be put to them.

In a quiet place, set the Mannaz rune stone where you can see it, and breathe deeply until your mind and spirit are at rest. Lower your eyes to the rune and look at its shape, so much like that of a suspension bridge. All that is missing is a straight line across the middle of the rune to represent the roadway connecting the two sides of the bridge.

Let the image fill your eyes and try to visualize the missing line crossing beneath the supports of the bridge. When you can see that line, close your eyes. The image will remain visible, probably with the colors reversed, behind your lids.

Picture the image slowly transforming from a simple line drawing to a real, three-dimensional bridge. Visualize the two vertical lines thickening into gray concrete pillars. See the two lines that cross each other becoming mighty cables strung from the pillars. Picture the horizontal line swelling to become a solid, secure concrete roadway.

Below the bridge is an abyss, a bottomless chasm—the chasm of disagreement, antagonism, and misunderstanding. You want to cross that void very badly. You know it is the only way to resolve the hurtful quarrel in which you are trapped.

Now visualize the bridge swinging around, so that the right hand end comes toward you, almost as if it was inviting you to step out onto its surface and walk across. Now that end of the bridge stops before you. See the hard, dark pavement, as real as the ground beneath your feet.

Lift your mental eyes. Across on the other side of the bridge is the person (or persons) with whom you want to end hostilities. He or she is small and distant, but you can make out the details.

Imagine yourself stepping out on the bridge. Feel your feet slapping down on the hard pavement. See the guardrails of the bridge stretching out on both sides of you. Continue walking forward. Over the side of the bridge you catch glimpses of the chasm of disagreement—stretching downward until it is lost in the mist.

The bridge is not long and you soon find yourself at its opposite end. See the person you have been disputing with standing there before you. Visualize her or him as completely as you can. What color is that person's hair? Eyes? The shape of the face? Mouth? Expression? How tall is she or he? What clothing is she or he wearing? What is her or his stance?

Now, visualize yourself stepping forward into the person's body, literally into her or his shoes. Don't be shy. See your self merge completely until your arms are where the other person's arms are, your legs where the other's legs are. Most important of all, find your head where the other's head is—looking out at the world from their eyes.

Try to see yourself as the other person would see you. Visualize yourself physically as he or she would visualize you—in detail. Ask yourself the previous questions. How would that person perceive your looks, intelligence, motives?

Carefully review the conflict from the beginning, the way you now see it through the other's eyes. Where does he or she see it as starting? What does the person see as the cause? What does he or she see as the basic areas of disagreement? Of agreement? In essence, how does the person see his or her side? How does he or she see yours? Why does he or she believe your position is a stupid one and his or hers the only right way to go?

Next, and of great significance, looking out at the world from that person's eyes, what are the places where he or she would be willing to negotiate, compromise, or come to an understanding? How does that person like to be approached in situations like this? What will set off the least number of defenses? Or disarm him or her altogether?

Finally, picture yourself stepping outside the person's body, turning so you are face-to-face. Now, knowing what you have just learned, what mutually acceptable compromise might you offer? And what would be the best way to present it to ensure acceptance?

By now you will in all likelihood know what to do to bring about a win-win solution for everyone. If it still isn't completely clear, sleep on the question. The answer will probably manifest itself in your dreams, or surface into your thoughts the next day.

Chapter 7

Runes of Finance and Prosperity

Do you have enough money? Do you wish for more? Or are you faced with an urgent financial crisis?

You might need money for any one of these reasons:

- To help fund a worthy cause—schools, charities, clinics
- To ensure others won't want for shelter, medical care, and the necessities in old age
- To pay for guilty pleasures, vacations, expensive electronic gear, new clothes, a hobby, or a high-performance sports car
- To meet a serious financial emergency—a hospitalization, the loss of investments, a relative's crisis
- To realize a lifelong dream, such as living in a retirement home by the sea or going into business for yourself
- To have something set aside for a rainy day

Whatever your reason for wanting money, when you don't have it, it hurts. Sometimes it just pinches and you have to economize. Other times, it's a disaster and you lose everything. Still other times, you "merely" yearn for what only money can buy.

Something as old and esoteric as runes might seem far removed from financial practicalities when you aren't as prosperous as you'd like, or when you desperately need a quick infusion of cash. But runes and money came into existence at almost the same time. In fact, as an alphabet, runes were used to keep track of the earliest financial transactions.

Because the runic system incorporates all the basic aspects of life, five runes are directly related to wealth and finance. That is 20 percent—which reflects the rune's recognition of the basic importance of money in human society. These five runes are: Fehu, which literally means prosperity; Uruz, which represents assets; Jera, the harvest or abundance and plenty; Dagaz, which symbolizes increase; and Othala, rune of possessions and inheritance. Meditate on any of these five runes when you want to deepen your understanding of how to create greater wealth. Or use them in magical ceremonies aimed at increasing your financial balance. You will also find these runes occupy critical positions in any reading about money problems.

Runes will show you how to make money, spend it more wisely, and earn greater interest when you save or invest. They can help you understand the things you do that sabotage your prospects of financial success, and capitalize on your personal financial strengths. If you want, they will also reveal your best short-term and long-term strategies for ensuring you will have the money you need when you need it.

Due to the specific relationship of each rune to some thing or quality, by using combinations of runes, every aspect of existence can be described and investigated.

—Nigel Pennick, *Magical Alphabets*

Freeing Your Financial Potential

What does prosperity mean to you? Most of us know how much money we *don't* have when we look at our bills every month. And most of us know how much money we *could* have when we see the way wealthy people live. Most of us have a dream of being better off financially—but we never do much about it. Instead, we settle for the familiar grind of working for a paycheck that just barely gets us through the month. Or if we are in business for ourselves, after we reach a comfortable plateau, we are so thrilled with our limited success, and so afraid of losing it, that we make no real effort to push it further.

Sometimes we try to expand ourselves financially and reach out toward riches—only to fail and fall flat on our faces.

Whether we try and fail or never try at all, the reasons are usually the same. Frequently, deep down we don't believe that we can become prosperous, that it takes some mental talent or secret knowledge we don't possess. Just as often, what holds us back from financial plenty or even financial sufficiency are our own self-defeating bad habits of finance and prosperity.

Your Financial Bad Habits and Runes

What self-defeating financial behavior patterns are you caught up in? Everybody has some monetary bad habits—even the world's richest people (they might just have fewer of them). It is these habits that block and restrict your financial potential.

Among the bad habits that keep most people from achieving genuine prosperity are ...

- Impulse spending.
- Lack of overall financial goals or plan.
- Not saving enough.
- Not saving regularly.
- Lack of a budget.
- Failure to make an effort to earn and attract more money.
- Failure to believe you can achieve prosperity.
- Believing you don't deserve prosperity.

If not for these financially self-defeating patterns, you would already have achieved prosperity. For, just as you have bad financial habits, you have good ones. You bought this book, so you have some money. You are probably eating and have a roof over your head and a job. People who have only self-defeating monetary behaviors don't have these—or are imminently in danger of losing them.

If your negative money habits were removed from the picture, your positive habits would carry you quickly forward to prosperity and sufficiency. You would have enough for your needs and a bit left over to be banked for an emergency. Now, imagine how much more you would achieve financially, if you could transform your bad monetary habits into good ones and add them to the positive habits you already possess.

If you are willing to make an effort to free your financial potential for achieving prosperity, the following method of reading the runes will help. This reading shines a powerful spotlight on financial bad habits. Study it carefully, and you will discover it illuminates your path to changing them, as well.

The reading is simple to use: It doesn't require the three circles, you merely throw the runes and read those that land facedown—these will indicate your self-defeating behaviors around money. You don't need to worry about the ones that land faceup at all.

Rune Reading: Identifying Your Financial Bad Habits

This reading was conducted for a gentleman I'll call Ira. Things were not going well for Ira. He was in his late thirties and was having a major financial crisis. According to Ira, he never seemed to have enough money or to be able to save any. He always seemed to be short of cash and one step away from being broke. He had once even had his car repossessed. Ira's financial woes seemed strange because he was the senior copywriter at a large advertising agency and had always received a substantial salary. Furthermore, he was unmarried, lived alone, and had no children. With plenty of money and few expenses, he should have been able to maintain a strong bank balance to help with such emergencies.

Recently, Ira had seen his dream home, on a bluff overlooking the Pacific Ocean, and purchased it. Because he had very little in the bank, he had been able to make only a small down payment, and was stuck with an abnormally high interest on his 30-year mortgage. He had been wildly ecstatic about his new home, purchasing new furniture, appliances, and other conveniences.

Then disaster struck. The founder of the advertising agency died and his heirs sold it to a rival agency. The new owners kept the accounts, but let all the employees of Ira's firm go. With only minimal savings in the bank Ira realized he would be facing foreclosure on his dream house within a few short months unless he found another job—and Ira was having a hard time finding one in the tightening economy. He networked like crazy and e-mailed job applications and resumes far and wide—without result.

Finally, Ira decided to see what insight the runes might offer him. I suggested the reading I felt would do him the most good. He would throw the stones and we would scrutinize those that fell facedown. These would provide clues to the financial bad habits that had precipitated his crisis. Hopefully, they would also provide suggestions for transforming those habits and help him extricate himself from his predicament. (Runes that landed facedown are shown shaded.)

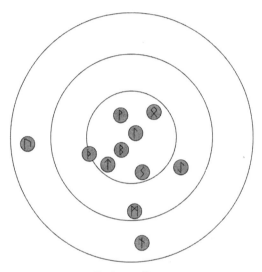

Ira's reading.

If you didn't already know that Ira was constantly in and out of financial difficulties, you could predict it from the number of occluded runes in this reading. Facedown runes signify the weak financial areas in his approach to life. With 10 of 24 of the runes symbols occluded, it is evident that when it comes to money, Ira will have a lot of difficulties and be lucky to break even.

Just making a list of the negative qualities related to finance associated with each of these 10 facedown runes is very revealing. Note the consistent themes that underscore the basic financial bad habits that led Ira into his current financial crisis:

- Eihwaz occluded—Lack of management, recklessness in finance, unrealistic goals

- Lagaz occluded—Misled by intuition into that for which you have no aptitude, doing the wrong thing, taking the easy way out, failure to use wisdom
- Wunjo occluded—Continuing difficulties, sorrow, unfavorable circumstances
- Berkana occluded—Lack of prudence, relief thorough restraint and timely action
- Kenaz occluded—Energy out of control, poor judgment
- Uruz occluded—The untamed self, lack of will power
- Tiwaz occluded—Extreme impatience, the darkness before the dawn
- Naudhiz occluded—A course of action that should be abandoned, hasty judgment leading to disaster, failure and despair, lack of what is desperately needed
- Sowilo occluded—Too much too soon, person who wants to be in charge and worries when she or he is not
- Othala occluded—Delay and frustration from trying to go too fast

Abstracting from this list, we find that over and over the reading informs us that Ira's sufferings are of his own making. They are due to financial behaviors that can be summed up as a lack of prudence, management, and self-control; poor judgment; being hasty, unwise, impatient, and reckless; and wanting too much too soon. Certainly all these relate to Ira's constant and compulsive spending of all his money—as quickly it came in.

The reading also reiterates the consequences of Ira's poor money habits. They include: Continuing difficulties, sorrow, unfavorable circumstances, actions that should be abandoned, hasty judgment leading to disaster, failure and despair, lack of what is desperately needed, and frustration. He had been experiencing some of these all along, and now he was experiencing all of them, all of the time.

And, as always, these runes offer tips on the steps Ira must take to put an end to his constant financial difficulties. First and foremost, he needs to change his financial bad habits. Ira must replace financial recklessness with prudence, learn to exercise self-control, and become better at managing his money (budgeting, planning, and saving). In brief, he must find a way to overcome his compulsive spending—even if it means seeking therapy or a 12-step group.

In addition to long-term issues, the reading seemed to hold out hope that Ira's immediate difficulties, which resulted from unemployment, were soon to be put to an end. We learn this from Tiwaz, one of whose meanings is the darkness before the dawn. This turned out to be true: Ira had a new job within the month.

I wish the outcome of Ira's story were as neatly wrapped up as a television drama. He disregarded the reading's entreaty that he change his financial ways. Ira didn't seek help, and when last heard of had lost his house, despite a well-paying position at a major advertising agency.

Rune #13: Eihwaz or Eoh

The yew tree's bark is rough/its leaves give shade/its roots sink deep below/its branches are heaven's support/Eternal it stands/guardian of the estate.

—*The Old English Rune Poem*

Eihwaz

Eihwaz (pronounced eye-waz) is your rune of the strength to uphold worlds. The yew tree (eihwaz) had great importance to the people of long ago. Yews stood in the yard beside the door and generation after generation would pass, but the long-lived yew endured—until its permanency made it seem the true "guardian of the estate." The towering yew's branches appeared to uphold the heavens and its roots grew so deep they must penetrate the underworld. For these reasons, the yew came to represent Yggdrasil, the world tree that supports the three worlds: Asgard (home of the gods), Midgard (Earth), and Hel (the underworld).

Rune Image: A yew tree

In Rune Reading

Faceup meanings: Ability to juggle or manage things in several arenas of life simultaneously, protection, management, control of finances or decision-making, achievable goals, difficulties avoided by wise foresight, timely action, dreaming, magic, life. *Tarot comparison:* The Hanged Man. *Astrological comparison:* Scorpio.

Occluded (facedown) meanings: Lack of management, vulnerability, recklessness in finance, unrealistic goals, failure in several arenas, lack of foresight, bad timing, spiritual and magical sterility, death. *Tarot comparison:* The Hanged Man reversed. *Astrological comparison:* Scorpio afflicted.

In Rune Magic

Use to: Protect people and projects from negative energies, remove obstacles, connect with other planes and realms, develop magical abilities, increase psychic dreaming, communicate with ancestors

In Rune Meditation

Use to: Develop spiritual endurance, understand world tree (of life), release fear of death, communicate between different levels of awareness

Rune Gods: Uller, God of Winter

Rune Totems: Dragons, horses, eagles, hounds, dolphins, wolves, ravens

Rune Herb: Mandrake

Rune Color: Dark blue

Coping with Financial Ups and Downs

Whether or not you have amassed a tidy nest egg for a rainy day, the unforeseen chance of Perdhro will still find ways to work financial emergency and even catastrophe into your life. Many of us, in fact, experience monetary ups and downs far too frequently for comfort. If you are part of that vast majority who are just able to make ends meet, then life is probably an unending series of financial shortfalls, tight corners, and disasters. You are sailing along on an even keel; you even have bit in the bank. Then bang! The unforeseen happens. You break your arm and are home on sick leave at three-fourths pay and with additional expenses. Or your sister suddenly needs money to pay emergency dental bills for your nephew.

The term "unforeseen" financial crisis is almost redundant. If you could foresee it, you would have taken steps to prevent the problem or to be better prepared for it. By the very nature of the beast, a calamity involving money is always an unwelcome surprise. Because it is something you weren't expecting, you won't be prepared, and you won't have a plan. And if it were easy to find a solution for, it wouldn't be a crisis. Instead, you don't know where to turn or see any way out. Things seem as black as they can be. The result is stress, worry, and despair. You feel overwhelmed and defeated before you even begin to look for a way out. Of course, this makes it even more difficult for you to take action or perceive a potential answer, often when it lies under your very nose.

However, a special way of reading runes can help you identify a viable way out of even the most catastrophic monetary crisis. It uses five stones arranged to mimic the shape of rune Dagaz, and frames the solution within the elements of the problem.

In a Dagaz reading, the first four rune stones represent certain aspects of the problem, and the fifth rune represents the solution. Because the first four runes are present only in their problematic aspect—as the cause of the difficulty—only their meanings when facedown are considered in the interpretation. The fifth stone points toward the solution, so only its significance when faceup (in its positive mode) is considered.

Rune Reading: Solving a Financial Crisis

This reading is based on the shape of one of the principle runes of finance and prosperity, Dagaz. By copying the shape of the rune, the reading draws down its energy to ensure the reading and runes will focus on your monetary issues. The runes with images are placed facedown, and five stones are drawn, and then placed at the five points in Dagaz where lines meet. These are the four corners of the rune and the center, where the "X" shaped lines that connect them cross.

In the Dagaz reading, the two stones forming the left-hand vertical line (1 and 3) show why you need money. This might seem evident if your car is totaled in an accident and the other driver doesn't have insurance and you are short the down payment on a new one. If that's all that is involved, the runes will reflect it. But, just as frequently, the runes will indicate unsuspected contributory factors, such as not having a comprehensive collision policy that would have helped pay to replace your car.

The two runes forming the right-hand vertical line (2 and 4) show the factors that caused your lack of funds. Such factors might include a relative who always needs money, a financial bad habit like failure to budget, or having fewer clients due to a recession. Again, you might think you know what those factors are, but sometimes you learn that they're different than you perceived. For example, the runes might point to the huge sum you spent last month to purchase the newest wall-sized flat screen television, when you had a very large screen TV already.

The fifth and central rune reveals the solution to your financial scarcity. It is here that you will discover a practical way of solving your problem, one that suggests how you can get the money you need.

Sample Reading

Recently divorced, Kathleen was an intelligent woman in her late twenties whose husband had run off with another woman. Kathleen was already working two jobs to support herself and her two young sons. It was a struggle every month just to feed the three of them and pay the mortgage on the house she and her husband had bought a few years earlier. Kathleen was determined to hold on to the house for the sake of the children, because she felt continuing to live there gave them a sense of stability and enabled them to remain in the same school with all their friends.

Then the sky fell on her, when her mother, who was living on social security, suffered a stroke. Although Kathleen's mother made an almost full recovery and moved in with Kathleen, which allowed her to keep an eye on the kids, she needed expensive drugs that Medicare and its supplements didn't cover. The burden of paying for them rested on Kathleen.

Already stretched thin financially before her mother's stroke, Kathleen felt she was facing an impossible task. She had barely been able to pay her bills while working two jobs. Kathleen knew she couldn't work additional hours, yet she desperately needed money to keep her mother alive. She decided to seek answers in a Dagaz reading.

In the first position (top left), representing a factor in the past shedding light on why Kathleen needed the money, was Berkana, which facedown signifies family problems and friction. This evidentially referred to the desertion by her former husband and their consequent divorce. This, of course, had been a major factor in putting her in such a difficult financial bind.

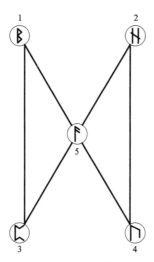

Kathleen's reading.

In the second position (top right), representing a factor in the past shedding light on the cause of her not having the money she needed, was Hagalaz, which is symbolic of forces outside your control and of disruption by a natural event. It was saying her current financial embarrassment was not her fault. Both her husband's desertion and her mother's stroke had been forces outside her control and both had contributed to her current crisis.

In the third position (bottom left), representing a factor in the present shedding light on why Kathleen needed money, was Uruz, which occluded often means illness. Her mother's stroke was the biggest single reason for Kathleen's need for additional funds.

In the fourth position (bottom right), representing a factor in the present shedding light on the cause of her not having the money she needed, was Perdhro. As Perdhro facedown often indicates bad luck, it is another sign that her financial difficulties were not of her making. This was a relief to Kathleen, who tended to blame herself.

The Solution

Last, in the fifth position (the center), representing the solution to her financial emergency, was Ansuz. It is read as being faceup, because it represents a solution and not a problem. When Ansuz is interpreted as a rune of solution, it typically points toward networking, getting help and advice by communicating with another or others about whatever the problem is.

Kathleen had a tendency to keep her problems to herself. But she was persuaded that any embarrassment or shyness she felt about letting others in on her financial crisis was outweighed by the needs of her children and mother. She mentioned the situation to a few people at her different jobs, and was taken aback by the outpouring of support she received. One woman, whose mother had been in a similar situation, supplied the name of a local program that helped those who otherwise could not afford to pay for lifesaving drugs. Another friend knew of a job opening that paid as much as Kathleen's two jobs put together.

Ansuz can also mean tests or interviews, and in this case it signified a job interview. Kathleen got the position, then learned of a second one she could do from home over the Internet, while spending time with her family.

Rune #14: Perdhro or Peordh

The dice cup provides/amusement and diversion for/people after a hard day's work/when companions sit in leisure/in the dining hall laughing/as they play at dice.

—*The Old English Rune Poem*

Perdhro

Perdhro (pronounced perth-row) is your rune of luck, laughter, and fellowship. In the days before television, radio, and vaudeville, amusements were few, and men and women both passed the time at games of chance like cards and dice. The dice cup (perdhro) became a universal symbol for the cosmic laws behind fate, joy, and friendship.

Rune Image: Dice cup

In Rune Reading

Faceup meanings: Coming or presence of favorable luck, unexpected gains, destiny, something positive but hidden revealed, fellowship, conviviality, relaxation, laughter, the fool (or inner child), sexual compatibility, mutual attraction, strong psychic gifts. *Tarot comparison:* The Wheel of Fortune. *Astrological comparison:* Saturn.

Occluded (facedown) meanings: Unfavorable luck, unpleasant surprises and losses, something negative but hidden revealed, abandonment, antagonism, stress, sorrow, disappointment by another, sexual incompatibility, lack of attraction, rash experimentation with the occult. *Tarot comparison:* The Wheel of Fortune reversed. *Astrological comparison:* Saturn afflicted.

In Rune Magic

Use to: Direct cosmic laws, increase luck, grow investments, ensure good karma, divination, read your fate

In Rune Meditation

Use to: Comprehend the nature of cause and effect, develop the wisdom to make things work out right for you, understand where your present path might lead

Rune Gods: Frigga, Mother Goddess as Earth Mother; Mimir, God of Wisdom; the three Norns

Rune Totems: Wolves, pythons, kangaroos, dinosaurs, chameleons, tortoises, falcons

Rune Herb: Aconite

Rune Color: Blackish silver

Rune Magic: Becoming a Prosperity Magnet

The peoples of ancient times knew many secrets for attracting wealth. Both the Koran and the Christian New Testament contain a number of formulas for ensuring prosperity. The magical practitioners of most nations—Egyptian sorcerers, the Taoists, the Tibetans, the Knights Templar, the Mayan priests, and others—include spells for attracting money and amassing wealth. This explains the vast wealth and prosperity of many of the great nations of antiquity.

In modern, more materialistic, times, these secrets have been scoffed at and driven underground. Pulling money to you like a magnet when you need it was ridiculed as a pie in the sky dream, a fable even children would be too wise to believe. Those who preserved such beliefs and practices were branded charlatans, fools, and weak minded. Fortunately, the last few decades have witnessed a slow turn-around in this attitude. Financial gurus like Suze Orman, Marianne Williamson, and Anthony Robbins have proven that there is something more to these ideas than mere superstition or folk beliefs. In their own lives, and through the success of those who have heeded them, they have demonstrated that if one knows the secrets, it is possible to thrive and prosper even in economies that are in a downturn.

The secret of attracting money was also preserved in rune lore. In part, the symbol of Fehu is a runic microchip designed to attract and direct one of the fundamental cosmic forces behind prosperity and financial abundance. When you hold it in your hand, you are really holding a highly energized magnet that will draw into your sphere the many opportunities for making and receiving money that surround us every day. We are normally unaware of these opportunities, or they seem so remote that we believe they are closed to us, or brush pass unrecognized—or we lack sufficient confidence in ourselves to believe we can succeed like the others we've seen achieve financial sufficiency.

For example, one very close friend, Jeffery, a book editor, had lost his job in a downsizing. Jeff had two teenagers to support, and a wife who was ill much of the time, so he sent out resumés to every book publisher in the city where he lived. He received several calls from companies telling him that they didn't have a current opening, but that his qualifications were so superior, they would keep his resumé on file.

Finally, on the very day his savings were about to run out and he had to have a job or else, Jeff thought to try the power of Fehu. Literally that afternoon, the president of a large publisher of books and magazines phoned. The man said that they had no openings in their book division, and Jeff braced himself for another "but we loved your resumé and will keep it on file" ending. He could hardly believe his ears when the man told him, instead, that they were starting up a new tourist magazine and, because Jeff had edited a number of books on travel and great cities, wanted to know if he would be interested in becoming its editor in chief.

The barbarians from the north place as much importance on auguries and auspices as anyone. The way they read them is this: They cut slips from the branch of a tree and designate them by cutting certain figures (runes) into them. Then they throw the slips randomly across a white cloth. Afterward a priest (vitki) interprets the slips. If the augury prohibits some action, they desist and ask no more that day. If it is favorable, then they ask further about the matter.

—Tacitus, Roman historian (circa 80 B.C.E.)

The Fehu Money Ritual

Use this ritual when you ...

- Need money quickly.
- Want to strengthen long-term prosperity.
- Would like to seal the financial success of a venture.

To perform the ceremony, you should have the Fehu rune stone, a light red candle, and a bit of the herb nettle for your incense burner. In the right time and place for you to conduct a magical ritual uninterrupted, light the candle and incense. Sit or kneel on the ground and place the rune before you.

Empty your mind and spirit of distracting forces by breathing slowly to clear them of interference and make them a channel for Fehu's energy. When you are prepared, focus your mind on the rune and say:

In the name of the Aesir,
I invoke Fehu!

Take Fehu in your left hand (so its energies will be closer to your heart). Raise it above your head to better receive the cosmic forces the rune controls. Picture the energy pouring down from above into the rune. Say:

Let the energy
of this rune
imbue my life.
Fehu, obey me
at the Gods' command!

At this point in the ritual, your hand and arm should begin tingling as the cosmic forces of abundance and prosperity pour into you attracted by the rune. Or the stone may become warm as it charges with runic energy. Still holding the Fehu rune stone above you, say:

May the energy of Fehu
miss no opportunity
to fill me with abundance.
May it attract prosperity
from everywhere.
Through Fehu,
may I never
feel want's pinch.

Fehu!

When you say the rune's name again at the end, you should feel the energy leave your body. The tingling will stop or the temperature of your rune stone return to normal. The cosmic forces of prosperity linked to Fehu are being instantaneously disseminated through the atmosphere, to begin their work of directing opportunities and money to you.

Thank the gods and the rune for their aid. Say:

Thank you, Aesir,
thank you, Fehu,
for this blessing.

Breathe deeply to clear yourself of any residual energies and still your mind. Then snuff out the candle, but let the herb burn itself out.

With Fehu's aid you have just turned yourself into an incredibly powerful prosperity magnet. Throughout the next hours, days, and weeks you will find money and the means for making it coming at you in multiple unexpected sources. Be prepared for phone calls, e-mail, encounters with strangers—all to practically deliver checks to your door and put them in the bank for you.

Rune Meditation: Releasing Inner Abundance

Jera is the rune of harvest. Prosperity lies in rich harvests, and that is what this rune represents. Meditate on it whenever you find yourself in need of a financial harvest. It will reveal unsuspected sources of highly remunerative work, ways of using what you know to generate cash, even money you might be owed or that others are waiting to give you.

Get comfortable and relaxed for meditation when you can be sure you will not be interrupted. Quiet and still your thoughts with a few slow, calm breaths. Remember, never hurry this part of the process, it is essential to a successful meditation.

When you feel ready, focus your eyes on Jera on the stone's surface. Visually contemplate the image of the rune for a few moments, then close your eyes. When you do, the rune symbol—two right angles interlocked in zigzag fashion—will remain white or pastel against the blackness of your closed lids.

Visualize these zigzagging right angles growing upward for a foot or so, like an animation on television. They will look something like the path a skier takes downhill—full of short, sharp angles as he or she cuts back and forth—or like a zigzag watercourse designed to slow the flow of a torrent.

The result will also look like a cartoonist's outline sketch of the way the seeds on a stalk of wheat grow out of each other. Visualize the zigzagging row of interlocked right angles filling out into three dimensions, turning pale yellow, becoming the seeds on a wheat stalk. See the tiny tufts at the tips of the seeds, the long golden stem that supports the wheat.

Picture your wheat stalk as one among tens of thousands. See a vast sea of ripe, golden wheat stretching unbroken toward the horizon in every direction. Each individual stalk is swollen with ripeness, the seeds so huge they are about to burst forth from their pods and spill to the earth.

Now, visualize each of the dozens of tightly interwoven seeds at the end of each stalk transforming into a tightly rolled one hundred dollar bill. See the whole field sprouting one hundred dollar bills. Tens of thousands of bills. Millions. Far more than you will ever need in your lifetime.

This vast field of bills is at its ripest point. As you watch, the hundred dollar bills swell further and burst free from the stalks. They rain on the ground by the dozens at the base of every stalk—as far as the eye can see. It is a rain of greater wealth than the world has ever yet seen.

On the back of each bill is a way you can obtain far more than one hundred dollars. It is a secret known only to your subconscious. It may be something you have never thought of, or an idea that has flashed across your mind before that you ignored.

See yourself walking up to the nearest stalk. You reach down and pick up one of the bills. Picture turning the bill over. What is the suggestion for getting the money you need that has been printed there? Sometimes when you do this meditation, you will actually see the words printed on the back of the bill. Other times, the suggestion will surface as words in your mind.

If the words are out of focus, the back of the bill is blank, or you don't understand what you read there, remain patient. Frequently your own anxiety about money will interfere with reception and cause static the same way a storm does with your car radio. It might take a few hours or days for the message to become clear.

Typically, when it is delayed, one of these runic messages will pop into your mind unexpectedly when you are thinking hard about something else. Perhaps it will come just as you are falling asleep at night or for a daytime nap. It can even manifest itself in your dreams.

Chapter 8

Runes of Business and Success

Do you manage a business? Do you own one or dream or starting one? Do you work for one and want to rise higher or be more productive? If professional success or what it brings matters to you, runes can be your allies, mentors, and cheerleaders.

Business was no less central a part of life in the days when runes made their initial appearance in the land. Trade, produce, manufacturing, investment, service industries, arts and crafts, and public works were thriving institutions even then. According to rune lore, the ancients symbolized the energies that underlie business and success in eight key runes. These eight runes have the power to carry you to success in your business, profession, or career. Their wisdom will coach you through or around any bad patches that lie ahead, and mentor you on the best ways to achieve your goals. They also release potent forces, through magic and meditation, that swing the tide of events in your favor and optimize your chance for success.

The runes of business and success are Fehu, which is abundance; Uruz, which increases business opportunities; Ehwaz, which is all about partnerships; Dagaz, which sees ventures off to good start; Ingwaz, which engenders successful conclusions;

Othala, which is wealth and property; Wunjo, which is circumstances turning in your favor; and Tiwaz, victory. Call on them for business, career, or success help.

Here are just some of the aspects of business and success runes can help you with:

- Advancement—For an individual or organization
- Competition—Countering and surmounting competition
- Management—From motivating others to resolving conflicts between team members
- Productivity—Making a department or a business more productive
- Clients—Winning them, keeping them happy
- Motivation—Getting it and keeping it
- Finance—Cash flow, profits, stopping losses
- Marketing—Yourself, services, product, company
- Strategic planning—Short- and long-term
- Negotiation—Knowing which issues are open to compromise and which aren't

Runes of victory though must know, if victory thou wantest.
—*The Elder Edda*

Maximizing Your Success Potential

If you are like most people, you have a dream of succeeding that involves something meaningful to you. Typically, people who think of themselves as having a career, profession, or being in business, want to succeed. Most men and women in dead-end jobs dream of finding a better one, with some promise of advancement and the "big money."

Even people who are content to be cogs in a company, who put in their eight hours and go home, have dreams of success. Their dreams just lie outside the boundaries of their work—in a lifestyle, hobby, civic work, church, family, art, or in just enjoying a comfortable, easy-going life.

What is your success dream? Is it ...

- To one day be promoted to CEO of your company or elected to public office?
- To retire wealthier than Bill Gates?
- To make enough that you will never have to worry?
- To win award or recognition for your efforts?
- To become a major pop star, best-selling writer, or performer?
- To make the major contribution to your company or organization that you know you are capable of and to be rewarded with the position and financial benefits it deserves?
- To become wealthy while doing something you can do sitting on the houseboat in Florida?

Whatever your dream of success is, whether it is a good week's sales, a good month's work, a good year for your business, or a lifetime goal— do you know how to make it happen? Do you have a valid strategy for getting there? Do you know what the greatest obstacle is to that success? What the strongest asset you have in your corner is? Or the most important thing you need to know to make your success a reality? If the answer is no, a traditional rune reading I call the Mirror of Success will identify these things for you. Heed its insights and you'll maximize your potential for success.

The Mirror of Success Reading

In this reading, seven rune stones are arranged in the shape of the kind of hand-mirror people used in ancient times. Look into the Mirror of Success reading and you can see your path to future business or personal success. It sums up at a single glance the challenges to your success and how you can surmount them to achieve your goal.

In the Mirror of Success reading, you begin with the 24 stones that bear rune images turned facedown, and choose 6 stones from among them, one at a time. You lay the first three rune stones down in a vertical line, with the first at the bottom and the second above it, and the third at the top— to form the mirror's handle. The first rune represents elements that have prepared you for success, the second shows where you are on the path to success, and the third shows the major challenge to success you face or will face (it reflects a problem, so it is interpreted as if it's facedown).

The fourth rune goes just above and to the left of the top of the handle (third stone) to become the left side of the frame of the mirror, and the fifth just to the right of the top of the handle to make the frame on the mirror's right side. The sixth stone goes in the center just above the two stones forming the sides to become the top of the frame. The fourth rune signifies your success weaknesses (and is also read as if occluded); the fifth shows your success strengths; and the sixth rune points out the strategy that will carry you to your success.

What about the seventh rune stone? Why were you only asked to draw six? What goes in the blank space in the frame to act as your mirror?

The twenty-fifth rune stone, Wyrd, is the blank stone, the Rune of Fate or Wishing Stone. Its blankness serves as a mirror in which you will perceive the final key to your future success.

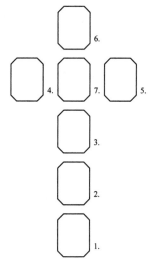

The Mirror of Success reading.

Rune Reading: Seeing Your Success in the Mirror of Success

Sit down at a table large enough for you to set out all your rune stones and still have space to arrange seven stones in the shape of a hand-mirror. Locate the blank stone and set it aside. Then, place the others facedown on the table, shuffle them around and mix them up at random like a card deck.

Relax your breathing for several moments. When you feel you are in a receptive state for receiving heavenly guidance, extend your hand over the stones and say:

Runar radh rett radh. (Runes bless me with good guidance.)

Don't try to consciously move your hand and pick; wait for it to move by inspiration. If you do, you will be directed to the right runes every time. Then, as your hand is guided, pick them up, turn them over, and place the runes as follows:

- First rune, directly before you as the base of the handle
- Second rune, directly above it as the middle of the handle
- Third rune, directly above it as the top of the handle
- Fourth rune, above the third to the left as the frame
- Fifth rune, above the third to the right as the frame
- Sixth rune, capping four and five as the frame's upper edge
- Seventh rune (blank), in the middle of the frame between five and six

To interpret a Mirror of Success reading, begin with the rune at the base of the handle, the first one you selected. Read the runes upward, in order, as you would a paragraph or page. Then try to put the message of the individual runes together into a whole. The first position shows elements that have prepared you for success. The second shows where you are on the path to success. The third shows a major challenge to your success. The fourth shows your principle success weakness. The fifth shows your principle, success strength. The sixth shows your key success strategy.

Now, read the stones from the bottom up, and interpret them according to the meanings of the individual runes. Keep in mind that as both the third and fourth runes reveal trouble areas, you read them as if they were occluded.

161

Lastly, lay the blank rune stone, Wyrd, in the blank spot in the frame where the mirror goes. Look into this mirror and you will see anything else vital to ensuring your future success. The following reading should help give you a fuller sense of what this process is like.

Sample Reading

The woman I will call Amber was in her late thirties. She was a member of upper-level management in a large charitable organization. She loved her job, and was valued by everyone she worked with for her ready empathy and problem-solving abilities. But Amber wasn't content. She had a dream. She had spent 15 years working for the same organization, and much as she loved it, she wanted to kick loose.

Amber was an omnivorous reader, especially of books about social, medical, and psychological problems. Most of the books she read had dissatisfied her. She felt the books that described problems like alcoholism, manic-depression, heart disease, and the like lacked clear, concrete advice for dealing with them. Most of the books that did provide step-by-step suggestions failed to explain their causes clearly.

Deep down, Amber had long dreamed of starting a small publishing company, one whose catalogue would be devoted exclusively to self-help books that were both informative and filled with practical advice. Nearing her forties, Amber felt that if she didn't begin implementing her dream soon, it would be too late for her to start over in life. She had saved enough to live inexpensively for several years and start her publishing company.

On the other hand, she had a wonderful, secure job. If the publishing company failed, she would be forced to return to the job market and compete against young twenty-somethings fresh out of school and brimming with all the newest information. She could be much better off just standing pat and holding on to her present job.

What Amber wanted the runes to tell her was whether she would be wiser to quit her job and go into publishing for herself, or stick where she was for the time being. In short, would she be successful as a publisher? After agreeing that a Mirror of Success reading might supply the answers, Amber drew the following runes:

1. Elements that have prepared you for success (base of handle): Ehwaz, reliance on others, working in tandem

2. Where you are on the path to success (mid-handle): Ingwaz, successful ventures and accomplishments

3. The major challenge to your success (top of handle): Sowilo, doubt, lack of motivation, failure

4. Your success weakness (left frame): Algiz, vulnerability, deception by others, ventures that should be entered cautiously or not at all

5. Your success strength (right frame): Lagaz, rune of emotions, the unconscious, the fluid in life

6. Your key success strategy (upper frame): Perdhro, taking advantage of every lucky break, capitalizing on good fortune

Then she placed Wyrd (the Wishing Stone or Stone of Fate) in the center of the frame, between runes five and six.

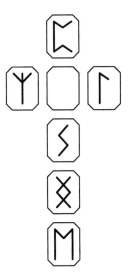

Amber's Mirror of Success reading.

As we looked over the reading together, here is what we saw: If Amber left her present employment and started a publishing company, all the interpersonal skills she had acquired over the years through working with others would prove key elements in preparing her for success in her new field of endeavor. For that matter, she was already well down the path to success in publishing or any business venture she attempted, although she didn't realize it, due to all the successful ventures and accomplishments she had already totaled up in her current job. Amber's most serious success challenge would be to overcome her lack of faith in her own ability to succeed (which in part was what brought her to the runes and had kept her from acting on her dreams sooner). Unless she could overcome this, Amber would find it difficult, if not impossible, to make a success of the publishing company she dreamed of founding.

Her most serious success weakness, which she would have to guard against carefully, was her vulnerability to deception by others (the result of the compassionate heart that led her into charitable work in the first place). As a result, each contract and agreement she undertook as a publisher should be entered into cautiously or not at all. Amber's greatest success strength if she went into publishing would be her intuition, emotions, unconscious wisdom, and flexibility. Finally, her most effective strategy for ensuring a publishing company's success embraced qualities that were already an innate part of Amber's character (which itself seemed a good omen to her), laughter and fellowship, her ability to win friends and get along with people.

At this point Amber placed the seventh rune, Wyrd, in the center, its unmarked surface symbolizing the mirror. I instructed her to reflect on all the runes had disclosed to her so far, and then to look at the blank stone for a minute. Wyrd, I explained, would reflect back to her mind's eye an image of her future success in which she would learn anything further she needed to know.

I asked Amber to describe any image or impression that came to her while staring into the blank rune. "I see Lois!" she exclaimed. Lois was a close friend, the charity's retired CPA, who shared many of Amber's values, but was more hardheaded about business matters. Amber felt this was a sign that she should consider asking Lois to become her partner and run the business side of things.

Lois accepted her offer, and the two ran the publishing firm Amber founded for several years, until Lois' passing. At that point, Amber sold the company to a larger publisher and began a third successful career as a writer.

Rune #15: Algiz or Eolh

Elk's Sedge grows in the marsh/where it flourishes by the water./Its burrs pierce/and its stems burn/the unwary when they grasp it./This is protection.
—*The Old English Rune Poem*

Algiz

Algiz (pronounced all-jeez) is your rune of protection, guardianship, and the difficult path made easy. Like thorn bushes, the plant Elk's Sedge (Algiz) had sharp burrs that inflicted excruciating pain on anyone foolish enough to grab one or venture far into a patch. Elk's Sedge grew thickly along the lakeshores of Northern Europe, creating a barrier between the peoples of early times and the fish and water they needed for cooking. Fortunate were those who dared the shores and escaped its clutches. Hidden in it, even the elk and waterfowl were safe from hunters. For the men and women of this age, Algiz became the living embodiment of the energies of sanctuary, help, and good or ill fortune.

Rune Image: Branches of the Elk's Sedge plant

In Rune Reading

Faceup meanings: Protection, sanctuary, haven, guardianship, aid, counsel, heavenly guides, timely premonitions of disaster, prickly problems overcome or avoided, suffering in a good cause or rewarded, success in difficult ventures. *Tarot comparison:* The Moon. *Astrological comparison:* Cancer.

Occluded (facedown) meanings: Vulnerability, deception by others, lack of aid, ignoring heavenly counsel, prickly problems you cannot easily solve, suffering to no purpose or without reward, ventures that should be entered cautiously or not at all. *Tarot comparison:* The Moon reversed. *Astrological comparison:* Cancer afflicted.

In Rune Magic

Use to: Protect you or another from ill-fortune or difficulty, create a sanctuary area safe from negative energy, attract timely counsel or assistance, ease suffering and pain, launch and support important but risky ventures

In Rune Meditation

Use to: Increase emotional strength and resistance, enter a mental safe-haven when you are suffering emotionally, understand the ways of good- and ill-fortune, seek counsel from a higher power

Rune Gods: Hemdal, protector of Asgard, God of Light; the Valkyries

Rune Totems: Elk, deer, snow geese, bison, ducks, mountain lions, foxes, wolves

Rune Herb: Angelica

Rune Color: Rainbow

Determining Your Future Success

What most books on business, success, and motivation won't admit is that you can't always succeed. You can succeed most of the time, you can succeed more often than not over the long term, you can have a triumphantly successful life.

But sometimes you don't succeed. Things go wrong, you make a mistake, the unforeseeable occurs, the obstacles are simply too great. Instead of things working for you, they work against you. Quite often, it's through no fault of your own—it is just that you can't win all of the time. Some people call this lack of success "failure" or "losing"; others call them "setbacks" or "reversals." No matter what you call it, wouldn't you avoid wasting the time and effort involved if you could? Or if you couldn't avoid it, but knew it was coming, wouldn't you react better, protect yourself better, and recover better?

There is no need for you to guess or hope or go forward blindly—or lose months and years on something that isn't going to succeed. Not when you can learn ahead of time whether or not your efforts will bear fruit in the future, and what factors will undo them. Better to discover the truth now and redirect your time and energies toward goals that you can achieve.

Knowing success lies ahead also fires motivation. Don't you always work with a whole heart when you believe what you are doing is going to turn out well? If you were so tired you couldn't sit up straight, wouldn't you find the energy for two more hours of work, or to resolve that one last seemingly insurmountable obstacle—if you were certain it would carry you to success?

Whether it is in a business, career, or personal situation, you can take a photograph of how your efforts are going to play out, and whether they are likely to pay off, with this very special method of rune reading. With this reading, you also use three circles. But, here the inner circle is the Circle of Current Manifestation—showing what is working for or against your success efforts at the present moment. The middle circle is the Circle of Immediate Manifestation—it shows what will be working for or against your success efforts in the near future. The outer circle is the Circle of Future Manifestation—it reveals how your efforts will play out over the long-term.

Rune Reading: Spotting the Patterns of Success

Three friends, Ruben, Zane, and Shawn, had formed a partnership, ReSeated, Inc. They planned to market a wonderful product: bench covers of a new ultra-durable plastic that would give new life to old wooden and concrete bus stop and park benches. It would save municipalities money in replacement cost, and was ecological because it kept older benches in service longer, reducing the use of raw materials to manufacture new ones.

With backing from a group of investors, the three had samples made, a product brochure printed, and opened offices in Boston. Ruben, who had been VP of marketing at his own company, set out on the road with Shawn, their enthusiastic plastics expert, to solicit sales. Zane held things down at the office, along with two secretaries.

The three partners, who were very different in background and temperament, meshed well and the future for ReSeated looked bright. Everyone who saw their product demonstrated was converted and wanted to purchase the covers for their own benches. ReSeated should have been a big success.

However, the trio had overlooked one vital fact. Coming from corporate backgrounds, they had failed to appreciate just how long state, county, and city governments take to make a decision. In some cases, it would be as many as three years before a decision could be made. Sometimes six months or a year was all it took. A few municipalities could and did reach decisions quicker, and some substantial orders came in. But, it was clear that it would take far longer for the company to turn a profit and go out of the red than the partners had estimated. They would have used up all their capital before then, and their backers were not willing to underwrite them further.

Naturally, the three men were very discouraged, and were debating whether they should go further. Zane, who was a student of runes, advised they try a rune reading. I suggested the three partners, Ruben, Zane, and Shawn, hold the 25 rune stones together and cast them onto the three circles. (Runes that landed facedown are shown shaded.)

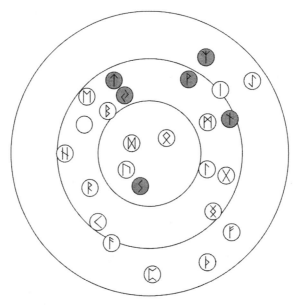

The ReSeated, Inc. reading.

Circle of Current Manifestation

If you didn't know the company was off the drawing board and had become a reality, you could guess that was the case by the presence of Uruz and Othala, two of the four stones that landed in the Circle of Current Manifestation. They tell us that ReSeated, Inc. is not just an illusion, dream, or wish. The company exists—it is an actuality. Uruz, the physical, and Othala, home, point to the company having a physical home—and it did, a suite of offices in Boston.

Dagaz in the inner circle bespeaks the harmony and mutual accord between the company's trio of principals. Faceup, this rune's meanings include balance between seemingly opposite forces. And certainly the three men were a study in contrasts.

The only cloud over ReSeated's inner existence is, of course, Sowilo facedown. Representing the energies of victory, power, and motivation when faceup, here Sowilo signifies that the company isn't making a large enough profit yet to sustain itself. This in turn led to the consternation and decline in motivation that brought the three partners to the runes.

Circle of Immediate Manifestation

Fourteen stones have fallen into the company's Circle of Immediate Manifestation. This is nearly two-thirds of the runes and tells us that the immediate future for the company is going to be very busy and event-filled. Of these 14, 10 are faceup, and only 4 are occluded, a strong hint that their business and cash flow will turn more positive than negative soon.

There aren't any conspicuous lines in the middle ring, or anywhere else in the reading, but there is one square, signifying forces that work inharmoniously together. The corners of this square are Berkana and Ehwaz faceup, and Tiwaz and Jera occluded. The four runes almost seem to signify a stalemate or stand off, with the negative energies of Tiwaz and Jera counteracting those of Berkana and Ehwaz.

I explained that Berkana's associations were nurturing, children, birth of a person or idea, a fortunate outcome. Ehwaz, I said, represented a steadfast partner with good judgment, harmonious collaboration with another, marriage, change for the better, and opportune period for initiating new ventures involving other people. Zane thought that these runes referred to the actual birth of the company as a successful entity, and that they should not give up because they had begun it at the right time.

However, I pointed out Tiwaz and Jera facedown as the opposing corners of the square would tend to retard progress in the immediate future. Occluded Tiwaz signifies lack of success, dark before the dawn, loss of money and power, weak will. Jera occluded signifies scarcity, delay, and effort without reward. Ruben felt this was a sign that while things were slow at the moment, it was the darkness before the dawn and that if they held out, things would be better.

Significantly, opposite this square in the lower left of the middle ring is a triangle, a very positive configuration, that tends to counter any negative effects of Tiwaz and Jera. The triangle is formed by Gebo, Lagaz, and Ingwaz all faceup, their energies unblocked.

Gebo, of course, is favorable meetings and connections. Lagaz symbolizes intuition and the unconscious. Ingwaz is the rune of favorable partnerships. To Shawn, favorable meetings suggested all the positive response they were getting. Ruben felt it might mean they would meet additional backers. Shawn also thought the runes were saying they were right to follow their intuition and start the company.

Other faceup stones that augur well for the partnership's immediate future are Kenaz, creative fire; Raidho, good luck; Mannaz, successful relationships with others; and Hagalaz, smooth sailing, trouble turned around. These far outweigh the potential trouble areas represented by the two remaining facedown stones: Wunjo, delayed harvests; and Naudhiz, unfulfilled needs.

Another important stone, the Wishing Stone or Stone of Fate, Wyrd, also lies within this circle, perhaps signifying that the three partners will still be wishing for success in the immediate future.

Yet another interesting feature of the reading is the way Isa lies on the border between the Circle of Immediate Manifestation and Future Manifestation. As Isa means both immobility and release from immobility, this seems to imply that after a long, slow birthing for the company in the immediate future, just a bit further ahead it will make a sudden transition to profitability and success.

Circle of Future Manifestation

The inference that there is success in ReSeated's future seems supported by the presence of four faceup runes in the outer circle and none that landed facedown. The faceup runes are Fehu, prosperity, property, wealth; Anza, communications (business communications, Shawn thought); Perdhro, good fortune (financial success, Zane believed); and Thurisaz, protection and freedom from worry (which sounded good to Ruben).

Both Algiz and Ehwaz lie beyond the outer ring, signifying the energies they represent will not play a significant role in the company's future.

Ultimately Zane and Ruben decided to stick with the partnership. Shawn decided he didn't want to invest the additional time it would take to make the company a success and sold his interest to his two partners. Two years later, after a long, slow startup period, ReSeated, Inc. went into the black, just as the reading had suggested.

Rune #16: Sowilo or Sigil

The shining of the sun/is the prayer of sailors/when they sail far out/upon the fishes' bath/until they return/in safety to the shore.

—*The Old English Rune Poem*

Sowilo

Sowilo (pronounced so-whee-lo) is your rune of victory, power, and motivation. The radiant energy of the sun (sowilo) was considered the source and protector of all life in the eras where runes first saw use. Its rays caused plants to grow; they lit the world so that danger became visible at the first approach and could be avoided. The sun, believed to be carried across the sky in a chariot, was a blessing to hunters and fishers alike, for only by its light could they find their way back home in safety. Victorious over the dark and cold of night, the sun was seen as the emblem of success, openness and fair-dealing, and the inner radiance of motivation and spiritual growth.

Rune Image: The flaming spokes of the wheels of the solar chariot

In Rune Reading

Faceup meanings: Victory shining forth, success, fair play in the light of day, causes, goals, and paths, material and spiritual power or increase, will power or motivation to overcome all obstacles, taking charge, power to control, transformation, spiritual illumination. *Tarot comparison:* The Sun. *Astrological comparison:* The Sun.

Occluded (facedown) meanings: Failure, injustice or double-dealing in the darkness, wrong causes, misperceived paths, worry leading to lack of motivation, anxiousness when not in control, diminished vitality and health, spiritual darkness. *Tarot comparison:* The Sun reversed. *Astrological comparison:* The Sun afflicted.

In Rune Magic

Use to: Make certain the success of any venture, work healing energy, fire motivation and will-power when you need them, increase healing energy, super-energize any magical working, awaken psychic centers and chakras

In Rune Meditation

Use to: Develop will power, germinate psychic abilities, achieve enlightenment

Rune Gods: Sol, God who drives the chariot of sun; Sol, his female original and counterpart

Rune Totems: Peacocks, chameleons, parrots, groundhogs, swallows, robin redbreasts, camels, lizards

Rune Herb: Mistletoe

Rune Color: Sunshine gold

Rune Magic: Magnetizing Your Life for Success

Ensure business and professional success now. Magnetize your life for success with this traditional magical ceremony, long used to release the energies of accomplishment and victory. With the aid of their guardian gods, the forces of three runes—Dagaz, Ingwaz, and Wunjo—will pave the path to success for you.

The energies of Dagaz will see all your efforts get off to a successful start. Those of Ingwaz will guide them to successful conclusions. And Wunjo is the sense of joy you will feel at everything turning out successfully.

You will need candles of three different colors, each one of the colors harmonious with the three runes. For incense, you will also want to make a special blend of the three herbs harmonious with these runes. For Dagaz, these are sky blue and clary sage. For Ingwaz, they are oak wood white and ragwort. For Wunjo, yellowish gold and flax.

When it isn't practical for you to find or use all these items, use only one candle and one herb for incense. If possible select yellowish gold and flax. Otherwise, just use whichever of these herbs and colors you can obtain. The only really essential thing is to have some harmonious light and some harmonious herb.

Pick a time to work your ritual when you will be undisturbed and a site where you feel comfortable performing magic. Take a pinch each of the three herbs, and blend the sage, ragwort, and flax together. Set your incense burner in a safe location, place a small pinch of this blend on your incense burner, and carefully light it.

Separate Dagaz, Ingwaz, and Wunjo from the other rune stones and lay the remainder aside. Place Dagaz just to the left of you, Ingwaz in front of you, and Wunjo just to the right. This creates a channel or circuit down which the ritual's runic energies can run—from a successful beginning, to a successful conclusion, to the joy of Wunjo afterward.

On the far side of each rune stone, in a safe location, place and light the candle whose color is harmonious with that rune. Kneel, sit, or stand as you are most comfortable, and settle yourself with deep breathing. After you have settled into a calm, receptive state, suitable for accumulating and channeling the runes' energies, take Dagaz in the hand closest to your heart (the left hand).

With Dagaz in left hand, say:

In the name of Ostara,
I invoke Dagaz!

After a few moments, the rune stone should begin to grow unusually warm in your hand, or a tingling sensation will occur in your left arm—sometimes both. This is a sign that the rune's deity has heeded you and is releasing to your control the cosmic forces Dagaz channels. Return the rune to its original position and replace it with Ingwaz in your left hand. Say:

In the name of Ing,
I invoke Ingwaz!

Again, within a minute or two, you will feel the stone warming or experience a tingling current of energy running up your arm from your left hand. Lay Ingwaz back in place, pick up Wunjo (also with your left hand), and say:

In the name of Frey,
I invoke Wunjo!

When the stone warms, and you sense the rune's deity has opened its energies to you, you may set it back in its place. Then say:

Thank you, Ostara.
Thank you, Ing.
Thank you, Frey.

Take all three stones and hold them in your cupped hands. Lift your hands as high out in front of you as is comfortable, directing the forces they are charged with back into the world to contribute to your success (or that of a loved one) according to their natures. Say:

Let the energy
of these runes
flow through me.
May the energy of Dagaz
see all my ventures
off to a successful start.
May the energy of Ingwaz
guide them to
a successful ending.
May the energy of Wunjo
bring an occasion
for celebrating successes.
Ostara bids you obey me.
Ing bids you obey me.
Frey bids you obey me.
Dagaz! Ingwaz! Wunjo!

As you have been speaking, the warmth should have begun to fade and any tingling should subside. This is a sign that the energies of the runes, directed by your instructions, are pouring from the runes to carry out your intentions and are already active in your behalf. Express your sense of gratefulness to the rune's deities, and say:

Thank you, Ostara,
thank you, Ing,
thank you, Frey,
for this blessing.

Take a minute to return to normal by breathing deeply several times. Extinguish the candles, and put the three stones back with the rest. If it is not dangerous, let the incense burn itself out, otherwise, snuff it out at once.

Use this for general success in life or success with a specific venture, such as business, romance, or a test. The results will astonish you!

The runes are an ancient Scandinavian source of wisdom. When faced with a question, you can ask for "the right course of action" and then draw a rune. [Runes] provide not only a "yes or no" answer, but additional insights into the factors that will impact the outcome of your decision.
—Bernice L. Ross, Ph.D., *Three Strategies for Making Smarter Choices*

Rune Meditation: Bathing in the Light of Victory

It's a fact that to succeed—you must *believe* you can succeed. Yet, it's natural to lose faith in your own success from time to time. No matter how strong their belief in themselves or how high their motivation, everyone has periods when they begin to doubt, run out of steam, or find their motivation has gone to pot.

This loss of faith in your success is the number one threat to that success. As long as you are convinced you can't, you will never try to chug up the hill and become the little engine that could—and did! How do you get back that belief when you have lost it? The ancients had a solution: a meditation called Bathing in the Light of Victory. This meditation draws down the power of Tiwaz, rune of victory, to recharge your belief system. It uses Tiwaz's spear-like shape as a key for aligning yourself with its runic energies.

Find a good place for meditation, and set the Tiwaz rune stone where you can look at it comfortably. Relax first by breathing slowly and deeply for a few minutes until your mind is at rest. Close your eyes and count to 10, then open them and let them rest on the rune Tiwaz.

The long upright line is like the shaft of a spear with the two short lines meeting at the tip like the spear's point. Keep your eyes on this line, let it absorb into your retinas—until it is all that you see. When everything else but the rune image is a blur, close your eyes.

You should still be able to see Tiwaz's image vividly as white on black, or as a jet-black spear shape floating against gray. Visualize the line that makes the shaft turning into real wood, solid, round, and polished until it gleams. Picture the tip becoming the silvery-iron of a spear's tip.

Visualize the image growing in size until it is as tall as the top of a person's head. The base of the shaft rests on your floor, the metal tip gleams on high. The spear looks strong and protective, the very symbol of victory.

Focus on the shining tip of the spear. Its burnished iron catches the light. Picture the gleaming point of brightness reflected from the tip.

In your mind's eye, see this gleaming point grow brighter and brighter. This is the Light of Victory, and it shines on you and through you. Its radiance penetrates your skin and bathes you with the energy of Tiwaz, until your whole body tingles and is charged with the forces of unconquerable success.

By this place in the meditation, you should feel hopeful and rejuvenated. At least some of your motivation, confidence, and belief in your success should have returned. If it hasn't yet, continue visualizing yourself being bathed in the Light of Victory until it does.

Open your eyes when you feel ready. Turn to this meditation to recharge your belief in your success any time you feel it sagging. Remember, if you believe you can—you can!

Chapter 9

Runes of Love and Romance

Are you looking for love and don't seem able to find it? Have you just found it and want to keep the flame blazing bright and hot—always? Is there a new person in your life and you wonder if he or she could be that special someone? Have you been together for a while, and wish you could reignite the original chemistry that excited you both? Has trouble surfaced in your current love relationship that you don't know how to heal?

Men and women—gay or straight, married or partnered—have longed for love, fallen in love, and had lover's quarrels since time began. These truths were as fundamental millennia ago when the runes first appeared in the land as they are today. There is almost nothing we need more than intimate, romantic, sexual love. There is also nothing that causes us more confusion, conflict, or contradiction. Ultimately, sexual love is more important to most women and men than success, wealth, business, background, religion, and family.

The runes reflect this knowledge, for 11—nearly half of all the 24 rune symbols—have meanings connected in some way with sexual love and sexual pairings (marriage or domestic unions). The 11 runes of love and sex are: Fehu, Thurisaz, Ansuz, Kenaz, Gebo, Wunjo, Naudhiz, Tiwaz, Berkana, Ehwaz, and Ingwaz.

These runes, and the others, can help you find love, keep love, and make it grow. They can show you the way through the inevitable troubles that surface in any relationship, and point the way to deeper harmony, intimacy, and passion.

Fulfilling Your Need for Love

Whether you call him or her Mr. Right, Ms. Right, your soul mate, that special someone, husband, wife, or life-partner, finding your soul mate transforms existence and lights up your whole world. It gives greater meaning and enjoyment to everything you do. It bestows the miracle of giving and receiving love, without which life feels empty and futile.

If you have been seeking a soul mate and not finding one, or have kept thinking you've found Ms. or Mr. Right, only to have them turn out to be very wrong, maybe the problem is that you have been looking for the wrong kind of person. There are times when we don't know what is good for us, and the search for true love can be one of those times.

Or you might have met someone, felt a spark, and be wondering if they could be your soul mate. Or you might be in a relationship with someone you felt was your soul mate at first, but now are having second thoughts.

You don't need to fill out complicated personality surveys at an expensive dating service to discover the signs that will tell you if the person you have just met fits the ideal profile of your soul mate. An ancient rune reading technique can do the same thing free and in less than 20 minutes. Instead of filling out forms, all you need to do is throw the rune stones.

Kiss me, for I am troubled with love.
—Love magic inscription, circa 1200 C.E.

Rune Reading: Identifying Your Soul Mate

You only read the faceup stones in this traditional runic approach to creating a portrait of your soul mate. Set the blank stone, Wyrd, aside and cast the other 24. Ignore those that fall facedown—they represent qualities that aren't needed for someone to be your personal Ms. or Mr. Right.

Runes that land with the image side up reveal the qualities a person has to have to be your ideal soul mate. These are usually qualities you lack, such as patience or assertiveness. Or else they are qualities needed to act as a counterbalance to qualities of yours, such as the caution needed to balance your impulsiveness.

Sample Reading

Shirleen was 32, strikingly attractive, and held a responsible position in her city's Department of Public Works. She owned her own home, had nice clothes, money in the bank, and a wide circle of friends. What she didn't have was the one thing Shirleen wanted most—a soul mate.

She had been through a number of boyfriends, some lasting a year or two, some only months. At the time Shirleen became involved with each of them, she thought "this is the one" only to be disappointed. The result was that at 30, she had begun to wonder if something was wrong with her. "Why can't I find my soul mate?" she asked.

Shirleen's choices were suggestive in themselves. One boyfriend had been a doctor who was devoutly religious. Another, a mechanic at the garage where she'd had her car repaired after an accident who liked to party. Yet another had been an unemployed, divorced father. Another, a career military man who was in AA.

These men were all so different from each other. There was no common "type"—nothing to connect them. Shirleen might have selected them at random by throwing darts. It was evident that Shirleen simply latched onto the first man to come along—and hoped he was her soul mate. She had no independent concept of what her soul mate would be like. Shirleen hadn't stopped to think about what qualities he would need to have for her to be happy—and for him to truly be her soul mate. "I want him to be good to me," was all she could articulate.

I suggested that, rather than a problem reading with the three circles, Shirleen try a reading that would reveal the essential characteristics of her ideal soul mate. Runes that landed faceup would show the qualities in a man that would best support and nurture her. And, in turn, they would show the sort of man whom she could best support and nurture with her love.

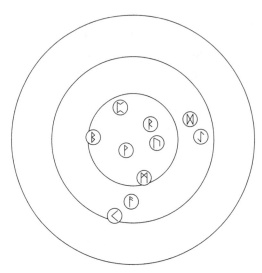

Shirleen's reading (shows faceup stones only).

Characteristics of Shirleen's Soul Mate

An interesting group of personality traits emerged when Shirleen threw the rune stones. Berkana, Kenaz, Ansuz, Mannaz, Wunjo, Perdhro, Raidho, Uruz, Dagaz, and Eihwaz fell faceup. These runes said she should look for a man who ...

- Is nurturing and giving (Berkana).
- Has a solid job and career (Kenaz).
- Is a good communicator with something valuable to say (Ansuz).
- Is personable and got along well with others (Mannaz).
- Is upbeat and positive (Wunjo).
- Is a winner rather than a loser (Perdhro).
- Is someone who enjoys travel, change, and meeting new people (Raidho).
- Is healthy and a good worker (Uruz).
- Is calm and unruffled, with a talent for peacemaking (Dagaz).
- Is organized and together and able to help others get organized and together (Eihwaz).

When Shirleen heard the traits associated with these runes, she brightened considerably. Each one, she said, struck a chord. Either it was essential for a good relationship (such as being nurturing), or matched exactly her own interests (such as an interest in travel), or it complemented her weaknesses (such as being organized, which she said she wasn't).

Put together like that, Shirleen saw that she had been on the wrong dating and relationship path. She had been too easily satisfied, with no clear idea what she really wanted or needed in a man. Now, in the portrait runes had painted, she recognized her ideal man. "It's funny," Shirleen said. "The runes knew what my soul mate would be like, even when I didn't!"

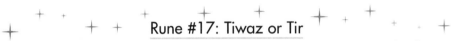

Rune #17: Tiwaz or Tir

A spear point shines like beacon./It spells victory over enemies./It faithfully protects the people./Raised on high/it is the sign of justice/straight and unfailing.

—*The Old English Rune Poem*

Tiwaz

Tiwaz (pronounced tea-was) is your rune of success and fair dealings. The spear point (tiwaz), shining above the warriors in times of trouble, was a sign of protection and a promise of victory. Held upright by the guards of a sovereign's court, it became a symbol of justice and rewards.

Rune Image: A spear point

In Rune Reading

Faceup meanings: Victory, success in competition, defense, or risk-taking, loyalty, self-sacrifice, fairness, justice, order, deserved increase in money and power, leader or ruler, strong will, motivation, positive masculine energy. *Tarot comparison:* Justice. *Astrological comparison:* Libra.

Occluded (facedown) meanings: Failure, lack of success, dark before the dawn, betrayal, selfishness, injustice, loss of money and power, weak or unfair leader, weak will, negative masculine energy. *Tarot comparison:* Justice reversed. *Astrological comparison:* Libra afflicted.

In Rune Magic

Use for: Bringing to pass justly deserved success, commanding order to your benefit, quick recovery from illness, victory in a lawsuit, building spiritual energies

In Rune Meditation

Use for: Discovering the key to success in any endeavor, developing spiritual will, perceiving equitable solutions, building leadership qualities

Rune Gods: Tyr, God of Battle and Martial Honor

Rune Totems: Hawks, wolves, owls, falcons, bears

Rune Herb: Sage

Rune Color: Bright red

Moving from Heartbreak to Happiness

Finding that one special someone doesn't mean walking off hand-in-hand to a movie-cliché happy ending. Love exists in the real world, and even the best of relationships experience stresses and strains sometimes. Problems, illness, or debt arise that create friction—or differing needs and ways of communicating—or even expressing love—lead to frustration and resentment.

You have had arguments and fights with your loved one—times when you were furious or so hurt you were emotionally cold to each other for days—everyone has. You might have argued over money, sex, priorities, behaviors, child-rearing, goals, or leisure time. Sometimes the things you say to each other, or the constant frustration at your loved one's inability to share your point of view, cuts so deep that you feel almost incapable or forgiving or forgetting.

When you and your lover end up in a dispute, have a falling out, blow up at each other, or fall to disagreeing and can't seem to find your way back to agreement, when your hearts are aching and hurt, runes can sort it all out for you, heal your wounds, and bring you back together in a spirit of loving reconciliation.

Love, heartache, and lover's quarrels are as old as love itself. The earliest myths, legends, and records tell of divorce, separations, jealousy, conflict, bitterness, and reconciliation among lovers. Men and women, their amours, and the hot passion of love—which occasionally turns to the hot passion of anger—have been the same throughout history.

Mostly when we find ourselves on the outs with the person we love most in the world is because of one or more of the following flashpoints of intimacy.

Ale-Runes must thou know to make maidens love thee.
—*The Elder Edda*

Communication

Often, even when two people love each other deeply, and agree on most issues, they wind up in heated disputes or unintentionally hurt each other because of differing communication styles. Women and men are said to have different ways of communicating, but the truth is, every person has his or her own communication style. What to say, what words to use, whether or not to say anything, even body language, are the result of background and experience.

You might say, "I love you!" in words. Someone else might say it with a glance or a touch, or by planting a garden for a loved one. If verbal confirmation of your lover's affection for you is what you crave, a touch or surprise vacation might leave you frustrated. Or you might feel that new facts warrant bringing up a topic the two of you had settled, whereas your lover becomes angry, feeling that you are simply trying to argue her or him to your point of view.

Outside Stresses

Problems involving family, finance, illness, job loss or transfer, and an unforeseen crisis all place enormous additional emotional pressures on you and your lover. Making an intimate relationship grow and thrive is difficult enough in normal circumstances. Otherwise, half of all marriages would not end in divorce.

Add to the typical daily strains of two very distinct individuals trying to get along during a prolonged and expensive illness; the stress can generate arguments, sexual dysfunction, and resentment—it can even lead to divorce. The same is true for the emotional tension generated by a job-related move to a new town and the readjustment it involves, as would be the case if you lost of all your most valued possessions in a fire or hurricane.

Sex

Sex is cited by couples as one of the most common causes of relationship and marital breakup. It's easy to understand why: We are sexual beings, and we most generally fall in love and want to be with someone due to emotional and sexual attraction.

Good sex with someone who deeply loves and cares for you supplies an essential emotional validation and source of life-affirming pleasure that is vital to mental, spiritual, and physical health. Without a deeply satisfying sexual relationship, we question our worth and our attractiveness. Life feels less than fully satisfying, even empty.

So many things can go wrong with sex that it takes hundreds of books to cover them all. You have probably had conflict with a lover over how often to have sex, or something you wanted to try in bed that your partner didn't (and vice versa). And after a time, when the newness and excitement of exploring each other's bodies has begun to wear off, there's the danger of one or both of you becoming bored and losing interest in the other sexually.

The Intertwined Hearts Reading

Why break up when you can make up? Thousands of years ago the Vitka, who held the secrets the runes in those days, had a way of helping intimate partners overcome the confusions and divisions to which the human heart is prone, discover points of agreement, and rekindle their original sense of passion and harmony. This approach to rune reading empowered couples to resolve even seemingly unresolvable impasses and disagreements. Use the same technique when you find yourself and your lover butting heads and you, too, can move from heartbreak to happiness. Called the Intertwined Hearts reading, it only takes 5 runes and 15 minutes.

The Intertwined Hearts reading is an extremely powerful tool for discovering solutions to the problems that sometimes arise in the course of an intimate relationship. Most approaches to using runes as a means of resolving conflicts between romantic partners are a "one size fits all" type of thing. That is, they take standard rune (or even Tarot) layouts and simply apply them to lover's quarrels.

Based on the shape of intertwined hearts, this rune reading acknowledges the fact that when two people fall in love and form a couple, each person's heart merges in part with the heart of the other. The result is that in intimate relationships each of us incorporates a bit of the other into our own sense of self and identity. This is the miracle of two becoming one—and it is a critical, but often overlooked, aspect of any relationship. You acknowledge this fusion whenever you speak of "we" and mean the two of you as a unit. You say, "We went on vacation." Or, "We hated the play." Or, "Why can't we agree about sex?"

Typically, when we are entangled in a conflict with an intimate partner, we are unaware of this aspect of the relationship. We consider the problem solely in terms of "me" and "you." We see the issue as what "I" feel/think versus what "you feel/think."

We rarely, perhaps never, pause to get in touch with the part of our lover that we have incorporated in our heart. We fail to factor it into the equation. When was the last time you were in the middle of an argument with your loved one and paused to ask yourself what role the bit of them in you is playing or what it thinks or feels?

The Intertwined Hearts reading brings this crucial factor into focus using only five runes. These runes are arranged to form the tops and tips of two intertwined hearts.

The first two rune stones, at the tip of the heart, reflect how you see the problem and how your lover views it. The third and fourth runes, at the dip of each heart, represent the part of her or him in you and the part of you that is in him or her. The fifth rune, which marks the point where the two tops of the hearts intersect, reveals the one key point they can both agree on with their whole hearts.

Rune Reading: Illuminating and Resolving Romantic Difficulties

The preparations for the Intertwined Heart reading are simple. First, have clearly in mind the issue causing you and your lover to disagree.

Second, on a large sheet of paper draw two intertwined hearts. Third, lay all your rune stones, except Wyrd, the blank stone, facedown and mix them around, so you have no idea which stones are where. Fourth, relax with deep breathing so that your mind is still enough to sense and respond to heavenly guidance when you select the five stones.

Finally, before you begin picking your runes, take a few moments to put yourself back in touch with your feelings of love for your partner. Think about what it was (and is) that made you fall in love with him or her. Recall what your budding love for your partner felt like then (and what it feels like now, when generally all is going well and you experience that love more intensely). This is the same state the Intertwined Hearts reading draws on and it is vital you be in tune with it for a truly powerful reading.

When you have done this, hold your hand over the scattered rune stones and say:

Runar radh rett radh. (Runes bless me with good guidance.)

Wait until you feel your hand being moved or moving itself and let it pick up the stone it reaches for. Turn this stone over and lay it on the bottom tip of the heart on the left. Repeat the process with the second stone, and lay it on the bottom tip of the heart on your right. Repeat again, and place the third rune stone opposite the second, where the top of its heart dips to form a "V." Repeat again, and set the fourth stone opposite the first, where the top of its heart dips to form a "V," but a bit to the left of it. Allow your hand to be guided a fifth time, turn this stone faceup, too, and place it where the two hearts intersect at the very top.

When you begin to interpret the runes you have drawn, keep the following guidelines in mind.

Meaning of the Two Hearts

The heart whose lower point projects to the left represents your heart. The rune you place at its tip shows your heart's position on the matter that brought you into contention. The other heart, whose lower tip projects to the right, represents your lover's heart. The rune that you place there represents his or her heart's position.

Meaning of the Intertwined Hearts

Notice how the "V" at the top of your lover's heart is deeply intertwined into your heart? This represents your point of access to the part of your lover you have taken in to your heart, and the rune there provides access to unique insights into her or his thoughts and feelings about the conflict that divides you. Likewise, the "V" at the top of your heart is deeply intertwined into your loved one's heart, and the rune there will provide access to unique insights into your thoughts and feelings about the matter.

Meaning of the Top Rune

If you look closely, you will see that the one place where the lines of the two hearts meet symmetrically and blend is at the very top. At the other points where the lines of the hearts meet, they do so at cross-purposes, the way lovers often do. Only at the top do they intersect harmoniously, and the rune here shows the one place where your heart and that of your lover intersect harmoniously on the difficulty that has put you at cross-purposes. It is here that you will discover an approach to working things out that you can both agree on with your whole hearts.

The only other item you need to remember when interpreting your Intertwined Hearts reading is that because the first four runes you draw represent problem areas or areas of contention, you look to their meanings when occluded for insight. However, because the fifth or top rune poses a probable solution, you read it in terms of its positive associations.

Sample Reading

Rebecca and Pete had been married for four years. Both were young urban professionals. Rebecca was the director of advertising sales for the local newspaper; Pete was the weatherman on the local nightly television news show.

Though Rebecca and Pete were dedicated to their jobs, both also wanted children. However, Pete was reluctant to start a family because he felt Rebecca was always putting her job before family and he felt she should put family first if they were going to have a baby. Rebecca felt that without her job they would never be able to afford the things they wanted for their children or to send them to decent schools, and that she had to be doubly businesslike because she was surrounded by highly competitive men who wanted her job.

The most recent source of friction, as far as Pete was concerned, had occurred a few weeks earlier, when Rebecca had missed her own sister's wedding. A business emergency had called her out of town the night before, and Pete was certain she could have delegated someone to go in her place. Rebecca believed that the crisis, which involved the paper's second biggest advertiser, had called for her direct involvement.

The tension between Rebecca and Pete was beginning to carry over into the bedroom. The pair made love less frequently. "Even if Pete didn't use condoms," Rebecca said, "the way things are, we do it so seldom there wouldn't be much likelihood of us having a baby now."

Using the Intertwined Hearts reading, Rebecca drew the following rune stones: In the first position, lower left, representing her take on the dispute, was rune Hagalaz. Hagalaz generally symbolizes disruptive forces with the potential to be transformed. Facedown, Hagalaz suggests limitation, delay, forces outside your control, inauspicious time for new starts or risks, disruption by a natural event.

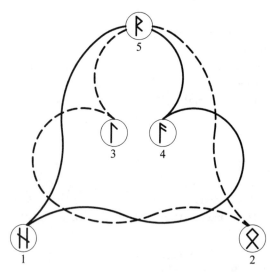

Rebecca's Intertwined Hearts reading.

Rebecca admitted that these were all feelings she'd had about having a baby. In terms of her job, and the income it brought in, she was afraid that bearing and rearing a child at this stage in her life would limit her career and delay her rise up the corporate ladder, and that it is not the time to risk all that. Rebecca felt she would be at the mercy of forces outside her job—the baby—that she couldn't control; she was afraid that her life, in short, would be disrupted by a natural event.

In the second position, lower right, representing her husband Pete's point of view on the problem, was Othala. This is the rune that embodies the energies of family, home, descent, and inheritance. The rune Rebecca had unknowingly selected seemed to reemphasize how important family was to Pete, explaining the strength of his feelings on the subject.

In the third position, representing how the part of Pete she had incorporated into her own heart felt about their conflict, was Lagaz. Typically, Lagaz represents the oceanic power and depths of the unconscious. When it relates to problems, Lagaz often indicates someone being misled by intuition into doing the wrong thing, taking the easy way out. Here, it seems to suggest Pete felt Rebecca was wrong in following her feelings about motherhood and family, taking the easy way out, and would regret it later.

In the fourth position, representing what the part of her Pete had incorporated into his heart had to say to him, was Ansuz. Rune of communication, when it is occluded Ansuz indicates someone who is not being listened to, as well as bad advice and verbal interference by others. Rebecca felt both that Pete was not hearing her and that he was being pressured by his family to pressure her to have a baby.

Lastly, in the fifth position, representing an approach to resolving their conflict that both Pete and Rebecca could both agree on with their whole hearts, was Raidho. Journeys both geographic and spiritual are at the heart of rune Raidho. As a rune of solution, we look to the rune's positive meanings. Among them are differences where happy compromise is possible (exactly what they were seeking!), plus change, motion, progression, rhythm, and natural cosmic cycles.

The Old English Rune Poem reminds us that "travel broadens everyone." This seemed a hint that if they could break away from their ingrained mindsets, routines, jobs, and family, the couple might be able to resolve their impasse. Although Rebecca was deeply involved in her career, she admitted Pete was even more important to her, and said she could agree to take a week or two off for a vacation—and she was sure Pete would.

Change, progression, rhythm, and natural cosmic cycles played a role in their vacation—and in easing away the tension between them. Somewhere on the slopes of Mount Shasta, Rebecca told friends later, she realized she did want Pete's children. Nine months later, they had a daughter, and Rebecca was working from home for the same company, as a consultant.

Rune #18: Berkana or Beorc

The branches of the birch/cast nurturing shade on all the families of the forest/provide concealment to the smallest of creatures./In winter it is bare and stark as death./In spring the birch bursts gloriously forth/with its canopy of richest green again.

—*The Old English Rune Poem*

Berkana

Berkana (pronounced bur-kan-a) is your rune of nurturing, family, and regeneration. The birch tree (berkana) was a constant reminder of the miracles of life, death, rebirth, and protection to the women and men of long ago. Its bark was made into clothing, cabin shingles, and even canoes. Rich in green leaves, it afforded shade in summer, as well as haven to the squirrel, chipmunk, owl, and sparrow. During the winter, barren of leaves, bark peeling, it seemed dead beyond hope of rebirth—but in spring, it miraculously burst forth once more.

Rune Image: Two leaves growing on a birch branch

In Rune Reading

Faceup meanings: Nurturing, protection, concealment, mothers, children, family celebrations, rebirth, growth, fortunate outcome, positive feminine energy, birth of a person, idea, or endeavor. *Tarot comparison:* The Empress. *Astrological comparison:* Virgo.

Occluded (facedown) meanings: Domestic difficulties; bad family news; a ruptured relationship; lack of nurturing or growth; an unfortunate outcome that

can be avoided through prudence, restraint, and timely action; negative feminine energy; hibernation of a person, idea, or endeavor. *Tarot comparison:*
The Empress reversed. *Astrological comparison:* Virgo afflicted.

In Rune Magic

Use to: Protect and conceal self or other from harmful influences, bring harmony to a household, generate spiritual or physical rebirth after negative experiences, send or receive nurturing energy, invoke female energy

In Rune Meditation

Use to: Revitalize wearied or dormant spiritual energies, perceive the moment
as the mother of all things; bring creative ideas to life, especially when they
have been stalled

Rune Gods: Holde, triple Goddess of birth, life, and death

Rune Totems: Squirrels, eagles, chipmunks, owls, jaguars, anacondas

Rune Herb: Lady's mantle

Rune Color: Dark green

Rune Magic: Enhancing Compatibility and Chemistry

If things aren't going well for you and that special someone, if you are at
arm's length over a dispute, if the passion appears to be cooling, or if
your aim is merely to intensify desire and add an extra spark to your
lovemaking—or if your problem is that you see a special someone and
want to attract her or him—then this bit of runic magic is just what the
love doctor ordered.

You'll use three of the most potent runes of love and romance—Gebo,
Ingwaz, and Dagaz—to kindle greater intimacy, harmony, and desire in
your relationship. You can do this rune magic by yourself—or with your
lover. Whichever approach is yours, the result will be an upswing in
compatibility and chemistry.

All that's involved in this ceremony is saying a few words, drawing two
interlocked hearts, and then inscribing Gebo, Ingwaz, and Dagaz in each
heart. Before you begin, you will need a deep blue candle, the herb heartsease, an incense burner, a sheet of blank paper, and a pen with red ink.

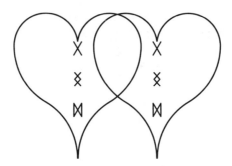

Runes' love magic hearts.

In a time and place suitable for working magic, light both your incense and candle. Sit comfortably with the paper and pen before you. As always, begin with a relaxation routine of deep, slow breaths to empty your mind and spirit so that you can serve as a conduit for the cosmic energies linked with runes.

Then say:

Freyja, Goddess of Love,
Frey, God of Spring,
bestow your blessing
on this worthy work.

Sit for a moment and wait until you feel a subtle shift in your spiritual state or body, signifying that the deities have directed some of their energy to supplement yours. Pick up the pen. Say:

Fill this pen
with the power of love.
Let that which it pictures
reflect heavenly truth.

When you feel an energy or vibration move into your hand, or it begins to move by itself, draw with red ink two large hearts interlocked, side-by-side. Say:

Freyja and Frey,
let these two hearts
become our hearts,
as closely intertwined.

Beginning with the heart that is to your left (the closest to your own heart), inscribe rune Gebo separately within each heart. Say:

May Gebo in these hearts
become Gebo in our hearts.
May the give and take of love
be in our relationship
and in our bed.

Beginning with the heart that is to your left, inscribe rune Ingwaz separately within each heart. Say:

May Ingwaz in these hearts
become Ingwaz in our hearts
May there be
ever abundant desire
and fulfillment
between us always!

Beginning with the heart that is to your left, inscribe rune Dagaz separately within each heart. Say:

May Dagaz in these hearts
become Dagaz in my heart.
May our energies be balanced,
harmonious,
and may magnetic attraction
lie between us.

Pause, and visualize your lover. As you do, you should experience warmth growing in your heart, and a feeling of both intense spiritual and physical yearning for the unique being that is him or her. Any animosity, resentment, or unhappiness you have been feeling toward her or him should have vanished.

If you are doing this ritual alone, for both of you, over the next few days or weeks, you will notice a change for the better in both your attitude and your partner's. Although your loved one was not part of the ceremony, he or she will also find his or her heart growing warmer toward you, along with greater physical desire for you, and increased feelings of harmony. If you are experiencing relationship difficulties, the change in your lover will either lead to—or result from—his or her discovery of a compromise that helps dispel the cloud that has been casting its shadow on your love for one another.

Conclude the ritual by saying:

Thank you
Freyja, Goddess of Love,
Thank you
Frey, God of Spring,
for bestowing your blessings
on this worthy work.

Now snuff out the candle. Your rune magic ritual is complete.

If the two of you have been fighting over a sensitive issue, you will be pleasantly surprised to find yourselves seeing eye to eye. If you have been having trouble communicating, you will discover you are both hearing and understanding and agreeing with each other more frequently. If sex hasn't been what you wanted it to be, all the old fire and magic will return.

Rune Meditation: Exploring True Intimacy

Whether you have been in a relationship for years or just days, this meditation will guide you into the development of deeper intimacy and interconnectedness than you ever dreamed possible. Your meditation will be centered on Gebo, the rune of sexual love, sexual union, and sexual harmony. Gebo's very shape conveys the idea of connection, two paths intersecting, even one person lying across another—in short, all that we associate with sexual love and union. Even today the memory of this rune survives in our culture—when we sign a note with "XXXXX" to symbolize kisses.

Rune Gebo's meaning of interrelationships and generosity conveys much of what we believe a loving sexual union should be like. So do its other associations, such as a favorable meeting, the harmonious intersection of forces, relationships, people working to achieve a common goal, gift, giving, giver, generosity, charity, and gratitude. And, of course, the tarot card that represents the same energy is titled The Lovers.

In magical rituals, Gebo is used in love and sex magic of all types. You can employ the powers it controls to attract a soul mate, to enhance lovemaking, to ensure fertility and conception, and more. Gebo is essential in that most sacred of all sex magic ceremonies where lovers become the living embodiment of the union of the god and goddess.

In meditation, Gebo aids you in better understanding relationships, deepening harmony, replacing frustration and anger with compassion and empathy. It is especially effective in exploring harmony, intimacy, and interconnectedness between lovers. That is what you will be doing with rune Gebo in this meditation.

In a quiet place, lay rune Gebo before you, then breathe slowly and deeply a few time to calm and center your mind.

Just as you can read the runes for an individual, you can read the runes for a couple or those involved in any relationship—lovers, friends, parents and children, even business partners.

—Deon Dolphin, *Rune Magic*

Two Paths Crossing

Look down at the Gebo. At first, you will see the image as two lines crossing. If you stare at it a little longer, you are likely to begin seeing them more metaphorically as two intersecting paths or roads.

Meditate for a while on how your relationship with your lover is like two paths that cross. Think about your lover's life up to the moment the two of you met. What is it that made your lover the person he or she is and someone who would love you? Knowing their background, think about what it was in you that your lover saw and found irresistible.

Think about your life up to the moment you met. What is it that made you what you are and someone who would fall for your lover? Think about what it is in him or her that you saw and found irresistible.

Contemplate the effect your paths crossing had on both your lives. How has your lover changed you? How have you changed your lover? How has the direction of each of your life paths changed as a result of meeting and joining together?

Think about the way your paths crossed. Was there something almost magical and predestined about it? Perhaps your lives had almost intersected before. You might have both known the same people or visited the same city at the same time. Or there might have been something almost pre-destined about the way your paths finally crossed. For instance, did you meet because one of you changed your mind on impulse, suddenly going to an event he or she had definitely decided not to attend? Or was it because you both took completely different routes to work than normal and encountered each other along the way?

If there was something magical about your coming together as a couple, contemplate how you felt when you first learned about it. Did you feel that your relationship was "meant to be"? That it was a romance destined by fate to happen?

How do you feel about that meeting now? The same? Different? Meditate on your answer for a time.

Close your eyes and breathe deeply to clear your mind and recharge your body for the next portion of the meditation.

Where Two Become One

Open your eyes and return them to the Gebo symbol. Look at it again, and see it not as two lines crossing—but as two separate triangles or diamond-shapes with four points defining the two shapes. Two distinct forms that meet and touch only at a single point.

Meditate on how your union is like these triangles. You are two distinct entities who can meet and know each other only at one place. That contact point is the intimacy your passionate love for each other and sexual union makes possible.

Think about yourself as an individual separate from and different than your lover. What makes you different? How are you different? What is most unique about you? What distinct characteristics make you "you"?

Think about your lover as an individual separate from and different than you. What makes her or him different? How is your lover different? What is most unique about him or her? What distinct characteristics make your lover the person he or she is?

Now, contemplate the place where your two separate lives touch and become one—the intimacy that allows you to drop the emotional barriers we keep raised for the rest of the world and merge and give and take, both in bed and out of it. What does that intimacy look like to you? What does it smell like? What would it feel like if you could touch it? What are the emotions you experience when you are naked in each other's arms and that intimacy surrounds you?

The Face of Love

Now that you are in touch with your positive feelings of love and intimacy for your partner, shift your attention to the image on the Gebo rune again. There is a third way to see the rune. It can also be a stylized frowny-face.

The middle, where the lines meet, could be the nose. The upper "V" could be slitted, intently frowning eyes. The lower, upside-down "V" would be the mouth turned in unhappiness.

Visualize this stylized frowny-face turning into your loved one's face. Picture their real face when you have seen them this unhappy. If your lover was before you now, and this was how his or her face looked, what would you be willing to do to change his or her frowny-face into a smile? What would you be willing to sacrifice or do differently to see them happy again?

Contemplate those thoughts for a few minutes. By now you should be feeling intense intimacy and love for your special someone.

Take some slow breaths. Look away from Gebo, to break contact with it. Get up, stretch, stir around. But don't rush the process. Allow yourself to exit from the meditational space at your own speed.

At the moment when you next see your partner, whether they have a smiley- or frowny-face, summon those feelings back again. Let the intimacy in your heart ignite greater intimacy in your loved one's heart. Show her or him what you are feeling.

Do whatever it was you knew you would be willing to do to put a smiley-face on her or him. If you do, you will find the bond between you deeper than ever.

Chapter 10

Runes of Power and Magic

For millennia the power of the runes has been invoked to aid, guard, and heal. Soldiers went into battle with magic runic symbols on their armor to strengthen their sword arm, ward off deadly blows, and quicken recovery from wounds received. Lovers gave each other rune charms to ensure fidelity and passion whether they were together or apart. Business owners carved them over the doorways of their shops. Parents wove runes of luck, health, and success into their children's garments.

You can use rune magic the same way. You can create powerful ceremonies, talismans, charms, and spells that will help you and your loved ones lead better, happier lives. You can release the cosmic forces associated with the runes to ensure the success and safety of your own endeavors and those of people and institutions dear to your heart.

Every rune is magical. Every rune can be—and is—used in rune magic. Every rune holds unlimited power. But some runes more magical than others. The special runes of magic and power strengthen the magic in ceremonies and help awaken your own inborn magical and psychic abilities. These runes are: Uruz, which strengthens magical power in general; Ansuz, which acts on telepathy and other psychic abilities associated with communication; Naudhiz, whose powers increase clairvoyance and divination; Eihwaz, which opens the way to psychic dreaming and tapping into the ancestral wisdom of the unconscious; Sowilo, which supercharges any magical working and aids in awakening psychic centers and chakras; Berkana, which helps perfect your magical skills; and Ehwaz, which boosts interpersonal psychic powers, such as empathy.

Unlocking Your Runic Powers

You already possess every talent and ability you need to work powerful, effective rune magic—or any other type of magic. You were born with them. Everyone is—the same way everyone, including you, is born with the ability to add two and two, the ability to learn to speak their native tongue, and the ability to learn to walk.

Of course, we all receive these gifts in different measures. Some of us are better at walking and become marathon runners. Other people are better at talking and become great speakers, sales people, ministers, or politicians. And some women and men, of course, grow up to be great mathematicians and scientists.

Similarly, although everyone is born with magical abilities and psychic powers, we all receive different ones in different proportions. What are yours? Do any of these sound familiar?

- You have very good luck, the ability to almost will traffic lights to change for you, big business deals to go through, or just the outfit you need in a store window to go on sale when you need it.
- You were gifted with a strong sense of empathy that allows you to tune in accurately on the feelings and emotions of others.
- You often know what is going to happen before it happens.
- You have an intuitive sense of how automobile engines work, computer programming language, how to get along with children, just how to hit a tennis ball so it goes where your opponent won't be next, or something else considered equally uncanny by your peers.

Chances are, you either recognized one of the above, or they caused you to think of a talent you do have.

You can work far more powerful rune magic if you know what your personal magical gifts are. For instance, yours might be clairvoyance, empathy, magical power, or psychic dreaming. Once you identify them, you have a guide to what runic rituals, charms, and spells you would find easiest to work.

Runes wilt thou find,
And rightly read,
Of wondrous weight,
Of mighty magic.
—*The Elder Edda*

You would also know where your powers are weakest and could use the knowledge to compensate for them during ceremonies. For example, your weaknesses might be divination, magical skill, or telepathy. By adding one of the runes that releases that ability to any rune ritual that requires it, you could strengthen yourself temporarily in that area—and work magic as potent as that of anyone born with an extra measure of it.

This next rune reading technique will help you discover where your magical abilities are strongest and weakest, so that you can unlock the runic powers that reside within.

Rune Reading: Identifying Your Magical Talents

This is a very simple reading that uses only seven rune stones: Uruz, Ansuz, Naudhiz, Eihwaz, Sowilo, Berkana, and Ehwaz. You simply throw them. The runes that land faceup tell you which psychic and magical powers you have, and the ones that land facedown reveal where your magical abilities are weakest.

Sample Reading

The reading that follows was done some years ago for a friend named Kelly. It clearly reveals where her psychic and magical abilities lie. Kelly didn't have a particular problem. She had been told by friends she seemed to be very psychic and magical, and she wanted to see if the runes confirmed what they said.

As you can see, five of the seven runes of magic and power landed faceup, indicating where her powers lie. These are: Ansuz, telepathy; Uruz, strong magical powers; Berkana, magical skill; Eihwaz, psychic dreaming; and Sowilo, awakened psychic centers and chakras. Read as a sentence, as with any other rune interpretation, they basically said that Kelly should have strong magical powers—and no wonder, because her psychic centers and chakras are awakened!—as well as skills. They also showed that she is both telepathic and able to tap into supernormal wisdom through psychic dreaming.

Kelly confirmed the accuracy of this reading as far as she was able. She had taken classes in yoga, which had included chakric exercises, so her psychic centers should have been awakened. She did have psychic dreams that gave her ideas for her business or told her of loved ones' deaths. And she did occasionally get telepathic flashes in which she knew exactly what her partner Alyson was thinking. As for magical skill, she had never tried it, so there was no way to tell how skilled she would be.

On the other hand, two runes landed facedown: Naudhiz, clairvoyance and divination; and Ehwaz, interpersonal psychic powers like empathy. Kelly said she never had precognitive flashes and rarely knew what others were feeling.

Altogether, this reading confirms that Kelly, like many people, had psychic and magical abilities she used unconsciously, but was consciously unaware of until they were pointed out to her. Once these gifts were identified, she was able to make far greater use of them.

Rune #19: Ehwaz or Eh

The steed is the pride/of the high and the mighty./Its fine points are the talk/of the famous and wealthy./To the restless/a source of release.

—*The Old English Rune Poem*

Ehwaz

Ehwaz (pronounced ee-was) is your rune of reliance on others, working in tandem, and harmonious partnerships. The taming of the horse (ehwaz) was an epical moment for humanity. Trade was made easier, people and heavy goods could be transported longer distances, and those with a restless foot and yen for distant places could satisfy it at last. Man and animal became one, working together. Soon the horse became the representation of the energy of work, working with a partner, and harmonious duos.

Rune Image: A horse's chest and legs

In Rune Reading

Faceup meanings: A steadfast partner, one with good judgment and commonsense, harmonious collaboration with another, work, marriage, leisure, vehicle, means of transportation, movement, physical change or relocation, change for the better, spiritual journeys, extending one's self into the world, sudden changes, opportune period for initiating new ventures involving another person. *Tarot comparison:* The Lovers. *Astrological comparison:* Gemini.

Occluded (facedown) meanings: An unhappy or treacherous partnership, misplaced trust in another, friction, lack of work, divorce, sudden change for the worse, immobility, poor time to begin anything involving the cooperation of another person. *Tarot comparison:* The Lovers reversed. *Astrological comparison:* Gemini afflicted.

In Rune Magic

Use to: Bring desired changes quickly, protect travelers, initiate soul travel out of the body, project an astral double, work sex magic, engender trust, loyalty, and harmony between two people

In Rune Meditation

Use to: Raise understanding of partners, lovers, or spouses, discover how to create harmony in relationships, comprehend the nature of duality

Rune Gods: Freyja and Frey as Cosmic Twins

Rune Totems: Horses, oxen, cattle, elephants, llamas, donkeys, dogs, cats, goats

Rune Herb: Ragwort

Rune Color: The white of oak wood

Using Rune Magic to Help and Heal

You may have some concerns about performing rune magic. Perhaps you're worried that it's black magic, or fear you will do something wrong and unintentionally bring harm to yourself or others. You may even worry that others might misuse it for selfish or malign ends. If so, you can say good-bye to your apprehensions. Rune magic can only be used for good. It can never cause harm. Only runes' positive and beneficial energies and meaning can be accessed or released through rune magic.

Rune's so-called "negative" or problematic aspects associated with occluded stones can never be channeled or released. They are not really rune energies at all—but only conditions that occur when a rune's energies are blocked or absent. Because they are blocked or absent, these conditions can not be channeled or released—there is nothing to channel or release.

Because you can only receive and direct positive energies with runes, you cannot harm anyone—either accidentally or intentionally. The most you can do is inadvertently set a different positive runic force at work in your life or that of someone else. Even that is not very easy. To send the wrong positive energy you would first have to mistake one rune for another, and then not notice the error throughout your preparations for the magical ritual, or during it.

When everything is said and done, all that would have happened is that you sent yourself or another, for example, energy for health and healing rather than for abundance and prosperity. It's a lot like blurting out "I love you" to a friend on their birthday, when you meant to say "Happy birthday." Both make the person feel better, so no real harm is done.

Besides, you are likely to notice your mistake with the runes sooner or later, and can then redo the ceremony correctly and release the energies of abundance and prosperity then. At worst, you have sent two positive forces into the world rather than one. Rather than "lighting just one little candle"—you'll have lit two. With rune magic, a mistake is actually a win-win situation for everyone.

Casting Spells for Protection and Good Fortune

If you have read any of the earlier chapters, you already have a fair idea of what goes on in a rune magic ceremony. But you may want to read this section anyway. It will serve as both a refresher course and to provide a list of the 12 steps common to all rune rituals.

If you have skipped right to this chapter, you are about to learn how to create and conduct your own magical rituals for channeling and directing the powers of runes. You will find everything you need to know to get started wielding the positive energy of rune magic to help yourself and others lead better, healthier, more rewarding lives. By the time you have finished this section you can go right to work using runic energies for healing, self-growth, prosperity, romance, and career and business success to make your deepest dreams come true—and more.

There are 12 steps to creating a ceremony to attract and release the magical powers of runes:

1. Have a clear purpose in mind.
2. Pick an appropriate rune.
3. Select an appropriate place.
4. Light the appropriate candle and herb.
5. Pause to breathe deeply and relax.
6. Hold the rune stone in your left hand.
7. Ask blessing of the rune's guardian deity or deities.
8. Request they send you the rune's energies.
9. Wait until you feel the runic energy.
10. Tell the energy who you want it to help and how.
11. Thank the deity or deities.
12. End the ritual.

Let's look at each step in more depth.

Have a Clear Purpose

This seems to go without saying. Why else would you perform a magical ceremony other than to make something happen; for instance, to attract a new lover for your lonely lesbian cousin? But as with success in any endeavor, in magic, having your goal clearly and firmly in mind is key to success. Nevertheless, many people begin ceremonies without a clearly defined purpose, which diffuses the runic energies so that little or nothing is accomplished. Have yours worked out ahead of time. There should be a concrete result you can visualize, as you will need to visualize it as part of the ritual.

Pick an Appropriate Rune

This is easy. Throughout this book (and summarized in Appendix A) are the meanings and energies associated with each rune. You will also find the key runes for health, communication, romance, career, prosperity, and developing your magical abilities mentioned at the start of the chapters devoted to those subjects.

For example, if you want to increase your prosperity or find a soul mate, any of the runes of finance or romance will do. But, if you want a soul mate who will enjoy working alongside you in your business, you might select Ehwaz. It is both a rune of romance and of partnership. Should you want to send healing energy to a sister, mother, aunt, or woman friend, you might pick Lagaz, which is a rune of both health and female energy.

Select an Appropriate Place

For rune magic rituals you want to pick a location similar to what you would need for meditation. It should be quiet and free of distractions and interruptions for as long as you will need to perform and complete the ceremony. Working magic and directing the forces released through the runes require intense concentrations—so avoiding distraction is a must.

The living room or bedroom of your home is fine, as long as no one else is likely to come by and you have turned the telephone, cell phone, and pager off. So is the backyard—or the midst of the deep woods, if you are comfortable performing magic there. Again, wherever you'd like to hold the ceremony is fine, as long as you are able to work in peace and quiet.

Light the Appropriate Candle and Herb

In the special boxes in each chapter describing the individual runes, you will find the name of the special candle color and herb that resonate best with each rune. Lighting the area around you with the right color helps in preparing you to receive the rune's energy. The wavelength of the color and the wavelength of the energy channeled by the rune are selected to be harmonious.

Burning a pinch of the special herb in an incense burner serves two purposes. One, it performs the same purpose as "smudging" among many Native American tribes. It purifies the area in which your ceremony will take place by purging it of discordant energy and effluvia, much like the "smudging" that precedes the rituals of many Native American tribes. In addition, the herb has also been selected because its scent is harmonious with the rune's energies.

Pause to Breathe Deeply and Relax

It is important to clear and still your body, mind, and spirit for working with rune magic. Just as distractions from the outside world can cause you to lose the concentration needed for directing runic energy for protection and good fortune, so can distractions from the inside. Stray thoughts, daydreams, emotions, worries—even thinking about what you want to accomplish—will all interfere with your focus.

That's why pausing for a few moments to breathe deeply, relax, and give your constantly busy mind a chance to settle down is so important. Breathe in and out deeply and slowly 10 times. If your mind is racing when you start, take 20 slow, deep breaths instead.

Hold the Rune Stone Over Your Head in Your Left Hand

The left hand is hand nearest your heart. Runic energies, being positive energies and forces for good, are accumulated in and directed by the heart. You get a better connection with these forces when they are received by the rune stone, and they reach your heart more quickly if you hold it in your left hand.

Because the energies directed by runes are cosmic forces received from the heavens, raising the rune stone above you acts like a lightning rod and attracts these energies to you. These forces are neutralized and dissipated by the earth, so it is very important to lift the stone as high as you can and still be comfortable, to get it away from the ground.

Ask Blessing of the Rune's Guardian Deity

Each rune has a deity or deities associated with it. These deities control the rune's power and can release to you the cosmic forces it channels. You must always ask them with great humility to open these energies to you.

You will find numerous examples of how to phrase this request in the "Rune Magic" exercises in the other chapters of this book. In general, however, you should be saying something along these lines:

Frigga, Mother Goddess, Mimir, God of Wisdom, bestow your blessing on this worthy work.

Except, replace the names of the deities above with deity or deities associated with the rune whose energies you have chosen to work with.

Request the Deities Send You the Rune's Energies

This can be very simple, but it must be stated explicitly. You must make a direct request to the rune's deities before they can act on it. Think of it as a heavenly "official request" form.

Just ask them to release the rune's energy to you. Again, you will find examples in the "Rune Magic" sections throughout the book. You might say:

Release to me the power of [name of rune].

Wait Until You Feel the Runic Energy

When the forces of the rune are released to you, they pass through the rune stone. The stone's reception of these energies, and the sign that they are being channeled to you, will typically manifest itself in the stone suddenly growing much warmer, or the hand and arm holding the stone might begin to tingle from the charge of energy being sent to you—or both.

This energy will flow down your arm and gather in your heart. At some point, you will feel the energy begin to overflow your heart, and decrease in intensity as it runs down from your hand. This means you have gathered the charge of positive runic force you need to conclude the ritual.

Tell the Energy Who You Want It to Help and How

Again, this does not have to be fancy. Just say explicitly what you want the energy to do. Once you do, you will feel the runic forces leave your heart in a rush, eager to be off on the beneficial task for which you have summoned them.

At the same time, picture in your mind's eye what it is you want the energy to do. Maybe you want to see a relative walking around healthy and full of energy again. Or maybe visualize yourself paying the hospital bill you desperately need money for. Visualizing the desired result helps impress it on the universe and creates a blueprint for the runic energies to follow in carrying out your desires.

Think of all this as the equivalent of pushing the "send" button on your e-mail program. You merely need to say something on the order of:

Let the energy of Lagaz sooth the aching heart of [name]. Heal the pain she feels over the breakup with [name].

Or whatever it is you want to see the runic energies accomplish.

Thank the Deity or Deities

It is a great favor for the gods to aid mortals. You should be appreciative of this. Never forget to express your heartfelt gratitude to them afterward— if you hope to work rune magic with their assistance in the future. And thank the rune, too.

You might say:

Thank you, Odin, All-father, thank you, Fehu, for this blessing.

Substitute the name of the rune you used in your ceremony and the name of its guardian deity or deities.

End the Ritual

Merely take a few deep breaths to calm and center yourself and release any remaining runic energies. Then snuff out the candle. If it is feasible, let the herb burn itself out in the incense burner.

Doing this formally closes the ceremony and ensures none of the energy leaks out of your spell. Your rune magic ceremony is over.

Rune #20: Mannaz or Mann

In their joy of living/people are dear to their loved ones./Yet each is fated to/depart from among them./It is heaven's decree that/our bodies return to the earth.

—*The Old English Rune Poem*

Mannaz

Mannaz (pronounced man-niz) is your rune of companionship, conviviality, and mutual aid. To the earliest humans, survival depended on the group. All the terms they had for describing the group they belonged to—homosapiens, Nez Perce, Nippon, Bantu—mean "our people" or "humanity" (mannaz). To be ostracized was to be condemned to death. As intimately interconnected and important to each other as they were, each person was loved dearly and held close to the heart. But not even all the power of love could hold a dear one back from death, which was seen as the will of the gods, and a deep wound in the body politic.

Rune Image: A person standing with his or her arms crossed

In Rune Reading

Faceup meanings: Humanity as a whole, people, companionship, colleagues, groups, organization, management, cooperation, a rise in social status, timely assistance or advice from others, empathy, seeing things from the other's point of view, the divine in the human, intelligence, an auspicious time for initiating projects involving others, an intriguing, interesting new person. *Tarot comparison:* The Magician. *Astrological comparison:* Jupiter.

Occluded (facedown) meanings: Lack of companionship, solitude, disorganization, fall in social status, no help from others, obstruction by others, failure to see others' point of view, lack of empathy, being too involved in a problem to be effective, blowing things out of proportion, need to heed good advice, poor time for new project requiring the cooperation of others, loss of social status, a new enemy. *Tarot comparison:* The Magician reversed. *Astrological comparison:* Jupiter afflicted.

In Rune Magic

Use to: Draw the aid, succor, or advice from others you need when you need it; ensure the success of a group undertaking; initiate others or form a magical group or coven; increase knowledge, memory, and wisdom; draw on the divine; develop the ability to read emotions and thoughts of others

In Rune Meditation

Use to: Perceive the divine and the human nature in yourself and others, develop empathy, understand others, comprehend the "why" of incarnation in human form

Rune Gods: Heimdall, God of Dawn and Light

Rune Totems: Bears, monkeys, gorillas, apes, gibbons, flying squirrels, dogs, beavers, cats

Rune Herb: Madder

Rune Color: Ruby red

Rune Magic: Making Runic Charms

You may know them as talisman, charms, amulets, obeah, or tines. They are objects inscribed with magical symbols (in this case, runes) that attract cosmic power for health, healing, luck, success, and warding off negative energies. For thousands of years, people of every culture have made talismanic charms to protect themselves and loved ones.

Because the idea is to draw positive energy to help someone or keep good luck coming their way, most charms are made to be worn or carried. That way the man or woman for whom the charm was made will receive the benefit of the energy on a regular basis. Pendants, bracelets, rings, stones, small wooden pieces called tines, slips of paper, even swords have all been used as amulets and objects of power.

Charms have also been painted on the sides of barns and carved in the ceilings of gothic cathedrals, as well as painted on cars, embroidered on clothing, and even tattooed on skin.

Technically, the charm is the inscription, those strange magical symbols. It is the charm or inscription that draws and focuses the magical energies. Charms have also been called spells, hexes, magic formula, and words of power. The talisman is the object the charm is written on. All the power lies in the charm, the same way the power lies in a printed electrical circuit. The talisman merely holds the charm, the same way the board a circuit is printed on holds it—so it can easily be put in place, stored, or carried.

The ancient rune masters known as Vitka made charms to draw runic energies from before the beginning of recorded history in Northern Europe. Runic charms have been found cut on bone amulets, stone pendants, knife blades, and the prows of Viking long-ships. In fact, rune magic was so widely spread that you can find early northern European relics inscribed with rune charms on display in museums almost everywhere.

Charms to Help Yourself and Others

Use runes to make your own charms and talismans to help yourself, your friends, family, business, hobby group, or sports team. They protect, heal, boost the odds of success, and more. You can even use rune charms to transform negative situations, people, and attitudes.

Rune charms are easy to make and don't take long. You don't need special skills. The only requirements are:

- A utensil to make the inscription (a pen, a paintbrush, or a dremel).
- Something to make the inscription on (a pendant, sheet of paper, or a stone).

What should you write your charm on? If it is for a building, business, or new car, inscribe it on the object you want to receive the runic energies. If it is for a person, inscribe it on something that is carried close to the body all the time, such as a piece of jewelry or a small sheet of paper that can be folded up in a wallet.

The Eddas present the runes as having been spells that could benefit gods and mankind, not as tools for divination.
—Maude Stephany

Creating Your Own Magic Formula

What do you write? You write down the combination of runes that is needed to attract the kind of energy you believe is needed most. That combination of runes is your charm.

For example, if you have a problem with a romantic relationship, you take some or all the runes of love and romance (Fehu, Thurisaz, Ansuz, Kenaz, Gebo, Wunjo, Naudhiz, Tiwaz, Berkana, Ehwaz, and Ingwaz) and inscribe them on your talisman. Or, you could write a more complicated charm with more specific runic "programming instructions."

If your problem is lack of a romantic partner, instead of just inscribing the runes for love, you could begin with Naudhiz (deliverance from distress), and follow that with a rune symbolizing what you need to deliver you from that distress, like Kenza (sexual desire). Then ensure the relationship will be lasting and fulfilling, you might include Ehwaz (auspicious partnerships). Finally, because you desire to meet such a person, add rune Gebo (meetings, interconnections, harmonious crossing of energies paths).

Here are three hints for creating a potent rune charm:

- Put Ehwaz immediately after the first rune to power the charm with dynamic energy.
- Put Wunjo immediately before the last rune for the happy conclusion you desire.
- Put Ingwaz after Wunjo at the very end to keep the runic energies sealed in your charm.

Finally, there are two ways you can inscribe the runes on a talisman: You can write them out like a sentence (rune scripts), or you can combine them into a single runic image (bindrunes).

Rune Scripts

These are simply the runes of a spell individually inscribed on a piece of wood, jewelry, or paper. Depending on the size and shape of your talisman, you can write them in a straight line like a sentence, or you can arrange them in a triangle, square, or two or more columns. Be guided by whatever fits the surface best, tickles your artistic fancy, or satisfies your sense of mystical geometry—or all three. There is no set rule. As long as you get the rune images on your talisman, you have done it right. This isn't something you can mess up.

The only rule for using rune scripts as charms is to check ahead of time so that you make your runes small enough that they all fit on your talisman.

Runic script for aid in romance.

Bindrunes

With bindrunes, rather than inscribing runes one after another, like the words in a sentence—you write the runes one on top of another. There's a little trick to it, however. The combination of runes you select needs to make a symmetrical pattern when superimposed on each other. Writing runes like this binds their energies into a single, powerful whole. This makes your runic charm especially potent, one whose effects will be seen early and prove profound. In ancient times it was said, "Mighty is the talisman that bears a bindrune."

How do you pick runes that will fit over each other and result in a harmonious design? One guideline is to pick runes with strong vertical lines that run straight up and down. Another tip is to look for angles and crossing lines that might blend together symmetrically.

For example, say you are creating a charm to boost the immune system of someone fighting a severe illness. You might notice that two runes of health and healing, Tiwaz and Lagaz, both have a strong central vertical line and short lines coming down at a the same angle from the top. These would certainly fit over each other harmoniously. Furthermore, Othala rises to a point in the center with two short lines coming down at an angle from the tip. It appears as if it, too, might blend with Tiwaz and Lagaz to make a bindrune.

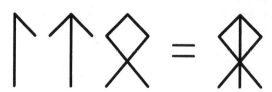

Bindrune for health and healing.

Your first attempt at combining runes might go astray. That's normal. It usually takes a few minutes, and several tries, to arrive at just the right design for a bindrune. The effort will repay itself, however—bindrunes are one of the most powerful ways of focusing and directing the cosmic energies of runes handed down to us from the Vitka.

One caution when devising bindrunes: Don't overdo it and try to superimpose too many runes on one another. Instead of greater power, you will end up with greater confusion of runic energies. Here is definitely one case where less is more. Many runeologists say three is the ideal number of runes to combine in your bind runes. Remember the importance of the number three in magic as discussed in Chapter 2. Two runes is too few; there is greater harmony and resonance when three are combined than four or five or more.

Consecrating Your Charms

To ensure the rune charm receives the energies you desire and succeeds in working the good fortune you desire, use the following ritual to consecrate your charm as you make it. *The New Merriam-Webster Dictionary* defines consecrate as "to make or declare sacred" and "to devote solemnly to a purpose." In this ceremony, you will both invoke the sacred and devote the charm exclusively to positive forces.

Before starting on any rune charm, place all the implements needed to make it before you. Making a magical charm is sacred business, and requires you be in a quiet, centered mood. Take several relaxing breaths, then say:

I invoke Odin,
I invoke Freya,
I invoke the Aesir,
and the Vanir.
Grant me my boon
guide hand and heart,
bind the runes' power
through my art.
May this charm's powers [state purpose for which the talisman is being made].
May it help only
and never work harm.

Inscribe the charm on whatever object you have chosen for your talisman. As you do so, visualize what it is you want the charm to accomplish: Guard a friend in a dangerous job from harm, help you learn what you need to pass that real estate license examination, attract the money your church needs for a new air conditioning system.

When you have finished, say:

I thank Odin,
I thank Freya,
I thank the Aesir,
and the Vanir,
for granting this boon,
for guiding my hand,
for binding the runes' power
to this charm.

Rune Meditation: Developing Runic Telepathy

You can use rune magic to help people more effectively if you truly know their thoughts and feelings and what it is they really need. You can do this if you develop your inborn ability to use mental telepathy. You have probably heard about mental telepathy. This is the ability to receive thoughts, feelings, and impressions from the minds of other people.

You might even have experienced it; millions of people have, according to reports. You might have picked up the phone to call a family member at the exact moment she was dialing you. You might have turned to say something to a friend just as he turned to say the same thing to you. Or—and this is often the most convincing example of telepathy for most people—you might have replied to something a friend said, only to learn that she never said it—she just thought it, and you "heard" her thoughts as clearly as if they were spoken.

You might never have experienced mental telepathy and are convinced that it doesn't exist. Or, if it does, that it was left out of your make-up when you were born. You might have never felt a premonition or had a psychic experience in your life.

Whichever describes your situation, your telepathic and psychic abilities will benefit from meditating on Sowilo, the most powerful of the runes relating to magic and paranormal. Sowilo is powered by the molten, inexhaustible energies of the sun itself. Meditating on it is ideal for anything involving illumination, especially inner vision—for example, telepathy and our other psychic capacities.

If you already have some ability to pick up the feelings and thoughts of others, Sowilo will strengthen and refine it. If you have never had a psychic experience before, or don't think you can have one, meditating on Sowilo will prove a revelation. It will activate the sector of the brain where your telepathic circuits lie, and you will begin to tune in on what others are thinking.

To develop your inborn telepathy, you will need the Sowilo rune stone and a quiet place to meditate. Lay the rune down faceup where you can see the image comfortably and clearly. Relax and calm your thoughts for meditation by sitting quietly and breathing slowly for a minute or so.

After you feel centered and ready for meditation, bring your attention to the rune stone in front of you. Focus your eyes on the image. It looks a bit like a "Z" cut by Zorro on a wall, or perhaps like an angular "S." The long slanted line is actually one of the spokes of the wheel of the solar chariot. The two short arms are really the rim of the wheel. They are all you can see because the wheel is spinning so fast.

When you perceive rune Sowilo this way, the spoke will seem to spin round and round in your mind's eye. The arms become the flashing circular rim. Close your eyes when this sensation first begins to manifest. Visualize the wheel spinning, spokes and rim an almost invisible blur from the speed.

What you are seeing is the dark, shadowy blur of the wheel spinning. Now, picture a tiny pinpoint of intense white-hot light at the center of the blurred, shadowy wheel. The light is a flame so hot and intense that it burns through the center of the wheel rapidly.

Behind it is the blinding incandescence of the sun, setting fire to the wheel. Blazing through the center, it flames outward in a circle and burns upward along the spokes, consuming them as it goes—until it reaches the rim, burns that away, and is revealed as the blinding disk of the sun.

It is so bright it almost blinds you. But rather than squinting or fighting against the brilliance, accept it. Accept the searing bolt of visualized sunlight into your eyes. Picture it blazing through your eyes and into your optic nerves.

Visualize the sun's incandescent energies racing along your optic nerves, entering your brain. Picture the nuclear-powered brilliance lighting up your brain. Every part, every nook and cranny, is illuminated and charged by the sun's inexhaustible light.

You can feel it, your whole brain lit and awake, with the sunlight pouring into your wide-open eyes. Even the portion of your brain where your telepathic and other psychic abilities are lodged—which otherwise resides in darkness—scintillates with this energy. (You will probably feel this part of you being activated or powered up as a strong tingling somewhere inside your head.)

Sit without moving for several minutes, picturing the sun's light pouring in and illuminating the telepathic portion of your brain.

Now, visualize the light slowly fading, growing dimmer. Its spinning disk grows slower. Gradually you see it slow until the disk becomes rune Sowilo and spins to a stop. Open your eyes and look at the actual rune before you.

Take several breaths. The meditation is over. Stand and stretch.

Your innate telepathic capabilities should have been woken. Don't try to force them by consciously and intently trying to read the mind of everyone you meet. You will only strain your developing powers and possibly block them.

Besides, mental telepathy doesn't work like that. Instead, give it time to develop. The impressions will begin to come to you. You won't need to reach out for them. The quieter and more receptive your own mind, the faster your telepathic powers will manifest and the clearer the reception will be.

Chapter 11

Runes of Future and Fate

Can future events be foretold? And, if so, are those events inexorably fated to happen? Or can they be changed for the better? People have asked these questions throughout human history. Great works of philosophy have been written to expound the answers. Religions have risen and fallen as a result of the quality of their answers to these questions.

When you read the 25 runes again and again over the years, you will discover that they serve as a book of priceless wisdom with their own answers to these questions. This book of runic wisdom tells us that although the shape of future events can be glimpsed, those events as pictured are not inexorably fated to occur. Runes show us, instead, that through our attitudes and actions we create our own future.

When runes reveal a happy or difficult period ahead, that doesn't mean you get a free ride if the happy future was in your reading, or that you are doomed to face difficulty if that's what your reading pictured.

Alter your actions and attitudes in the present, and you alter the outcome in the future. Get involved with shady associates, slack-off at work, and party all night, and the brilliant career shown by your rune reading will go right down the drain. Get in therapy, go back to school, and change your lifestyle—you'll become a success, and the trouble-filled future predicted for you by the runes will never come to pass.

However, runic powers over future and fate extend far beyond mere divination and steering a course away from difficulty. Runes are bound to the very cosmic forces that produce the universe and control its ceaseless progression from this moment to the next through the future. Through rune magic and meditation with the nine runes of future and fate, you can gain access to those forces and literally shape your own future.

All the runes are linked to future and fate in some sense, of course. But nine concern it very directly. The nine runes of future and fate are: Naudhiz, coming difficulty that can be averted; Berkana, a fortunate outcome; Perdhro, luck, karma; Wunjo, the tide turning in your favor; Hagalaz, good time to launch new projects; Isa, a time of stagnation when nothing can be accomplished; Dagaz, opportune time to get new projects off to successful starts; Uruz, shape events into the pattern you desire; and Wyrd, the Rune of Fate and Wishes (the blank rune).

Of course, to shape your future the way you want, you need to know where you are now. This is not always an easy thing to do. Sometimes you are very clear about where you are and what is going on in your life. Other times, you feel almost completely out of touch with yourself. When you are out of touch with yourself, runes can show you the things you can't see. With a clear picture of now, you can begin creating your own picture of the future.

When You Don't Know What to Ask

Sometimes when people come to runes for a reading, they don't really know what it is they want to know. They don't have a specific question in mind. Instead, they are motivated most often by a vague sense of dissatisfaction. They have a nagging feeling that something is out of kilter with their life, but they can't put their finger on it. They want the kind of counsel runes can give them—but they aren't sure what they need counsel about. When they arrive for a reading, they tend to say, half-apologetically, "I don't even know why I'm here."

Naturally, they worry that if they can't formulate a clear question, they won't get a clear reading. This concern causes some people to give up before they begin and never consult the runes. But both reactions are based on an incorrect premise.

Actually, if there is an issue in your life that you need to know about, runes will show it to you clearly, no matter how vague your question. Runes are always more in touch with the cosmic forces affecting your life than you are—or can be. They illuminate vividly many things about your life that you can ordinarily see only dimly, if at all, or as the Bible puts it, "as through a glass, darkly."

Runes will even point you toward the area of your life you should focus on in your reading. Try the Focus Stone reading the next time you find yourself in this situation. It's a lifesaver if you are someone who would feel more confident consulting the runes if you had a clearer idea what you should be asking about.

The Focus Stone technique uncovers the most crucial concern active in your life at the time of the reading. When you yourself don't know, it answers the question of what your question for the runes should concern. In other words, it shows you what the focus of your reading should be.

In Norse spirituality, instead of helpless predestination, fate meant a destiny created by earlier actions.

—Danaan Parry

Rune Reading: Finding What You Most Need to Know

Sit down where you are guaranteed solitude for the duration of this reading. This will be a Three Circles of Self reading, so have ready at hand a rune cloth or sheet of paper with the three circles in front of you, and the pouch or other container where you keep your rune stones. However, before you commence the actual Focus Stone reading, inhale and exhale slowly several times.

When you feel the slight change within your head and heart that signals you have entered the relaxed condition required to receive runic counsel, open your eyes and say:

Runar radh rett radh. (Runes bless me with good guidance.)

Reach into your rune pouch or box, and take the first rune stone your fingers find waiting for them. This is your Focus Stone. The issues it represents are what you need to focus on in your life right now.

If you haven't memorized the meanings of all the runes yet, find the entry describing the rune you picked for a Focus Stone in its "What You Need to Know About the Runes" entry. Read through it carefully until you see how it applies to your current situation. The remainder of your reading will focus on and apply to that one issue.

Lay the Focus Stone aside for a minute and cast the rest of the runes on the Three Circles of Self. Allow the stones to come to rest, then position your Focus Stone in the exact center of the inner circle—at the focus of the reading. (If another rune has landed there, place your Focus Stone next to it so they touch.)

Then read the runes following the guidelines given in earlier chapters. Look for ...

- Stones that are facedown.
- Two or more stones touching (multiplies their powers and they work as one).
- Lines of stones (key qualities).
- Triangles of stones (runes' energies work harmoniously).
- Squares of stones (runes' energies work inharmoniously).
- Rectangles of stones (runes' energies are unstable).
- Stones at opposite ends of reading (runes' energies oppose each other).

Sample Reading

Arthur had asked for rune readings several times when he had crises in his life or a specific question he wanted to answer. But this time, he only had a nagging feeling of unquiet and restlessness that he couldn't shake and couldn't understand. It plagued him all day at work and at night when he was home in his bachelor apartment.

Arthur had held a well-paying job as the chief financial officer of a small health-care company. He had studied math and science in college, and was drawn to the mental world of numbers. Although he didn't have many friends, he was very well off financially and dated frequently, but none of the relationships ever lasted long. "I think they found me boring," Arthur said sheepishly. "I was always talking about cash flow, deferments, off-shore tax shelters. It's what I know."

Otherwise, Arthur seemed to lead an exceptional life many people would envy. Because he couldn't seem to put his finger on what was wrong, I suggested the Focus Stone reading might help us locate the cause of his current sense of anxiety and dissatisfaction.

When Arthur drew his Focus Stone, it was Naudhiz. It's hardly surprising that Arthur had a sense that something was wrong. Naudhiz as the Focus Stone signifies a problem, and so only its meaning when occluded is consulted: Here this hints that a vital need at the center of Arthur's life was going unmet.

Arthur threw the other 24 runes; 16, nearly two-thirds, were faceup. When he placed Naudhiz in the center, they formed one of the most unusual and powerful configurations I have ever seen.

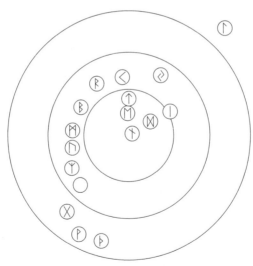

Arthur's reading—shows only important stones.

In this reading, a single, very, very long curving line of stones starts down at the bottom of the Circle of Outward Self and winds all the way up through the Circle of Conscious Self until it reaches the top of the Circle of Inner Self, where it dips down to the center of that circle to include Naudhiz and then swings upward and backward to finish high in the Circle of Conscious Self with Jera.

Only a few rune stones fell facedown, and they were so scattered, that it was evident whatever problems they represented were of minor importance compared to the vast line of positive runes. I have felt safe in omitting them from this diagram so that the true scope of the line of curving runes, and the vast amount of territory it occupies can be appreciated.

Here, listed from the bottom up, just as they appeared in Arthur's reading, are the 16 runes and the qualities they represent:

- Jera—An abundant, well-earned harvest
- Isa—Rest and stock-taking
- Dagaz—Slow but steady increase and growth, balance
- Naudhiz—Needs fulfilled, love, and the heat of passion
- Ehwaz—Steadfast partner, marriage
- Tiwaz—Victory, success
- Kenza—The guiding, ever-present, spiritual light
- Raidho—Luck and fellowship
- Berkana—Family, children
- Mannaz—Friends, admirers, help
- Uruz—Strength, health, overcoming obstacles
- Algiz—Protection, sanctuary, success in difficult ventures
- Wyrd—Favorable fortune, happy future
- Gebo—Relationships, generosity, sexual union
- Wunjo—Joy, end to troubles, hopes fulfilled
- Thurisaz—Safety, opportunities in difficulties

In most readings, a line suggests a person's best qualities. This one signified that all the wonderful qualities represented by these runes were hovering just on the edge or Arthur's life. But, significantly, they are held apart by Naudhiz. In short, there was something essential missing from his life that Arthur needed to nourish him or make him happy. Arthur couldn't enjoy any of the wonderful things that were hovering all around him until he found it. What is this quality? Or, to turn the question around, is there anything in this reading that offers us a clue about what might be missing?

When you look at the reading with this in mind, Lagaz in the upper-right hand corner immediately stands out. The rune lies well beyond the rim of the outermost circle. In other words, it is missing from the reading. This might be a strong hint that Lagaz is the vital ingredient that Arthur needs to enjoy his life again. Lagaz is the rune of the unconscious, emotion, love and fear, intuition. This seems to make sense, as Arthur was very caught up in the rational, nonfeeling side of himself.

Arthur needed to change his lifestyle, get in touch with his emotions, fall in love, and make friends. Until he did, his sense of unease, of something indefinable being wrong with his life, would continue. Oddly, when Arthur tried this by attending some workshops on emotional intelligence, he met and eventually fell in love with a woman who was the comptroller for another company in the field of health-care services, who shared many of his interests and values.

Rune #21: Lagaz or Lagu

The large bodies of water seem unending/when people venture out/on an unsteady craft./High waves terrify/and the surf-steeds/fail to heed the bridle.
—*The Old English Rune Poem*

Lagaz

Lagaz (pronounced lag-az) is your rune of emotions, the unconscious, and the fluid in life. To our ancestors, large bodies of water (lagaz) were a source of bounty. Their depths held fish, which provided nourishment, oils for light, and bones for tools. Their surfaces bore trading vessels that increased prosperity. But large bodies of water were also known to be powerful and dangerous: In hurricanes, floods, and torrential storms their turbulent surfaces could snatch ships down into the depths and even drown those on shore in their sleep.

Rune Image: An ocean wave

In Rune Reading

Faceup meanings: Primal waters, primal power, primal emotions, love and fear, the unconscious, intuition, imagination, psychic ability, guidance from a higher power, sympathy and understanding, ability to deal with whatever comes, memory, learning, going with the flow, tide turning in your favor, female fertility, the primal cycle of life, birth, and death. *Tarot comparison:* The Star. *Astrological comparison:* The waxing moon.

Occluded (facedown) meanings: Misdirected emotions or emotional turbulence, an unfortunate birth or death, difficulties either through being misled by your intuition or failing to heed your instincts, being carried in the wrong direction, creative bankruptcy, stormy seas ahead, time to batten down the hatches and wait and see, or be swept away by the flood, disloyalty from someone you love. *Tarot comparison:* The Star reversed. *Astrological comparison:* The waxing moon afflicted.

In Rune Magic

Use to: Calm an emotional situation, draw on the enormous emotional forces of the unconscious, buoy yourself or others through difficult situations, gather power before a magical ceremony, wash away negative energies and self-destructive habits, increase vitality and life force

In Rune Meditation

Use to: Understand and integrate feelings and desires, tune into your or others' unconscious thoughts and motives, stir the creative unconscious, become attuned to the birth-life-death cycle

Rune Gods: Njord, God of Sea, Wind, and Summer; Ran, Goddess of Ocean Storms and the Drowned

Rune Totems: Beaver, otters, seals, whales, dolphins, seagulls, ducks, swans

Rune Herb: Leek

Rune Color: Deep blue green

Learning What Your Future Holds

Would you like to know your future? Most people would? Few men or women, if given the opportunity, could resist a peak behind the veil Norn Skuld holds across future, to discover what fate holds in store for them.

Will you be ...

- Surrounded by friends or friendless?
- Employed or out of work?
- Well off or struggling?
- Living your dreams or filled with regrets?
- With a special someone or alone?
- Satisfied with life or unfulfilled?

For thousands of years people have tried to peer into the future. They have used tarot, astrology, I-Ching, tea leaves, omens, palmistry, runes, crystal gazing, ritual dance, and peyote, to list only a few. All of these are good ways to catch glimpses of your likely future, but runes are certainly one of the best.

In tarot readings, for example, you typically use no more than seven to a dozen of the full 78 cards. Thus you filter out about four-fifths of the deck's potential message. In most rune readings, however, you throw all 25 rune stones—and therefore reap one hundred percent of the potential message.

Vitka, the ancient scholars of runelore, were highly adept at helping people discern their future fate in the runes. With a modified three circle reading, they showed men and women what their lives would be like in the immediate, near, and far future, given their current actions and attitudes. You can use the same reading to discover what your own future holds.

Rune Reading: Determining What Lies Ahead

This next reading provides a glimpse of what you can expect over the next few weeks or year, the next several years, and a decade or more beyond. You'll learn what's coming your way. When it is over, you will know what good things to expect and what troublesome ones to steer clear of.

Be prepared. Have your runes at your side and spread out your rune cloth (or a large sheet of paper with three large concentric circles on it) before you begin. In this reading, rather than the three circles representing three aspects of the self, they represent your immediate, near, and far future.

Place yourself in the proper state for beginning a rune reading with breathing or other relaxation techniques. Open your mind and heart to the aid of the gods. Then beseech them for it. Say:

Great Odin, who brought
these runes
from the darkness
to light our way
guide my hands
direct my mind
that I might sup
of their wisdom.

Now, fill your cupped palms with the 25 runes and cast them over the three circles. You interpret this reading the same way you do any full three circles reading. Remember to look for whether runes are faceup or down, as well as patterns and shapes.

When you have identified the patterns, determine which circles the stones landed in. This will tell you when in the future you can expect to encounter the configuration of forces represented by the runes.

- If the stones lie within the Circle of Immediate Future, look to the coming weeks, months, or year.
- If the stones lie within the Circle of Near Future, look to the next several years.
- If the stones lie within the Circle of Far Future, look a decade or more ahead.

If you feel intimidated by interpreting this reading or are confused over just how to apply it, the following sample reading offers pointers that might help.

Sample Reading

Rhonda and Ahn had met a year earlier and were very much in love. With the help of a good therapist, Rhonda had overcome the damage done by growing up in an alcoholic family and transformed herself into an up-beat, loving young woman, with many friends and a wonderful job as the principal of a small private school. Ahn was the son of an immigrant, who had earned a degree in pediatric medicine and had opened an office not far from Rhonda's school.

The couple's wedding was scheduled for spring, and because of their different backgrounds, they wondered what a rune reading could tell them about their future life together. Because it is always best to have the person being read for cast the stones, and the reading was for Ahn and Rhonda as a couple, I asked them to hold the runes together. They did and then threw them together. (Runes that landed facedown are shown shaded.)

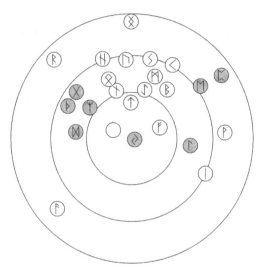

Rhonda and Ahn's reading.

Oddly, only four runes fell in the center circle. The majority of the remaining 21 stones landed in the middle ring, with a bare handful scattering themselves around the Circle of Far Future. This suggests that the couple's life is going to be relatively uneventful in the immediate future, but is about to become very busy in the near future. These stones also suggested that things would settle back down again for Rhonda and Ahn in the distant future.

Circle of Immediate Future

If you didn't already know this was a future reading, you might guess it. The clue is the way the giant triangle radiates out from Jera to Tiwaz, then spreads out, as if the ramifications of some action spreading into the future, to include eight more stones, encompassing all of two circles and bridging the boundary to the third.

In the very center of the Circle of Immediate future is facedown Jera, which is also the first rune of the great triangle, along with Tiwaz and Fehu, faceup, and the Wishing Stone or Rune of Fate. The presence of the blank rune here in a future reading suggests how deeply the couples wishes and fate are focused on the immediate future, which is understandable with their impending wedding just ahead.

The presence of Jera in the very center of the reading suggests that abundance will be central to their relationship (as does the presence of Fehu, another powerful rune of abundance nearby). Tiwaz, rune of triumph faceup, follows Fehu as the second rune of the triangle. It almost seems to imply that after Rhonda and Ahn have experienced the triumph of their wedding, abundance and much more (represented by the other eight stones in the great triangle) will come into being.

Circle of Near Future

The presence of 14 runes, more than half, in the center ring shows that the pair's life will become very active in the near future. Of these 14 rune stones, 8, or more than half, are part of the great triangle, pointing to it and the events of the Near Future as a major focus of their coming life together.

The energy of Tiwaz (marriage) in the Immediate Future crosses into the middle ring, like an atom colliding into other atoms or a billiard ball hitting a pair of balls. Then that impact sets off two different chain reactions down the runes on the right- and left-hand sides of the triangle.

After examining these runes, several themes shed light on the shape of Ahn and Rhonda's future together. As the energy imparted by Tiwaz travels up the left-hand side it activates the energies of rune Naudhiz, whose positive associations include passion, emotional need, and deliverance from difficulty. Then it activates Othala, which usually points to family, home, roots—all of which were the natural outcome of their prospective union. Othala has another meaning that bears favorably on their marriage: opportune time to advance projects and prospects quickly and effortlessly. And finally it activates the energies of Hagalaz, which bestow the ability to transform potentially destructive forces to beneficial ends, opportunity, smooth sailing, and, again, time for a new undertaking, plus, good luck through a natural event.

As Tiwaz's energy runs along the great triangle's right side, it switches on rune Eihwaz, the ability to juggle or manage things, protection, management, control of finances or decision-making, achievable goals. All are keys to a successful marriage, family life, child rearing, and the financial abundance promised by Jera. The next energy circuit to be opened is Ehwaz, whose meanings are a steadfast partner with good judgment, harmonious collaboration, marriage, change for the better, spiritual journeys, and, for the third time, an opportune period for initiating new ventures, in this case, especially those involving another person. Then the energy opens up Kenaz, which points to sexual passion, the guiding, ever-present, and an auspicious moment for beginnings. These, too, are essential qualities of a wonderful relationship.

Last, Tiwaz's energy courses together from the two upper corners of the triangle (Hagalaz and Kenza), activating Uruz (strength, healing, courage, tenacity, strong emotions, potential to organize, make things happen, overcoming obstacles) and Sowilo (success, fair play, material and spiritual increase, motivation to overcome all obstacles, taking charge). Here, again, are qualities every marriage ideally should have.

The repetition of the auspiciousness of the time, coupled with their planned nuptials, indicated that this marriage was meant to be and would get off to a wonderful start.

Significantly the entire upper side of this triangle (Halagaz, Uruz, Sowilo, Kenaz) also bridges the border between the center and outer circles. What this suggests is that the energy of Rhonda and Ahn's marriage, once released, extends from the immediate, through the near and into the distant future. In other words, it will endure.

Near Future Troubles

Notice all the near future events not part of the great triangle are represented by occluded runes: Dagaz, Thurisaz, Gebo, Algiz, and Lagaz. This group of runes represents potential trouble areas the couple should watch out for and be prepared to cope with in the near future. The trouble areas they should be wary of are:

- *Dagaz*: Endings (divorce?) caused by failure to grow, turning away from the spirit, lack of balance, dwelling on problems, and failure to use the inner strength to make things better

- *Thurisaz*: Letting vulnerabilities, obstacles, problems, lead to mutual destruction, barriers, enmity

- *Gebo*: Missed connections, unharmonious relationships, greed, sexual incompatibility

- *Algiz*: Lack of aid to each other, ignoring their own higher self, the frustration of problems they cannot solve

- *Lagaz*: Emotional turbulence, being carried in the wrong direction, disloyalty from someone you love

Although these are all challenging issues for any couple to face, the grouping of 10 stones that forms the great triangle brims with such overwhelming positive energy that Rhonda and Ahn ought to easily ride out whatever storms the near future might bring.

Runic divination or "rune casting" is not "fortunetelling" in the sense that one actually sees the future. Instead, runes give one a means of analyzing the path that one is on and a likely outcome. The future is not fixed. It changes with everything one does. If one does not like the prediction, one can always change paths.

—Ingrid Halvorsen, *Runes: Alphabet of Mystery*

Circle of Far Future

In the outer circle are seven stones, five faceup and two facedown. Here is a strong hint that the circumstances of the couple's far future will be significantly more positive than negative.

The five runes that landed faceup indicate that in their far future the duo can look for: Wunjo, an end to their troubles, hopes fulfilled, winds shifting in your favor, turning things around, fellowship, harmony; Ingwaz, successful conclusions, good fortune, deliverance, the power to easily overcome difficulty, fertility; Raidho, pleasant journeys, happy compromises, change, progression lay ahead; Isa, stillness, rest, taking stock; and Ansuz, the pair would be able to communicate well with each other into the distant future. This was a wonderful forecast for any marriage.

The only blot on this otherwise happy picture of their far future was Mannaz and Perdhro occluded. Perdhro suggested they would have to face some unfortunate event or piece of news. Mannaz warned them to be prepared for a crucial problem in the distant future to come from interference by others—possibly from their respective families, as they were people from very different backgrounds.

However, with factors like good communication, courage, tenacity, a sense of fair play, and the motivation to overcome all obstacles, theirs appeared to be a very happy, fulfilling future life as a couple.

Rune #22: Ingwaz or Ing

Brave Ing was first/among the people./When he voyaged East/across the uncharted ocean/others followed/and named him hero.

—*The Old English Rune Poem*

Ingwaz

Ingwaz (pronounced ing-was) is your rune of successful ventures and accomplishments. Even today, many people never venture far from the place where they were born. In early times, when the world beyond the village or kingdom was unknown, thought to be full of monsters, and certainly filled with robbers and enemies, anyone who ventured far away was considered courageous. Often these adventurers brought back news of new lands with which the people could trade and prosper. They grew legendary as great heroes (ingwaz) and came to symbolize achievement, male energy, milestones that changed life for the better.

Rune Image: A hero in victorious stance, legs spread wide, arms lifted to sky

In Rune Reading

Faceup meanings: Successful conclusions, good fortune, deliverance, the divine in the human, hero, higher-self, teacher, power to easily overcome difficulty, relief, milestone events, a new, exciting phase of life, male energy and fertility. *Tarot comparison:* Judgment. *Astrological comparison:* The dark moon.

Occluded (facedown) meanings: Lack of closure, unsuccessful conclusions, the ignoble in humanity, the lower self, a false leader, difficulties not easily overcome, the same old same old in life, lack of or misdirected male energy. *Tarot comparison:* Judgment reversed. *Astrological comparison:* The dark moon afflicted.

In Rune Magic

Use to: Store and transform energy for magical workings, perform sex magic and fertility rituals, bring an important venture to a successful conclusion, ensure a satisfactory result at the end of a spell, release energy suddenly in an intense burst

In Rune Meditation

Use to: Deepen meditation, center yourself, explore nature of different energies, contact the higher self, understand and master the forces of change

Rune Gods: Ing, Earth God, first Dane to contact the Norse

Rune Totems: Cows, horses, oxen, doves, eagles

Rune Herb: Self-heal

Rune Color: Amber

Rune Magic: Shaping the Future You Want

Make your future turn out the way you want it to be when you make rune Uruz the focus of this powerful ritual. In magic, you release the forces behind Uruz to shape events into the pattern you desire. No other rune has such influence over the future. With Uruz, you can make all your dreams, wishes, and hopes for the future come true.

For the Uruz future-shaping ceremony you will want to have available the rune Uruz, a dark green candle, sphagnum moss, and an incense burner.

Be sure you will remain completely undisturbed for at least half an hour. Light your candle, then do the same with a pinch of the moss in your burner. As the vibratory wavelengths of the color of the candle and the incense are harmonious with the energy of Uruz, they create an atmosphere around you through which this energy can easily flow.

Lay the Uruz rune stone before you. As always, before you begin your rune ritual, use deep breathing to quiet your thoughts and feelings, and bring you into the proper receptive state. Look down at the image on the stone, so that your attention is centered on it, and say:

In the name of the Vanir,
I invoke Uruz!

With your left hand, pick up Uruz. (This places the stone and its energies closer to your heart.) Elevate the stone as high above your head as feasible. As with old-fashioned broadcast television, you get better reception if you lift your antenna up away from the interference of Earth currents and human-made electromagnetic waves.

Then say:

Let the energy
of this rune
imbue my life.
Uruz, obey me
at the Gods' command!

At this point in the ritual, or within in a very few moments, you should feel the cosmic energies actually entering the Uruz stone. It will turn warm quickly or your hand and arm will tingle. With stone held high, continue and say:

May the energy of Uruz
miss no opportunity
to shape my future Fate
to heart's desire.
May I always receive
what is good for me.
Through Uruz,
May I never receive
what is bad.
Uruz!

As you pronounce "Uruz!" the rune stone will cool appreciably, and any tingling you experienced will leave your left arm. This is a sign that the energies of Uruz are already at work—shaping your future into the pattern you desire. Now is the time to sincerely thank the rune and its guardian gods. Say:

Thank you, Vanir,
thank you, Uruz,
for this blessing.

Rune Meditation: Empowering Your Future Self

What do you want to be when you grow up? What do you want to be now that you have been grown up for quite some time? Where do you see yourself in 5 years, 10 years, 20, 40? Where would you like to see yourself? Are they the same? Which life would you prefer? The one you think you'll be living or the one you imagine yourself living?

Everyone's vision of a "happy ending" for their life-story is different. What's yours? Whatever it is, how would you like the power to design your own future? The blank rune stone, Wyrd, can give it to you. And you can use it again and again to change, sharpen, and improve that design along the way.

Wyrd is the rune stone associated with the cosmic forces behind what we call wishes, dreams, the future, and fate. In this meditation, it becomes a gateway or portal through which you can create your own design for your life on the future.

As this is a particularly important and powerful meditation affecting your whole future, you will want to take extra pains to ensure you will be completely undisturbed throughout. Wait until even your noisy neighbor is gone and switch off every phone in the house. Hang a "Do Not Disturb" sign on your door, if that is what it takes.

Sit in a chair or the floor, whichever you find most comfortable. Lay the Wyrd rune stone where your eyes can rest on it naturally without straining. Have the future you want to see yourself in clearly in mind, then close your eyes and begin to breathe slowly in and out.

Stretch the amount of time you devote to relaxation and deep breathing out a bit longer than you did for the other meditations in this book. The importance of this meditation to your future cannot be overemphasized. Only when you feel your mind, spirit, and body are truly still and relaxed are you ready to start.

Open your eyes and look down at Wyrd. The stone is blank. There is no image there. All you see is a featureless circle or oval shape.

Try to visually ignore the surface. Allow your eyes to see only the shape—the outline—of your particular stone. Is it circular, oval, elongated?

Whatever your stone's outline, it is a boundary between the stone and the rest of the world.

Now, visualize the stone slowly dissolving away until an opening shows through to whatever lies beyond. Picture all that's left of the stone is its circular or oval outline (like the Cheshire Cat's smile in *Alice in Wonderland*). Through the hole where the stone dissolved, you see an opening—and through it you catch a glimpse of the future. It is the future the way you want it to be.

Visualize this opening growing larger, until it is as big as a large doorway. Mentally picture yourself standing up and stepping through that portal. You have just stepped five years into your future as you want it to be. What do you see?

Where are you living in this ideal future? How do you dress? What is your career or lifestyle? What is your source (or sources) of income? Who are your friends? Are you single, living with someone, or married? How do you spend your leisure time? What are the most important activities to you? What about you remains the same? What about you has changed? How happy are you?

When you can clearly picture all those elements of your life five years from now, ask yourself how you feel about what you see. Is there anything that could be improved? Anything you got wrong? Anything you now see wasn't right for you after all?

If there is something you feel should be changed, summon up the portrait of your life five years away, and change it. Visualize everything else remaining the exact same way, but with your income, friends, education, or leisure changed—or change it all, if you feel that is necessary.

When you feel your revised portrait of the future is closer to heart's desire, ask yourself the same set of questions again. If you are satisfied with the picture, impress it on your memory (this helps impress the blueprint of it on the cosmic energies of fate controlled by the Wyrd stone). If there are still improvements you see could be made, continue to alter it until you are satisfied with the result, then impress your finished picture of the future on your mind.

Take a deep breath to refresh yourself, then visualize yourself turning around and stepping back through the portal. Only, you have not passed back to the present. Instead, you have stepped five years further into your future as you would have it designed.

What does your life as you want it to be look like 10 years from today? What do you see? Where are you living? How do you dress? What is your career or lifestyle? What is your source (or sources) of income? Who are your friends? Are you single, living with someone, or married? How do you spend your leisure time? What are the most important activities to you? What about you remains the same? What about you has changed? How happy are you?

All in all, how do you feel about what you see? Is there anything you would change? Anything you would like to see improved? Anything you now see wasn't right for you after all?

Are you happy with what you see just the way it is? If not, keep working at this portrait of your future a decade hence until you are satisfied. When you are ready to sign off on it, pause to impress the picture on your mind.

Relax a moment, and picture yourself turning around and stepping back through the portal. Before you is your future the way you would like to see it 25 years from now. What is it you see?

Where are you living? How do you dress? What is your career or lifestyle? What is your source (or sources) of income? Who are your friends? Are you single, living with someone, or married? How do you spend your leisure time? What are the most important activities to you? What about you remains the same? What about you has changed? How happy are you?

All in all, how do you feel about what is in this picture? Is there anything you would change? Anything you would like to see improved? Anything you now see wasn't right for you? Make whatever changes are called for until you are content with your portrait of your life a quarter century from now. Impress the final picture on your mind.

In your mind's eye turn and step back through the portal a final time. This time you step back into the present moment, the moment from which you left. Visualize yourself sitting back down before the Wyrd rune.

Close your eyes and breathe slowly until you feel yourself return to normal. Then get up and move around to get your energy recirculating. Return the rune to your rune pouch or box.

It might seem that all you have done is exercise your imagination. But you have just performed one of the most powerful mental exercises known for impressing your personal desires on fate. You should soon begin to notice indications that the future is unfolding just the way you visualized it.

Chapter 12

Living the Runes

Runes aren't just a source of insight and solace during times of difficulty. Their connection to cosmic forces makes them a source of profound wisdom and guidance. Like Tarot, runes are like a book: a book of philosophy. Runes are the words in that book and rune readings are its sentences, paragraphs, and pages. Together they are a complete plan for successful living. As you read that book, you begin to absorb that philosophy and understand and heed its cosmic wisdom.

The more you act on this ancient runic wisdom, the better your own life becomes. The better your life becomes, the more you pay attention to the wisdom of the runes. The result will be a rewarding, fulfilling life, increased success, and the personal, intimate friendships and love you deserve.

In short, you will be the person you have always wanted to be—the person you deserve to be—the person you were born to be—the true you.

A Rune a Day ...

A rune a day keeps your difficulties at bay. No, it's not a famous folk saying, but it ought to be. The energies of a different rune rule each day of your life. Although all the forces signified by all the other runes will still be present, the energies of this one rune will predominate—like one voice or instrument will in a song. If Othala predominates, for instance, matters relating to parents and grandparents, or family property (your own and other people's), or a family trait, will play a large role in your day.

You don't have to guess what your day will be like, or which particular runic energy will predominate all day. The runes will tell you every morning, with your coffee. It's like getting a runic newspaper all about you—one that previews the basic theme of your day.

Taking five minutes every morning to discover your Rune of the Day gives you a look at what kind of energies, situations, and people you can expect to interact with during the day ahead. It tells you what kind of positive happenings to expect and what kind of negative ones to prepare for. It will even provide insights on the wisest way to handle both.

As the day progresses, you will find the symbol for your Rune of the Day appearing all around you. You may see it in a pattern in a rug, a street sign or billboard, the shape of a cloud or tree, or an advertisement. You will be surprised at how ubiquitous the image is.

As you become more familiar with this runic way of looking at the world, you will begin to recognize signs of the energies of the rune you have chosen in many of the day's happenings. If Mannaz is your rune, colleagues and strangers will aid you or offer good advice, while others work to actively foil your plans or cause you pain. Events at work, at home, even during a commute or leisure activities, will constantly remind your of your interdependence with others, and much of your day will be occupied in group or partnership endeavors.

Eventually, you will notice indications that the energies associated with your Rune of the Day are at work in your attitudes, behaviors, and actions. If you drew Algiz, you could discover yourself being prickly all day, or affording others sanctuary and guidance. You might even feel the rune's energies resonating inside you. When this begins to occur regularly, you are truly living the runes day by day.

The Seven-Day Rune Plan

If you're like most people, the idea of committing yourself to doing anything on a daily basis for a year, no matter how little time or effort it
takes, might seem daunting. Especially something as esoteric sounding as
drawing a Rune of the Day, whose rewards seem hypothetical at best.
No one wants to commit to a long-term project and then end up feeling
foolish because it didn't turn out to repay the time involved. But how
about a week? A few minutes every morning for just seven days? Would
you be willing to invest that little of your time to find out whether the
insights and counsel you get from your Rune of the Day is worthwhile?
That is all you have to commit to discover if it makes a difference in your
life. Starting tomorrow, as soon as you get up, reach into your rune pouch
or box. Your hand will be guided straight to your Rune of the Day.

At the end of seven days, evaluate the results. Has your life improved?
If you feel the effort isn't worthwhile—quit. But, if feel you reaped
rewards from drawing your Rune of the Day, is it too much to ask you
to invest three more weeks to fill out the month—and give it a real test?

Warning: Most people who try the seven-day plan discover such miraculous changes in their lives and such positive benefits that they go on to
the month—and find they never want to stop!

Rune Reading: Drawing Your Rune of the Day

As soon as practical after waking up, sit somewhere quiet, lay the 24
image runes facedown. Breathe deeply to center your mind so that it can
receive heavenly impulses, and say:

Runar radh rett radh. (Runes bless me with good guidance.)

Stretch your hand out over the runes and wait until it is guided to
pick up one of the runes. Turn that rune faceup and place it before you.
Quickly review what you know about the rune. (Flip back to the table in
Chapter 1 that lists the chapter in which each rune is profiled, or check
Appendix A to see all the runes at a glance.)

Ask yourself: What are its positive meanings and associations? What
are its associations when occluded? What positive events does it point
toward for today? What difficulties does it say you will face? What
counsel for surmounting them does it proffer?

Now, use pen and paper to draw the rune. Do this slo-o-owly. As you make each line, be conscious of the positive energy of the rune and that you are making a microchip circuit to attract that energy to your aid. Thank heaven for its aid in sending you this energy.

Fold the drawing up. Keep it somewhere on or near your person all day: in a pocket, billfold, purse, fannypack, or backpack. You want to be in contact with the circuit you have created as often as possible, so that you are constantly charged and recharged with the positive forces the rune is drawing down to you.

Rune #23: Dagaz or Daeg

Day, heaven's glorious light/is the gods' gift/to women and men./Its dawn is a cause/of rejoicing and hope/for poor and rich alike.
—*The Old English Rune Poem*

Dagaz

Dagaz (pronounced da-gauze) is your rune of light, enlightenment, and hope. Dawn and the coming of the new day (dagaz) seemed miraculous to the people of Northern Europe during the long nights of winter and the short, but glorious months of summer. Long, warm days meant rich harvests and fruitful hunting and fishing—all life stirred with new hope and promise. So day came to mean more than just another occasion of work and labor, it meant spiritual growth, the promise of something better, regeneration.

Rune Image: The rays of the sun

In Rune Reading

Faceup meanings: Day as beginning of rest of your life, self-renewal, one day at a time, literal as well as spiritual dawns, the present, now, slow but steady increase and growth, enlightenment, meditation, balance, between light and dark, between all seemingly opposite forces. *Tarot comparison:* Temperance. *Astrological comparison:* The half-moon, waxing or waning.

Occluded (facedown) meanings: Endings, in precipitate hurry, failure to grow, spiritual darkness or turning away from the spirit, lack of balance, constant dwelling on problems and obstacles that actually serves to attract them, the past, the inner strength to change things for the better exists but is not yet being utilized. *Tarot comparison:* Temperance reversed. *Astrological comparison:* The waxing or waning moon afflicted.

In Rune Magic

Use to: Focus the sun's energy to power a ritual or spell, ensure new projects will get off to a successful start, bring about desperately needed understandings and insights, increase abundance

In Rune Meditation

Use to: Merge with the alternating cycles of light, understand and balance opposing forces (in the world and in one's own life), cope with radical change, gain spiritual enlightenment

Rune Gods: Odin as all-seeing, all-knowing, enlightened inspirer of letters, science, the arts

Rune Totems: Eagles, horses, ravens, bears

Rune Herb: Clary sage

Rune Color: Sky blue

Steering by the Runes: The Annual Runic Cycle

You've probably noticed by now that your life seems to run in cycles. Doubtless you've experienced periods that are busy with activity, periods when things are stagnant and slow, periods when everything seems to go your way, periods when it is one catastrophe or hindrance piled on another, periods when your love life and sex life couldn't be better, and periods when they couldn't be worse.

Runes can provide you with a chart of what to expect when throughout the year. When your creative energies will be high, when is the best time make money, when you should be concentrating on children, or planning to complete that long-term assignment at work. Just as certain periods of time are ruled by the stars and planets in astrology, and the energies of a specific runes rule over your day, so the energies of each rune are activated during certain times of the year.

Two thousand and more years ago, the peoples who first used runes did not keep time in terms of "weeks." They thought of it in terms of the cycle of the moon—or a month of 28 days. This they divided into two bimonthly periods—each 14 days long—to represent the half month ruled by the waxing moon and two weeks ruled by the waning moon. The remnant of this custom can be found in England and the Continent where they still speak of "fortnights" (a period of two weeks).

The year they saw, not as we do of 12 months, but of 24 fortnights, each under the influence of the powers of one of the 24 rune stones with images. This annual runic cycle affects you, whether you know it or not. It explains why you sometimes seem to spend every moment warding off trouble and coping with problems, and why there are periods when you seem to be constantly interacting with others. Here is the annual runic cycle:

- **Fehu.** Rune fortnight: June 29–July 13
- **Uruz.** Rune fortnight: July 14–July 28
- **Thurisaz.** Rune fortnight: July 29–August 13
- **Ansuz.** Rune fortnight: August 14–August 28
- **Raidho.** Rune fortnight: August 29–September 13
- **Kenaz.** Rune fortnight: September 14–September 28
- **Gebo.** Rune fortnight: September 29–October 13
- **Wunjo.** Rune fortnight: October 14–October 28
- **Hagalaz.** Rune fortnight: October 29–November 13
- **Naudhiz.** Rune fortnight: November 14–November 28
- **Isa.** Rune fortnight: November 29–December 13
- **Jera.** Rune fortnight: December 14–December 28
- **Eihwaz.** Rune fortnight: December 29–January 13
- **Perdhro.** Rune fortnight: January 14–January 28
- **Algiz.** Rune fortnight: January 29–Febuary 13
- **Sowilo.** Rune fortnight: February 14–February 28
- **Tiwaz.** Rune fortnight: March 1–March 13
- **Berkana.** Rune fortnight: March 14–March 28
- **Ehwaz.** Rune fortnight: March 29–April 13
- **Mannaz.** Rune fortnight: April 14–April 28

- **Lagaz.** Rune fortnight: April 29–May 13
- **Ingwaz.** Rune fortnight: May 14–May 28
- **Dagaz.** Rune fortnight: May 29–June 13
- **Othala.** Rune fortnight: June 14–June 28

Sometimes it seems these periods and the energies that underlie them are working against you. Rather than their positive aspects manifesting, their disruptive and inharmonious ones appear. It feels like you are swimming against the tide. You and the time period are certainly not in tune.

But it doesn't have to be this way. When the energy of one part of the yearly runic cycle seems to be working against you, a powerful rune magic ritual can put you in harmony with the forces ruling that fortnight. Instead of having to fight them, you will mesh with them. Your way through the next 14 days will be made smooth.

When I choose to cast the rune stones, it is as if I am knocking on some ancient door. Without ever referring to a book, without switching my consciousness from knowing to understanding, from feeling to thinking, I experience my connection with something very old in me, very powerful, very solid. In time, as you become skilled in their use, you can lay the runes aside and permit the knowing to arise unfiltered, just as some dowsers use their bare hands to find water.

—Danaan Parry

Rune Magic: Synchronizing with Your Runic Cycles

You perform this ceremony on the first night of each of the 24 runic fortnights of the year. Your major requirements are the rune itself, and a quiet place where you can work magic without disturbance. You will also need a candle whose colors are harmonious with that of the rune, incense whose scent blends with it equally well when working magic, and an incense burner.

Light the candle and the incense. Stand upright, and place the rune whose fortnight is beginning in your left hand. Again, breathe in and out deeply and slowly until your mind, body, and spirit are themselves in harmony. Say:

Hail to thee, mighty [name of rune's guardian deity].
Hail to thee, mighty rune [rune's name]
whose time of earth-rule now begins.

Lift the stone and press it against your sternum over your heart. Say:

I beg thee,
let this rune
and my heart
be as one.
During its season,
let them beat
in harmony
and in time.
Let there be
no dissonance
between them.

As a sign that the deity and rune have heeded you, you should feel a warmth in the rune stone or your heart. If you feel it in the stone, wait a few moments and you will start to experience the same warmth enveloping your heart. When this occurs, you are ready to conclude the ceremony. Say:

Mighty [name of god],
mighty rune [name of rune]
take my thanks.
Henceforth,
for fourteen days
may [name of rune]
and I be as one.

Remain standing for a minute or so, until you feel the warmth leave the stone. Take a few breaths, then blow out the candle. As usual, let the incense burn itself out—if that is safe.

The warm feeling in your heart might last significantly longer than it does in the stone. If this happens, don't worry. It is not an indication that anything has gone wrong. Rather, you should take it as a sign that everything is going well. It means the energies of the rune and the energies of your heart are working in synchronicity. You should experience much smoother sailing through the fortnight when it rules, and much less friction. This is yet another way of living the runes that makes your efforts more productive and your life more successful. Your experiences, interactions, and intimate relationships, throughout the next two weeks should all take on a very positive aspect.

Rune #24: Othala or Ethel

The ancestral home/is very dear/to everyone./There people can enjoy/what they find comfortable and right./This is true abundance.

—*The Old English Rune Poem*

Othala

Othala (pronounced oth-aw-la) is your rune of parentage, family home, and inheritance. When our nomadic ancestors began to settle in one place to farm, land once claimed became the ancestral homestead (othala), passed down from generation to generation, where the whole extended family of brothers, sisters, in-laws, parents, and grandparents lived and worked and were interred. Thus the ancestral home became a symbol for all things associated with inheritance, from immovable property to those inborn traits of character we inherit from our ancestors.

Rune Image: The eves of a house with a lantern shedding light above it

In Rune Reading

Faceup meanings: Land, home, roots, inherited property, inherited character, help from family, opportune time to advance projects and prospects quickly and effortlessly, success. *Tarot comparison:* The Moon. *Astrological comparison:* The full moon.

Occluded (facedown) meanings: Difficulty or frustration at home or with property, lack of aid from family members, standing on your own two feet, problems as a result of trying to go too far too fast, success delayed and realizable only through thoroughness and attention to detail. *Tarot comparison:* The Moon reversed. *Astrological comparison:* The full moon afflicted.

In Rune Magic

Use to: Send healing energy to parents or relatives, protect material and spiritual possessions, support order and harmony in group endeavors, ensure financial gains or help, perform ceremonies on sacred land, contact ancestors and their knowledge

In Rune Meditation

Use to: Develop a team-attitude for group endeavors, develop a practical, down-to-earth attitude, understand family issues, come to terms with one's family traits

Rune Gods: Odin as all-Father, both male and female

Rune Totems: Bears, horses, wolves, cows, sheep, pigs, owls, ravens

Rune Herb: Gold-thread

Rune Color: Deep golden yellow

Rune Magic: Invoking the Wisdom of the Runes

Here is a second and even more powerful rune magic technique for living the runes. In it you will summon the wisdom of each of the 25 rune stones to contribute to your own. In effect, it is like putting the 25 wisest people you know to work as your permanent mentors and advisors.

All you need is sufficient room to lay out a magic circle with the runes, and sufficient privacy to conduct this most potent of ceremonies. You must also have a white candle, as white contains all colors (as you know if you have ever seen a beam of white light directed through a prism), and this ceremony invokes all the runes. For incense, use the herb known as all spice.

Lay out in a circle the 25 rune stones in order, clockwise, beginning with Fehu and ending with Wyrd, right on through to Othala. Light the candle and incense, and then step into the center of the circle.

Close your eyes and breathe slowly for a while, until your mind and body are calm and centered. Say:

Odin, All-father,
who hung nine days
and nine nights
above the netherworld
to win the mighty wisdom
of these runes,
grant my wish,
open to me the same mighty wisdom
which you won.

Pause for a moment to allow Odin to lend you his attention and place himself in resonance with your request. Then, repeat the following formula (it doesn't have to be exact, any desirable quality of the rune that you remember will do). As you say the name of each rune, shift your eyes to it, beginning with Fehu and ending with Wyrd. Doing so will take you clockwise in a 360° degree circle. Say:

Grant me
the foresight of Fehu,
the tenacity of Uruz,
the organization of Thurisaz,
the genius of Ansuz,
the flexibility of Raidho,
the insight of Kenaz,
the generosity of Gebo,
the joyfulness of Wunjo,
the timing of Hagalaz,
the deliberation of Naudhiz,
the restraint of Isa,
the judiciousness of Jera,
the decisiveness of Eihwaz,
the companionship of Perdhro,
the premonitions of Algiz,
the willpower of Sowilo,
the loyalty of Tiwaz,
the nurturing of Berkana,
the commonsense of Ehwaz,
the intelligence of Mannaz,
the creativity of Lagaz,
the divine connection of Ingwaz,

the balance of Dagaz,
the rootedness of Othala,
the cosmic vision of Wyrd.

Pause for a moment. You should definitely experience some kind of mental shift. Your brain might tingle, or feel clearer, or the world itself might look clearer, or you might feel like a mental light has been turned on. Your mind might even begin to race with thoughts.

The responses to this ritual take many forms. But, if you perform it several times a year, you should notice yourself becoming wiser, smarter, receiving more inspirations and productive brainstorms over a period of time. This is a sign that Odin, truly, has opened the treasure chest of runic wisdom to you, and that you are living your life by the runes.

In time, as you become skilled in their use, you can lay the runes aside and permit the knowing to arise unfiltered, just as some dowsers use their bare hands to find water.

—Ralph Blum, *The Book of Runes*

Rune Meditation: Being in Harmony with the Day

Every day is full of events, successes, failures, joys, heartbreaks, rewarding interactions with other people, frustrating interactions, work, family, and a hundred other challenges. All this can leave some people feeling frazzled, stressed, and burnt-out by nightfall. But it leaves others exhilarated, reinvigorated, and ready for what the next day brings. What's the difference? Why do some people end the day with their internal batteries recharged—and others are too drained to move? And how can you end your day feeling like the first group, and not in a state of collapse or despondency like the second?

Studies of people who survive and thrive on the day's challenges show they tend to feel more in harmony with what is going on around them—regardless of whether it is positive or negative. They tend to take things more in stride. At the close of a day when just about everything goes wrong, they view the events not as a catastrophe but as part of a natural cycle of ups and downs.

It is best to do this meditation in the early morning, not long after you have been guided to select your Rune of the Day. This will place you in harmony with the key energy ruling the day's events from the beginning. You will find your day going smoother, even when it is one problem after another, because instead of struggling against what happens you will accept it and move on.

If meditating in the morning isn't practical, meditate on the rune at the end of your day. No matter how you feel—jangled, exhausted, overwhelmed—about the way your day went, you will find yourself refreshed, centered, and with a greater awareness of any lessons or significance the events of the day hold for you.

In a location conducive to good meditation, lay your Rune of the Day faceup before you, and settle yourself comfortably. Breathe slowly and deeply until you feel you are in the proper state of inner quiet and relaxation to begin a meditation. Close your eyes for a moment, to allow them to relax and reset themselves.

Open your eyes and look at the symbol on the rune stone. Each one of the 24 rune images in some way represents some natural object, like a horse seen head-on (Ehwaz), an ox tossing its horns (Fehu), the crest of a wave (Lagaz), two paths that cross (Gebo), or a thorn (Thurisaz). What does the image on your Rune of the Day represent?

Look at the rune closely, until you can see how it resembles the object it represents. The two upright lines of Ehwaz, for instance, are the horse's forelegs, while the dipping lines are its chest and sternum. If you study it longer, you can begin to make out where the horse's head would be.

Now that you can see the resemblance, close your eyes. The outline of the rune will remain. Continue staring at this behind your closed lids, and visualize the rune slowly transforming into the object itself. For example, the tip of Lagaz becomes a wave of the ocean and sweeping across the horizon followed by an endless parade of other waves. Or Perdhro turned on its side becomes the gaming cup of a croupier.

Visualize that object for some moments until your mental picture is as clear as you can make it. Begin to meditate on the object and rune's meanings. Don't think about them so much as let the qualities and associations you've read about in this book surface in your mind.

Meditate on how those qualities manifest—both for good and seeming ill—in our world and in your life. You might see Lagaz in the flow of traffic on the freeway, in the ebb and surge of the stock market. You could find in Perdhro the fact that your car wouldn't start on your way to an important meeting, or in the way you ran into an old friend at the mall who knew of an ideal job just as you were looking for one.

Shift your attention to yourself. Meditate on how this runic energy manifests itself in you. You might perceive Lagaz in your easygoing flexibility or, conversely, in your stormy temper, or in the business intuitions that earned you raises and promotion. You might find Perdhro in the long series of disasters that occurred in your personal life last year, or your unusual luck at picking tickets that pay-off in the lottery, or your talent for making friends, even in your over-fondness for alcohol.

When you perceive how the energies of your Rune of the Day are part of you and the world that surrounds you everyday—of both the aspects you find pleasing and those you dislike—picture the object that your rune represents slowly metamorphosing back into its runic symbol. Visualize this image for a few moments; you should begin to notice something about the rune symbol you didn't notice before. It should be pulsing very slightly, like an electrical circuit with the energy traveling up and down the printed lines.

Picture your Rune of the Day slowly start to float toward you. It gets closer and closer. It passes into you. You should feel its runic energies blending and harmonizing with yours.

Wait a few more moments, then open your eyes and stand. As a result of this meditation, you will slowly come to realize that runes aren't a sometime thing, not just about an occasional reading or ceremony. Their knowledge, energies, and powers are all around you. They are part of you.

When you have a problem and need to go slow, you won't have to throw the rune stones to discover it. Hagalaz will whisper it to you. When your luck is about to turn bad or good, you won't need to read the runes. Perhdro will warn you ahead of time. When you are about to lose your temper, Uruz will whisper caution in your ear.

Eventually, following this wise council will become instinctive. When it does, you will find your whole life falling into place—romance, inner satisfaction, personal growth, financial abundance, respect, and more will all be yours. You will have become the person you always dreamed of being, your life the way you dreamed you life should be. That is the reward of living the runes.

Appendix A

Runes at a Glance

Fehu

1. Fehu: Rune of wisdom and prosperity

Uruz

2. Uruz: Rune of physical and mental health

Thurisaz

*3. Thurisaz: Rune of defense
and protection*

Ansuz

*4. Ansuz: Rune of communication
and knowledge*

Raidho

5. Raidho: Rune of travel and change

Kenaz

*6. Kenaz: Rune of creativity and
productivity*

Gebo

*7. Gebo: Rune of connection and
relationships*

Wunjo

*8. Wunjo: Rune of happiness and
harmony*

Hagalaz

*9. Hagalaz: Rune of karma and
opportunity*

Naudhiz

*10. Naudhiz: Rune of need and
deliverance*

Isa

11. Isa: Rune of stillness and waiting

Algiz

15. Algiz: Rune of guidance and aid

Jera

12. Jera: Rune of harvest and reward

Sowilo

16. Sowilo: Rune of power and motivation

Eihwaz

13. Eihwaz: Rune of management and foresight

Tiwaz

17. Tiwaz: Rune of victory and justice

Perdhro

14. Perdhro: Rune of luck and comradeship

Berkana

18. Berkana: Rune of nurturing and rebirth

Ehwaz

*19. Ehwaz: Rune of partnership
and work*

Mannaz

*20. Mannaz: Rune of humanity
and groups*

Lagaz

*21. Lagaz: Rune of emotions and
the unconscious*

Ingwaz

*22. Ingwaz: Rune of ventures and
achievement*

Dagaz

*23. Dagaz: Rune of balance
and self-renewal*

Othala

*24. Othala: Rune of family
and home*

Wyrd

*25. Wyrd: Rune of fate
and wishes*

Appendix B

Resources

If the rune lore in this book has whetted your appetite to learn more about the runes, or if you are interested in obtaining rune stone sets, pouches, or even runic card decks, the following list of books, mail order sources, and websites will help point you in the right direction.

Rune Books

Aswynn, Freya. *Northern Mysteries & Magick: Runes, Gods, and Feminine Powers.* Llewellen, 2002.

Blum, Ralph. *The Book of Runes.* St. Martin's, 1993.

Knight, Sirona. *The Little Giant Encyclopedia of Runes.* Sterling, 2002.

Mayer, John C. *Runework: A Practical Guide for Beginners.* Vanaheim Publishing, 1999.

Pennick, Nigel. *A Complete Illustrated Guide to the Runes.* Element, 2002.

Peschel, Lisa. *A Practical Guide to the Runes.* Llewellen, 2001.

Thorsson, Edred. *Futhark: A Handbook of Rune Magic.* Weiser, 1984.

———. *Runelore.* Weiser, 1987.

Rune Stone Sets

Beyond the Rainbow
Box 110, Ruby, NY 12475
www.rainbowcrystal.com
Rainbow Crystal rune sets: Stunning stones hand-carved and painted on glowing crystal.

Tara Hill Designs
P.O. Box 23074
55 Ontario Street South
Milton, ON L9T 5B4 CANADA
www.tarahill.com
Tara Hill rune sets: Hand-crafted rune sets in burnished wood. Also offers rune pendants and other rune talismans.

13 Moons Rune Stone
P.O. Box 294
Betterton, MD 21610
www.13moons.com
Lovely rune stone sets on a dozen different types of crystal, rock, even driftwood, plus pouches and books.

Reiki Council
420 Stone Road, Suite A1
Villa Park, IL 60181
www.reikicouncil.com
Quartz crystal rune stones: Radiant quartz sets that practically glow in the dark.

Rune Card Decks

Haindl "Rune Oracle." Created by Hermann Haindl. U.S. Game Systems, 1997. Strong metaphysical imagery and beauty.

Odin's Tree Rune Cards. Created by Cheryl Barnes. Music Design, 2000. Antique rune stone design.

Power of the Runes Deck. Created by Vomenix. U.S. Game Systems, 2003. Stunning metaphysical imagery.

Rune Vision Cards. Created by Sylvia Gainsford with Howard Rodway. Sterling Publishers, 2002. A very popular deck.

Soother's Rune Cards. Created by Soother's Books. Soother's Books and Music, 1999. One of the best.

The Book of Runes Cards. Created by Ralph Blum. Illustrated by Jane Walmsley. St. Martin's, 2001. A beautiful deck.

Rune Websites

Ankou's Page of Runes
my.execpc.com/~gronitz/futhark/index.html
Insightful account of runes and their background.

Arild Hauge's Runes
www.arild-hauge.com/eindex.htm
A Norwegian site, in English, with authentic rune lore and insights.

Lore and Saga
www.loreandsaga.free-online.co.uk/html/younger_futhork.html
Wonderful site. Covers many aspects of runes and Nordic culture.

Runes by Lady Moon
www.witchesrealm.com/rune/rune1.html
Excellent pagan/wiccan take on the runes, with other associated information.

The Anglo-Saxon Futhork
www.algonet.se/~tanprod/zerun31x.htm
Good overview site for beginners.

The Runemaker Group's Rune Information Page
www.runes.info
Many articles and links to other worthwhile sites.

The White Goddess
www.thewhitegoddess.co.uk/divination/futhorc.html
Excellent introduction to runes, and much associated magical information.

Index

J–K

N

W–X–Y–Z

The New Age way to get what you want out of life
The *Empowering Your Life* series

Empowering Your Life with Wicca

ISBN: 0-02-864437-9
$14.95 US/$22.99 CAN

Packed with advice and instructions, this book offers New Age Wicca techniques to help you get what you want most out of life, live joyously, and make each day sacred.

Available at all retailers in June 2003.

Empowering Your Life with Joy

ISBN: 1-59257-097-6
$14.95 US/$22.99 CAN

Easy-to-apply empowerment techniques help you carve a path through life's rough spots and find and embrace joy as an enduring reality.

Available at all retailers in September 2003.

Empowering Your Life with Dreams

ISBN: 1-59257-092-5
$14.95 US/$22.99 CAN

Provides a window into deeper levels of awareness by exploring the meaning of dreams and giving valuable insights into personal well-being.

Available in December 2003.